MW01609976

# CubaTravel Guide 2018

## AN ENTERTAINMENT DIRECTORY

### Where to Shop, Where to Dine, Attractions and Nightlife

EGP
Editorial

E.G.P. Editorial S.A., 2018

Cuba Travel Guide 2018

© Yardley G. Castro, 2018
© E.G.P. Editorial S.A., 2018

Printed in USA.

ISBN-13: 978-1545462379
ISBN-10: 1545462372

E.G.P. Editorial S.A., 2018

# INDEX

# WELCOME TO CUBA

Cuba is an island brimming with vibrant art, soul-stirring music and villages cloaked in colonial charm. Home to nine UNESCO World Heritage Sites and a population as warm and scintillating as its tropical climate and colorful arts.

Cuba, the biggest island in the Caribbean, is located at the entrance to the Gulf of México. Cuba's nearest neighbors are: to the East, Haití (77 kilometers), to the West, the Yucatan Peninsula (210 kilometers), to the North, Florida Peninsula (180 kilometers) and to the South, Jamaica (140 kilometers). The Bahamas are very near, toward the Northwest of the eastern end of Cuba. Formed by around 4,195 smaller keys, cays and islets, it covers a surface of 110,922 square kilometers and 1,200 kilometers of extension, on a mostly karstic and flat territory. Its nature, diverse and prodigal, shows wide variety of plants, animals and more than 280 beaches, Virgin Islands, grottos, caves, mountains, forests, savannas and marshes.

The island is divided into 15 provinces and one special municipality, Isla de la Juventud. Notable Cuba areas include rural Pinar Del Río, where tobacco farming builds economic momentum; seaside Santiago de Cuba, the country's second largest city next to Havana rife with colorful Afro-Cuban influence; and colonial Trinidad, a sleepy town designated a UNESCO world heritage site nestled between majestic mountains and the sea.

Cuba's population is richly diverse, with 11.2 million residents. Despite its Native roots, the most profound effects on Cuban culture are the result of European, African and North American influences.

## Climate

Moderate subtropical. The Cuban territory grazes the Tropic of Cancer, and due to its long and narrow configuration, on an east-west axis, it receives the refreshing action of the trade winds and the sea breezes. During the short winter, it is cooled by masses of cold air from the North; those cold fronts do not last long. The day and night temperatures differ less in the coastal regions than inland. The eastern part of the country has a warmer climate than the western part.

## Temperature

Average temperature 24, 6º C (76, 3º F) Summer average 25º C (77º F) Winter average 22º C (71, 6º F)

## Seasons

There are two, clearly defined: the dry season, from November through April; and the rainy season, from May through October. The average annual precipitation is 1 375 mm.

## Orography

There are three outstanding large mountain ranges. In the West, the Sierra de los Órganos; in the central part, the Sierra del Escambray; and in the southern region of eastern Cuba, the Sierra Maestra, where the highest point of the country is located, the Pico Real del Turquino, 1 974 meters above the sea level. Its longest river is the Cauto, with a length of 250 kilometers.

## History

Cuba was discovered by Christopher Columbus, on October 27, 1492. The conquest and colonization caused the extermination of the aboriginal inhabitants, due to which they imported black people from Africa to enslave them. The resulting mixture defined Cuba's population and culture. On October 10, 1868, the Cuban people began their struggle for independence from Spain, whose colonial rule lasted 4 centuries. United States intervened in the warlike conflict and established a pseudorepublic in 1902 until the 1st. of January of 1959, when the Revolution commanded by Fidel Castro triumphed, bringing essential transformations for the life of the country.

## Economy

The tourism is the main line. Other important industries are the sugar cane, tobacco, nickel, rum, coffee, and since a few years ago, the pharmaceutics and biotechnological lines.

## Education

Education is free and obligatory until the ninth grade. In 1961, illiteracy was eradicated and today the population has a high instruction level. Cuba's national system of education comprehends from day care centers for working mothers' children to universities disseminated throughout the whole country.

## Culture

A country prodigal in artistic and creative manifestations. It has made contributions to international culture with important names of writers, thinkers, dancers, musicians, painters, poets and singers. Cuban craftwork is interesting, with outstanding works in leather, vegetable fibers, wood, stone, metal and sea products. Cuba's cultural infrastructure consists of theaters, museums, art galleries and cinemas, where not only samples of the national wealth of all times are shown, but also of world art. It is the seat of important international events such as the Ballet Festival, the biennial of visual arts, popular music festivals and the Festival of the New Latin American Cinema, among others.

## Health

Cuba's health system is said to have one of the world's most complete programs of primary attention, the lowest of infantile mortality rate in Latin America and free services for all the people.

## Sports

Excellent Olympic results, a highlighted place in world sports and the massive and free practice in the country make Cuba proud and are counted among the achievements of the people in the past 40 years.

## Religion

Lay country with freedom of cults. Catholic and Afro-Cuban religions prevail, although other tendencies also exist.

**Payment Forms**

In tourist facilities and other service units, prices are set in Cuban Convertible Pesos (CUC). In Varadero, Cayo Largo del Sur, Jardines del Rey (Coco and Guillermo Keys), Santa Lucía and Covarrubias Beaches, and Holguín province (tourist resorts on northern coastline), you can also pay in Euros. Credit cards – except those issued by US banks or their branches in other countries – are accepted. Among those accepted are MasterCard, Visa International and CABAL. Cuban convertible pesos and coins equivalent to 50, 25, 10, 5 and 1 cents have unlimited legal course in the national territory. Cuban convertible pesos can be changed upon departure at bank offices at international airports and ports in Cuba. Traveler's checks, including those issued by US banks, are accepted.

**Official Commemorations**

Although they are not holidays, they are also considered important dates: January 28: Anniversary of the birth of José Martí, Cuba's National Hero, in 1853. February 24: Anniversary of the beginning of the War of Independence, in 1895. March 8: International Woman's Day. March 13: Anniversary of the attack to the Presidential Palace of Havana, by a group of revolutionary youths that sought to execute the tyrant Fulgencio Batista, in 1957. April 19: Anniversary of the defeat of the mercenary attack at the Bay of Pigs, in 1961. July 30: Day of the Martyrs of the Revolution. October 8: Anniversary of the death of Major Ernesto Ché Guevara, in 1967. October 28: Anniversary of Major Camilo Cienfuegos' death, in 1959. November 27: Commemoration of the execution of eight students of Medicine, by the Spanish colonial government, in 1871. December 7: Anniversary of Antonio Maceo's death in combat in 1896, an outstanding figure in Cuba's War of Independence against the Spanish colonial rule.

**Migratory Regulations**

Visitors should possess an effective passport or a trip document stating their name and the corresponding visa or Tourist Card, excepting those countries that Cuba maintains Free Visa agreements with. Tourist Cards can be requested at the Cuban consular representations. Also, in travel agencies and airlines. They are of two types: for individual tourists or tourists that travel in groups. The businessmen, journalists at work and natural of Cuba, non-residents or with another nationality, should get a visa.

## Sanitary Regulations

There are only restrictive sanitary regulations for visitors coming from countries where yellow fever and endemic cholera exist or have been declared infection areas by the World Health Organization. In such cases, an International Vaccination Certificate is demanded. Products of animal and vegetable origin have entry restrictions. Animals may be imported, previous presentation of the corresponding certificate.

## Electricity

The electric appliances endowed with round spikes should be brought with an adapter of plane spikes that are the type used for the plugs existent in the country. Electric current of general use is 110 V / 60 Hz, although in the recently constructed hotels it is 220 V / 60 Hz.

## Currency

The national currency is the Cuban Peso, which is equivalent to 100 centavos (cents). Notes can be of 1, 3, 5, 10, 20, 50 and 100 pesos. Coins can be of 1, 5 and 20 centavos, and there are others of 1 and 3 pesos. At the Bureaus of Exchange (CADECA) created to sell - buy Cuban Convertible Pesos, the exchange rate can vary now between $20.00 and $25.00 Cuban pesos to the Cuban Convertible Pesos (CUC). The exchange rate to the American dollar is fixed $ 1.00 CUC - $ 0.87 USD

# *TRAVEL TIPS*

You must be aware of some customs regulations before you travel to Cuba, for example: no weapons, explosives or pornographic magazines are allowed in the country; those tourists arriving from the States, either directly or from a third country, are not permitted to bring videocassette players. Tourist are allowed to bring, tax free, two bottles of liquor, one carton of cigarettes, personal belongings and jewels, photographic and video cameras, typewriters, sports and fishing gear. You can bring, duty free, up to 10 kilos of medicines in their original packaging.

Clothing should be light, mainly during summer, so it would be best to wear shorts, cotton and flannel outfits and sandals. As for winter, a light jacket or a fine wool sweater and closed comfortable shoes would do, mainly at night. You should also bring sunglasses and a bathing-suit and so that you can take a refreshing swim, and don't forget your sunscreen.

The voltage in most residential and trade areas, offices and hotels are 110 V / 60 HZ, though some facilities already have 220 V / 60 HZ. Wall outlets are for flat plugs.

You should not take urban transportation - like the "camel" -; they are always crowded and unreliable. You should take taxis or tourist buses instead, or walk when its short distances. If you want to go on a tour of the island, your best option is to rent a car. There are several car rental offices at the airports, hotels and tourist spots providing high quality cars and services.

You must show your passport and driver's license in order to rent a car. The driver must be at least 21 years old; the license could be international or from your country but at least a year old. It is not advisable to drive at night. You must also watch out for animals on the road and cyclists in urban areas when you are driving. Park the car in a safe well-lit place and do not leave anything valuable in it. You are liable for traffic fines; failure to pay would mean incurring a debt with the State. We recommend you buy a "Road Guide of Cuba" which is very helpful for finding your way around on the roads.

There is no need to be vaccinated to come to Cuba. Most hotels provide 24-hours health care services with specialists and nurses. There are specialized clinics for tourists in the main cities.

Though tap water is drinkable, we advise you to drink bottled water to avoid tropical illnesses.

Even though Cuba is a safe and has a low crime-rate, you should take some precautions to avoid being caught out by petty thieves, who are just waiting for the chance to grab any belonging such as wallets, photo and video cameras, pieces of luggage, handbags or shopping bags. Public peace is ensured in streets by lots of young police officers always willing to help in case you need them, though they do not speak English. You should take note of the following advice: do not take more money with you than you need; do not be careless with your belongings and purchases; take good care of your wallet and passport in crowded places, we suggest you keep them in your front pocket; check the bill at restaurants; get rid of so-called "tourist guides", they are not professional and many are not aware of Cuban history and culture, they just pretend to be nice to tourists in order to fool them; keep your jewels and valuables in the room safe.

Most hotels, restaurants, bars, shops, etc., take Visa and MasterCard credit cards, as long as they are not issued by American banks. However, you should have some cash on you just in case the machines are not working.

## *Shop, eat, relax and enjoy...*

# WHERE TO SHOP
## (VARADERO)

**8 000 Taquillas**
*Department store*
Ave. Playa e/ 53 y 54.
Cárdenas. Matanzas

**Josone**
*Department store*
Calle 1ra. e/ 58 y 59.
Cárdenas. Matanzas
Phone: (53 45) 66-7898

**Arenas Doradas**
*Department store*
Hotel Arenas Doradas.
Cárdenas. Matanzas
Phone: (53 45) 66-8332

**Kawama**
*Department store*
Hotel Kawama. Cárdenas.
Matanzas
Phone: (53 45) 66-7183

**Arte 63**
*Handicrafts*
Calle 63 e/ 1ra. y 2da.
Cárdenas. Matanzas
Phone: (53 45) 61-2156

**Kawama Sport**
*Department store*
Ave. 1ra. y 63.
Cárdenas. Matanzas
Phone: (53 45) 61-2934

**Arte Nuevo**
*Handicrafts*
Calle 63 y 2da.
Cárdenas. Matanzas
Phone: (53 45) 61-2888

**Barlovento**
*Department store*
Hotel Iberostar Barlovento.
Cárdenas. Matanzas
Phone: (53 45) 66-7701

**Barracuda**
*Department store*
Calle 1ra. y 60.
Cárdenas. Matanzas
Phone: (53 45) 66-3481

**La Casa del Habano**
*Cigar shop*
Calle 63 e/ 1ra. y 3ra.
Cárdenas. Matanzas
Phone: (53 45) 66-7186

**Brisas**
*Department store*
Hotel Brisas del Caribe.
Cárdenas. Matanzas
Phone: (53 45) 66-7622

**Vídeo Centro**
*Music*
Calle 28 y 1ra.
Cárdenas. Matanzas
Phone: (53 45) 66-7706

**Tortuga**
*Department store*
Hotel & Villas Tortuga.
Cárdenas. Matanzas
Phone: (53 45) 61-2066

**Galería de Arte Varadero**
*Handicrafts*
Calle 1ra. y 39.
Cárdenas. Matanzas
Phone: (53 45) 66-7554

**Bazar Hicacos**
*Handicrafts*
Calle 1ra. e/ 33 y 34.
Cárdenas. Matanzas
Phone: (53 45) 61-3663

**La Casa del Tabaco
Club Puntarena**
*Cigar shop*
Hotel Club Puntarena.
Cárdenas. Matanzas

**Bazar Varadero**
*Handicrafts*
Calle 1ra. e/ 44 y 46.
Cárdenas. Matanzas
Phone: (53 45) 61-2329

**Las Morlas**
*Department store*
Hotel Las Morlas.
Cárdenas. Matanzas
Phone: (53 45) 61-3913

**Bella Costa**
*Department store*
Hotel Bella Costa.
Cárdenas. Matanzas
Phone: (53 45) 66-7596

**Los Delfines**
*Department store*
Villa Los Delfines.
Cárdenas. Matanzas
Phone: (53 45) 61-4715

**Glamour**
*Boutique*
Ave. Playa y 29.
Cárdenas. Matanzas
Phone: (53 45) 66-7707

**13**

# WHERE TO SHOP
## (VARADERO)

**Marina Chapelín**
*Department store*
Carretera Las Morlas.
Cárdenas. Matanzas
Phone: (53 45) 66-7096

**Cabañas del Sol**
*Department store*
Carretera Las Américas.
Cárdenas. Matanzas
Phone: (53 45) 61-3466

**Meliá Las Américas**
*Commercial Center*
Hotel Meliá Las Américas.
Cárdenas. Matanzas
Phone: (53 45) 66-7600

**Caimán**
*Commercial Center*
Calle 1ra. e/ 61 y 62.
Cárdenas. Matanzas
Phone: (53 45) 66-7692

**Meliá Las Antillas**
*Department store*
Hotel Meliá Las Antillas.
Cárdenas. Matanzas
Phone: (53 45) 66-8470

**Caminos del Mar**
*Commercial Center*
Calle 12 e/ 1ra. y Playa.
Cárdenas. Matanzas
Phone: (53 45) 61-2835

**Meliá Varadero**
*Department store*
Hotel Meliá Varadero.
Cárdenas. Matanzas
Phone: (53 45) 66-7013

**Kiosko Artex**
*Music*
Calle 1ra. y 47.
Cárdenas. Matanzas
Phone: (53 45) 61-2249

**La Abejita**
*Souvenirs*
Calle 1ra. e/ 25 y 26.
Cárdenas. Matanzas
Phone: (53 45) 66-7736

**Bazar Cuba**
*Department store*
Calle 64 y 1ra.
Cárdenas. Matanzas
Phone: (53 45) 66-7691

**La Casa del Habano Varadero**
*Cigar, Rum and Coffee store*
Calle 39 y Ave. 1ra.
Cárdenas. Matanzas
Phone: (53 45) 61-4719

**Casa de la Miniatura**
*Handicrafts*
Calle 10 y Camino del Mar.
Cárdenas. Matanzas

**Grocery Plaza América**
*Market*
Ave. Las Américas km. 11.
Cárdenas. Matanzas
Phone: (53 45) 66-8181

**Galería Palma Real**
*Department store*
Ave. 2da. e/ 61 y 62.
Cárdenas. Matanzas
Phone: (53 45) 66-7898

**Caracol**
*Boutique*
Plaza Las Américas.
Cárdenas. Matanzas
Phone: (53 45) 66-8551

**Mini Super Bello Sol**
*Market*
Calle 63 e/ 1ra. y 3ra.
Cárdenas. Matanzas
Phone: (53 45) 61-2690

**Casa de Antigüedades**
*Handicrafts*
Centro Comercial "Plaza
América". Cárdenas. Matanzas

**Mini Super Cabañas del Sol**
*Market*
Carretera Las Américas.
Cárdenas. Matanzas
Phone: (53 45) 66-7185

**Casa de la Artesanía Latinoamericana**
*Handicrafts*
Calle 64 y 1ra.
Cárdenas. Matanzas
Phone: (53 45) 66-7691

**Mini Super Herradura**
*Market*
Hotel Herradura.
Cárdenas. Matanzas
Phone: (53 45) 66-7697

**Tienda Artex**
*Music*
Calle 60 No. 208 esq. a 3ra.
Cárdenas. Matanzas
Phone: (53 45) 66-7415

# WHERE TO SHOP
## (VARADERO)

**Mini Super Pelícano**
*Market*
Villa La Mar.
Cárdenas. Matanzas
Phone: (53 45) 66-7695

**Copey**
*Commercial Center*
Calle 3ra. e/ 61 y 63.
Cárdenas. Matanzas
Phone: (53 45) 66-7690

**Mini Super Playazul**
*Market*
Calle 13 e/ 1ra. y Playa.
Cárdenas. Matanzas
Phone: (53 45) 61-7867

**Coral Negro**
*Jewelry*
Hotel Sol Palmeras.
Cárdenas. Matanzas
Phone: (53 45) 66-7009

**Noi**
*Department store*
Calle 1ra. e/ 13 y 14.
Cárdenas. Matanzas
Phone: (53 45) 66-7632

**Cuatro Palmas**
*Department store*
Hotel Cuatro Palmas.
Cárdenas. Matanzas
Phone: (53 45) 66-7187

**Photoservice Calle 64**
*Photography*
Calle 64 No. 526, Varadero.
Cárdenas. Matanzas
Phone: (53 45) 61-3810

**El Encanto**
*Department store*
Calle 1ra. y 42.
Cárdenas. Matanzas
Phone: (53 45) 61-3632

**Plaza América**
*Commercial Center*
Carretera Las Américas km. 11
Cárdenas. Matanzas
Phone: (53 45) 66-8181

**El Monarca**
*Department store*
Ave. Las Américas km. 11
Cárdenas. Matanzas
Phone: (53 45) 66-7600

**Plaza de los Artesanos**
**Handicrafts**
Ave. 1ra. e/ 44 y 46. Cárdenas.

**Electrónica Granma**
*Department store*
Calle 31 e/ 1ra. y 3ra.
Cárdenas. Matanzas
Phone: (53 45) 66-7700

**Puerta al Sol**
*Department store*
Villas Punta Blanca.
Cárdenas. Matanzas
Phone: (53 45) 61-2362

**Feria Caracol**
*Department store*
Calle 1ra. e/ 53 y 57. Cárdenas.

**Punta Blanca**
*Department store*
Villas Punta Blanca. Cárdenas.
Phone: (53 45) 61-7871

**Fondo Cubano de Bienes Culturales**
*Handicrafts*
Calle 59 esq. a Ave. 1ra.
Cárdenas. Matanzas
Phone: (53 45) 66-7454

**Puntarena**
*Commercial Center*
Hotel Club Puntarena.
Cárdenas. Matanzas
Phone: (53 45) 66-7181

**Foto Express**
*Photography*
Calle 1ra. e/ 41 y 42.
Cárdenas. Matanzas
Phone: (53 45) 66-7015

**Romeo y Julieta**
*Department store*
Calle 63 e/ 1ra. y 3ra.
Cárdenas. Matanzas
Phone: (53 45) 66-7362

**Foto Vídeo Varadero**
*Photography*
Calle 1ra. y 42, Edificio Marbella.
Cárdenas. Matanzas

**Sol Palmeras**
*Commercial Center*
Hotel Sol Palmeras.
Cárdenas. Matanzas
Phone: (53 45) 66-7009

**Galería "Arte, Sol y Mar"**
*Handicrafts*
Ave. 1ra. e/ 34 y 36.
Cárdenas. Matanzas
Phone: (53 45) 61-3153

**15**

# WHERE TO SHOP
## (VARADERO)

**Super Club**
*Department store*
Hotel Breezes Varadero.
Cárdenas. Matanzas
Phone: (53 45) 66-7030

**Galería Club Amigo**
**Varadero**
*Commercial Center*
Hotel Club Amigo Varadero.
Cárdenas. Matanzas
Phone: (53 45) 66-8243

**Taller Cerámica CERVAR**
*Handicrafts*
Calle 60 esq. a Ave. 1ra.
Cárdenas. Matanzas
Phone: (53 45) 66-7829

**Tropical**
*Department store*
Hotel Club Tropical.
Cárdenas. Matanzas
Phone: (53 45) 66-7723

**Gaviota**
*Commercial Center*
Hotel Sol Sirenas-Coral.
Cárdenas. Matanzas
Phone: (53 45) 66-8070

**Tuxpan**
*Department store*
Hotel Tuxpan.
Cárdenas. Matanzas
Phone: (53 45) 66-7560

**Internacional**
*Commercial Center*
Hotel Varadero Internacional.
Cárdenas. Matanzas
Phone: (53 45) 66-7693

**Villa Cuba**
*Department store*
Villa Cuba Resort.
Cárdenas. Matanzas
Phone: (53 45) 66-7699

# WHERE TO SHOP
## (HAVANA COLONIAL)

**Almacenes Siboney**
*Department store*
Calle Monte esq. a Carmen.
La Habana Vieja. La Habana
Phone: (53 7) 862-1575

**La Bella Cubana**
*Department store*
Calle Oficios esq. a Lamparilla.
La Habana Vieja. La Habana
Phone: (53 7) 860-6524

**Amadeo**
*Department store*
Calle San Rafael y Monserrate.
La Habana Vieja. La Habana
Phone: (53 7) 863-6885

**La Casa del Café
Mamá Inés**
*Cigar, Rum and Coffee store*
Calle Baratillo esq. a Obispo.
La Habana Vieja. La Habana
Phone: (53 7) 33-8061

**Avenida del Puerto**
*Market*
Calle Oficios e/ Luz y Acosta.
La Habana Vieja. La Habana
Phone: (53 7) 860-6255

**La Casa del Habano**
*Cigar shop*
Hotel Conde de Villanueva.
La Habana Vieja. La Habana
Phone: (53 7) 862-9293

**Belén**
*Market*
Calle Compostela e/ Jesús María
y Merced. La Habana Vieja.
Phone: (53 7) 860-9475

**La Casa del Habano
Palacio de la Artesanía**
*Cigar shop*
Calle Cuba No. 64.
La Habana Vieja. La Habana

**Benetton**
*Clothes*
Calle Oficios No. 152 esq. a
Amargura. La Habana Vieja.

**La Casa del Tabaco
y del Ron**
*Cigar shop*
Calle Obispo e/ Bernaza y
Monserrate. La Habana Vieja.
La Habana

**Boutique Capitolio**
*Handicrafts*
Paseo del Prado y Teniente Rey,
Capitolio de La Habana.
La Habana Vieja. La Habana

**La Distinguida**
*Department store*
Calle Obispo e/ Bernaza y
Villegas. La Habana Vieja.
La Habana

**Casa Cofiño**
*Furniture*
Calle Neptuno e/ San Nicolás
y Manrique. Centro Habana.
Phone: (53 7) 33-8086

**La Equidad**
*Department store*
Calle Consulado y Neptuno.
La Habana Vieja. La Habana
Phone: (53 7) 863-3829

**Casa del Habano**
*Cigar shop*
Calle Mercaderes No. 120 e/
Obispo y Obrapía. La Habana
Vieja. La Habana

**La Felicidad**
*Department store*
Calle Monserrate esq. a
Lamparilla. La Habana Vieja.
Phone: (53 7) 860-8166

**Casa del Navegante**
*Nautical Charters*
Calle Mercaderes No. 115 e/
Obispo y Obrapía. La Habana
Vieja. La Habana
Phone: (53 7) 861-3625

**La Filosofía**
*Department store*
Calle Neptuno esq. a San
Nicolás. Centro Habana.
Phone: (53 7) 33-8603

**Casa del Tabaco**
*Cigar shop*
Hostal Valencia.
La Habana Vieja. La Habana
Phone: (53 7) 867-1037

**La Francia**
*Department store*
Calle Obispo No. 452 esq. a
Aguacate. La Habana Vieja.
Phone: (53 7) 867-1031

**Casa Pérez**
*Department store*
Calle Neptuno e/ San Nicolás y
Manrique. Centro Habana.
Phone: (53 7) 863-2380

# WHERE TO SHOP
## (HAVANA COLONIAL)

**La Metropolitana**

*Department store*

Calle Aguacate esq. a Obrapía.
La Habana Vieja. La Habana
Phone: (53 7) 860-0171

**Clubman**

*Department store*

Calle Obispo No. 514 e/ Villegas
y Bernaza. La Habana Vieja.

**La Taberna del Galeón**

*Cigar, Rum and Coffee store*

Calle Baratillo y Obispo.
La Habana Vieja. La Habana
Phone: (53 7) 33-8476

**Complejo "La Isla"**

*Department store*

Calle Galiano No. 307
e/ San Miguel y Neptuno.
Centro Habana. La Habana
Phone: (53 7) 33-8993

**Langwith**

*Animals, Accesories and Food*

Calle Obispo No. 410
e/ Aguacate y Compostela.
La Habana Vieja. La Habana

**Coral Negro Astral**

*Jewelry*

Calle Neptuno No. 362.
Centro Habana. La Habana
Phone: (53 7) 33-8424

**Los Marinos**

*Market*

Calle Egido y Monserrate.
La Habana Vieja. La Habana
Phone: (53 7) 862-1773

**Coral Negro Capricornio**

*Jewelry*

Calle Aguila No. 353.
Centro Habana. La Habana
Phone: (53 7) 33-8432

**Mercado Neptuno**

*Market*

Calle Neptuno e/ San Nicolás
y Manrique. Centro Habana.
La Habana
Phone: (53 7) 33-8619

**Coral Negro Gastón Bared**

*Jewelry*

Calle San Rafael e/ Consulado
e Industria. Centro Habana.
La Habana

**Monte y Aguila**

*Department store*

Calle Monte esq. a Aguila.
La Habana Vieja. La Habana
Phone: (53 7) 862-7528

**Coral Negro Gemenis**

*Jewelry*

Manzana de Gómez.
La Habana Vieja. La Habana
Phone: (53 7) 33-8381

**Moure**

*Department store*

Manzana de Gómez.
La Habana Vieja. La Habana
Phone: (53 7) 33-8323

**Coral Negro Gentry**

*Jewelry*

Calle Galiano No. 251.
Centro Habana. La Habana
Phone: (53 7) 33-8424

**Novator**

*Boutique*

Calle Obispo esq. a Compostela.
La Habana Vieja. La Habana

**Cuatro Caminos**

*Market*

Calle Monte No. 256 e/ Matadero
y Manglar. Centro Habana.
La Habana

**Palacio de la Artesanía**

*Commercial Center*

Calle Cuba No. 64.
La Habana Vieja. La Habana
Phone: (53 7) 33-8072

**Dominó**

*Department store*

Calle San Rafael e Industria.
Centro Habana. La Habana
Phone: (53 7) 33-8393

**Palacio San Miguel**

*Department store*

Hotel San Miguel.
La Habana Vieja. La Habana
Phone: (53 7) 862-7656

**El Cadete**

*Shoe stores*

Calle Monte No. 401.
La Habana Vieja. La Habana
Phone: (53 7) 33-8045

**Palais Royal**

*Department store*

Calle Obispo y Compostela.
La Habana Vieja. La Habana

# WHERE TO SHOP
## (HAVANA COLONIAL)

**El Clip**

*Watches and Jewelry Immitations*
Calle Obispo No. 501 e/ Villegas
y Bernaza. La Habana Vieja.
La Habana
Phone: (53 7) 861-4741

**Park View**

*Department store*
Hotel Park View.
La Habana Vieja. La Habana
Phone: (53 7) 861-3293

**El Cristal**

*Department store*
Calle San Rafael y Monserrate.
La Habana Vieja. La Habana
Phone: (53 7) 863-6885

**Parque Central**

*Department store*
Hotel Parque Central.
La Habana Vieja. La Habana
Phone: (53 7) 66-0890

**El Cristo**

*Market*
Calle Teniente Rey No. 503
e/ Cristo y Bernaza.
La Habana Vieja. La Habana
Phone: (53 7) 861-9070

**Peerlees**

*Department store*
Calle Neptuno esq. a Zulueta.
La Habana Vieja. La Habana
Phone: (53 7) 33-8179

**El Morro**

*Market*
Calle Cárcel No. 105 e/ Morro
y Prado. La Habana Vieja.

**Plaza**

*Department store*
Hotel Plaza. La Habana Vieja.
La Habana
Phone: (53 7) 860-8591

**El Palacio del Tabaco**

*Cigar, Rum and Coffee store*
Calle Zulueta No. 106
e/ Refugio y Colón.
La Habana Vieja. La Habana
Phone: (53 7) 33-8389

**Prado y Animas**

*Department store*
Paseo del Prado esq. a Animas.
La Habana Vieja. La Habana

**El Sol Naciente**

*Department store*
Calle Obispo esq. a Villegas.
La Habana Vieja. La Habana

**Puerto Carenas**

*Handicrafts*
Ave. del Puerto, Terminal de
Cruceros. La Habana Vieja.
La Habana

**Ferretería Neptuno**

*Hardware*
Calle Neptuno No. 753
e/ Lucena y Marquéz González.
Centro Habana. La Habana
Phone: (53 7) 33-8071

**Revert**

*Boutique*
Calle Obispo No. 403 esq. a
Compostela. La Habana Vieja.
La Habana

**Florida**

*Department store*
Calle Neptuno e/ San Nicolás y
Manrique. Centro Habana.
La Habana

**Saldos**

*Shoe stores*
Calle Obispo No. 504 e/ Bernaza
y Villegas. La Habana Vieja.
La Habana

**Fornos Chá**

*Boutique*
Calle Neptuno No. 1 esq. a San
Miguel. La Habana Vieja.
La Habana
Phone: (53 7) 867-1032

**Salón Crusellas**

*Perfumes and Silk*
Calle Obispo No. 522 e/ Villegas
y Bernaza. La Habana Vieja.

**Fundación Ron Havana Club**

*Liquor store*
Calle San Pedro No. 262 e/ Sol
y Muralla. La Habana Vieja.
Phone: (53 7) 861-1900

**Sancy**

*Jewelry*
Calle San Rafael y Amistad.
Centro Habana. La Habana
Phone: (53 7) 33-8322

**Galería "1903"**

*Handicrafts*
Hotel Palacio O'Farrill.
La Habana Vieja.
Phone: (53 7) 860-5080

# WHERE TO SHOP
## (HAVANA COLONIAL)

**Taller Arteylla**
Calle Galiano No. 202 esq. a
Virtudes. Centro Habana.
La Habana
Phone: (53 7) 66-6658

**Galería Los Oficios**
*Handicrafts*
Calle Oficios No. 166
e/ Amargura y Teniente Rey.
La Habana Vieja. La Habana

**Tienda Castillo de la
Real Fuerza**
*Cigar, Rum and Coffee store*
Ave. del Puerto esq. a O'Reilly.
La Habana Vieja. La Habana
Phone: (53 7) 33-8390

**Galería Soyú**
*Handicrafts*
Calle Oficios No. 6 e/ Obispo
y Obrapìa. La Habana Vieja.

**Tienda del Tabaco Hotel
Parque Central**
*Cigar, Rum and Coffee store*
Hotel Parque Central.
La Habana Vieja. La Habana
Phone: (53 7) 867-0890

**Habana**
*Boutique*
Calle Obispo No. 415 esq. a
Aguacate. La Habana Vieja.
La Habana

**Tienda Tema**
*Clothes*
Calle Galiano esq. a Virtudes.
Centro Habana. La Habana
Phone: (53 7) 863-5944

**Harrys Brothers**
*Department store*
Calle Monserrate e/ O'Reilly
y San Juan de Dios. La Habana
Vieja. La Habana
Phone: (53 7) 862-6882

**Topeka**
*Department store*
Calle Obispo No. 413 e/
Aguacate y Compostela.
La Habana Vieja. La Habana

**Humada**
*Electronics and Hardware*
Calle Obispo No. 502 esq. a
Villegas. La Habana Vieja.
La Habana

**Giselle**
*Shoe stores*
Calle San Rafael y Monserrate.
La Habana Vieja. La Habana
Phone: (53 7) 863-6885

**Tienda Tema**
*Handicrafts*
Calle San Rafael No. 101 esq. a
Industria. Centro Habana.
Phone: (53 7) 66-9488

**Vídeo Centro Ultra**
*Music*
Reina e/ Angeles y Rayo.
Centro Habana. La Habana

**Inglaterra**
*Department store*
Hotel Inglaterra. La Habana
Vieja. La Habana
Phone: (53 7) 33-8415

# WHERE TO SHOP
## (HAVANA CITY)

**17 y 26**
*Department store*
Calle 26 e/ 15 y 17, Vedado.
Plaza de la Revolución.
La Habana

**La Inesita**
*Clothes*
Calle Obispo No. 508 e/ Villegas
y Bernaza. La Habana Vieja.

**300 Aniversario**
*Department store*
Calle Martí No. 460
e/ Céspedes y Agramonte.
La Habana del Este. La Habana
Phone: (53 7) 97-0879

**La Isla de Cuba**
*Commercial Center*
Calle Monte No. 251 esq. a
Factoría. Centro Habana.
La Habana
Phone: (53 7) 66-9469

**3ra. y 0**
Department store
Calle 3ra. y 0, Miramar. Playa.
Phone: (53 7) 204-2551

**La Maison**
*Boutique*
Calle 16 No. 701 e/ 7ma. y 9na.,
Miramar. Playa. La Habana
Phone: (53 7) 204-1543

**5ta. y 112**
*Department store*
5ta. Ave. y 112, Miramar.
Playa. La Habana
Phone: (53 7) 204-7444

**La Mariposa**
*Department store*
Calle Tulipán y San Juan
Bautista, Nuevo Vedado.
Plaza de la Revolución.
Phone: (53 7) 881-0996

**5ta. y 42**
*Commercial Center*
Ave. 5ta. A e/ 40 y 42,
Miramar. Playa. La Habana
Phone: (53 7) 204-4321

**La Moderna**
*Department store*
Ave. 243 No. 27205 e/ 174 y 276,
Wajay. Boyeros. La Habana
Phone: (53 7) 55-6739

**5ta. y 96**
*Department store*
5ta. Ave. esq. a 96,
Miramar. Playa. La Habana
Phone: (53 7) 204-2075

**La Onda**
*Department store*
No. 162 Edif. A-55, Alamar.
La Habana del Este. La Habana
Phone: (53 7) 65-2502

**Aché**
*Department store*
Guanabacoa. La Habana
Phone: (53 7) 97-5387

**La Palma**
*Department store*
Edif. 34, Villa Panamericana.
La Habana del Este. La Habana
Phone: (53 7) 33-8520

**Almacenes Toyo**
*Department store*
Calzada 10 de Octubre esq. a
Calzada de Luyanó. Diez de
Octubre. La Habana
Phone: (53 7) 41-5777

**La Palma**
*Department store*
Calle Porvenir y Georgia.
Arroyo Naranjo. La Habana

**Almacenes Ultra**
*Department store*
Calle Reina No. 109 e/ Rayos y
Angeles. Centro Habana.
Phone: (53 7) 33-8608

**La Perla**
*Department store*
La Lisa. La Habana
Phone: (53 7) 33-0529

**Almendares**
*Department store*
Calle 49 s/n esq. 28,
Rpto. Kohly. Playa. La Habana
Phone: (53 7) 208-4747

**La Pradera**
*Department store* ˙
Hotel La Pradera.
Playa. La Habana
Phone: (53 7) 33-7471

**Amistad**
*Department store*
Calle 26 esq. a Zapata.
Plaza de la Revolución.
La Habana
Phone: (53 7) 830-1028

# WHERE TO SHOP
## (HAVANA CITY)

**La Premier**

*Department store*
Calle 11 esq. a 4, Vedado.
Plaza de la Revolución.
La Habana
Phone: (53 7) 33-3487

**Amistad**

*Market*
Calle San Lázaro e/ Infanta y
San Francisco. Centro Habana.
Phone: (53 7) 33-5832

**La Primera del Cerro**

*Department store*
Calle Santa Catalina y Duarte.
Cerro. La Habana
Phone: (53 7) 66-6361

**Arenas Modas**

*Department store*
Playa Guanabo.
La Habana del Este. La Habana
Phone: (53 7) 96-4293

**La Quincallera**

*Department store*
Ave. 51 e/ 118 y 120.
Marianao. La Habana
Phone: (53 7) 267-1612

**Aster**

*Laundrymat*
Calle 34 No. 304 e/ 3ra. y 5ta.,
Miramar. Playa. La Habana
Phone: (53 7) 204-1622

**La Rima**

*Department store*
Reparto Camilo Cienfuegos.
La Habana del Este. La Habana
Phone: (53 7) 95-3961

**Atlántico**

*Department store*
Hotel Atlántico.
La Habana del Este. La Habana
Phone: (53 7) 97-1359

**La Ruta**

*Department store*
Calzada de Managua y Mantilla
Arroyo Naranjo. La Habana
Phone: (53 7) 57-8083

**Bazar 22**

*Department store*
Calle 22 No. 503 e/ 5ta. y 7ma.,
Miramar. Playa. La Habana
Phone: (53 7) 204-1698

**La Silueta**

*Department store*
Calzada 10 de Octubre esq. a
Calzada de Luyanó.
Diez de Octubre. La Habana
Phone: (53 7) 57-7045

**Boulevar de Tiendas**

*Commercial Center*
Calle 3ra. e/ 78 y 80,
Miramar. Playa. La Habana

**La Sirena**

*Department store*
Ave. 51 e/ 132 y 134.
Marianao. La Habana
Phone: (53 7) 267-9076

**Capri**

*Department store*
Hotel Capri. Plaza de la
Revolución. La Habana
Phone: (53 7) 832-0511

**La Sorpresa**

*Department store*
Virgen del Camino. San Miguel
del Padrón. La Habana
Phone: (53 7) 91-7568

**Casa Bella**

*Department store*
7ma. Ave. esq. a 26,
Miramar. Playa. La Habana
Phone: (53 7) 208-9613

**La Sorpresa**

*Clothes*
Calle Obispo No. 520 e/ Villegas
y Bernaza. La Habana Vieja.
La Habana

**Casa Blanca**

*Boutique*
Hotel Tryp Habana Libre. Plaza
de la Revolución. La Habana
Phone: (53 7) 33-4011

**La Tríada**

*Cigar, Rum and Coffee store*
Complejo Morro-Cabaña.
La Habana del Este. La Habana
Phone: (53 7) 66-9154

**Casa de Antigüedades**

*Handicrafts*
Calle 36 No. 4704 esq. a 4,
Reparto Kohly.
Playa. La Habana
Phone: (53 7) 204-2776

**La Vigía**

*Commercial Center*
Marina Hemingway.
Playa. La Habana
Phone: (53 7) 204-6750

# WHERE TO SHOP
## (HAVANA CITY)

**Casa del Habano**
*Cigar shop*
5ta. Ave. No. 1407 esq. a 16,
Miramar. Playa. La Habana
Phone: (53 7) 204-1185

**La Volanta**
*Department store*
Ave. San Miguel del Padrón.
San Miguel del Padrón.
Phone: (53 7) 91-7989

**Casa del Tabaco El Espiral**
*Cigar, Rum and Coffee store*
Calle Paseo e/ 17 y 19, Vedado.
Plaza de la Revolución.
Phone: (53 7) 55-3270

**Las Brisas**
*Department store*
Villa Mirador del Mar.
La Habana del Este. La Habana
Phone: (53 7) 97-1354

**Casa del Tabaco La Cecilia**
*Cigar, Rum and Coffee store*
5ta. Ave. e/ 110 y 112, Miramar.
Phone: (53 7) 204-8062

**Lawton**
*Department store*
Calle 15 No. 475 e/ Concepción
y Dolores. Diez de Octubre.
Phone: (53 7) 98-4176

**Casa del Tabaco La Escogida**
*Cigar, Rum and Coffee store*
Hotel Comodoro.
Playa. La Habana
Phone: (53 7) 204-0308

**Le Salon**
*Decorations*
Calle 1ra. e/ Paseo y A, Vedado.
Plaza de la Revolución.
Phone: (53 7) 55-3705

**Casa Grande**
*Department store*
Calle Martí No. 12 e/ Pepe
Antonio y Div. Guanabacoa.
La Habana del Este. La Habana
Phone: (53 7) 97-6616

**Los Pinos**
*Department store*
Villa Los Pinos.
La Habana del Este. La Habana
Phone: (53 7) 97-1267

**Casa Sánchez**
*Department store*
Calzada de Bejucal s/n esq. a
Cervantes. Diez de Octubre.
Phone: (53 7) 57-8095

**Maisí**
*Department store*
Calle Infanta No. 1116.
Centro Habana. La Habana
Phone: (53 7) 33-5116

**Casa Suárez**
*Department store*
Calle San Rafael No. 202.
Centro Habana. La Habana
Phone: (53 7) 863-6269

**Mariposa**
*Department store*
Hotel Mariposa.
La Lisa. La Habana
Phone: (53 7) 204-9137

**Casa Verano**
*Boutique*
Calle 18 No. 4106 e/ 41 y 43,
Miramar. Playa. La Habana
Phone: (53 7) 204-1982

**Mégano**
*Department store*
Hotel Mégano.
La Habana del Este. La Habana
Phone: (53 7) 97-1330

**Casablanca**
*Department store*
Ave. 1ra. y 36, Miramar. Playa.
Phone: (53 7) 204-4918

**Mekong**
*Department store*
Ave. Santa Catalina e/
La Sola y Mayía Rodríguez.
Diez de Octubre. La Habana
Phone: (53 7) 40-7641

**Centro Veterinario Almiquí**
*Animals, Accesories and Food*
Calle 164 No. 506 esq. a 5ta. Ave.
Playa. La Habana
Phone: (53 7) 33-6127

**Mercadito H**
*Market*
Calle H No. 155 e/ Calzada y
9na., Vedado. Plaza de la
Revolución. La Habana
Phone: (53 7) 33-4362

**Club Le Select**
*Boutique*
5ta. Ave. esq. a 30,
Miramar. Playa. La Habana
Phone: (53 7) 204-4001

# WHERE TO SHOP
## (HAVANA CITY)

**Miami**

*Department store*

Calle Neptuno No. 460

e/ Manrique y Campanario.

Centro Habana. La Habana

Phone: (53 7) 862-5178

**Colorama**

*Department store*

Ave. 41 e/ 28 y 30. Playa.

Phone: (53 7) 204-4392

**Mini Super Caribe**

*Market*

Puente de Boca Ciega,

Playa Santa María del Mar.

La Habana del Este.

Phone: (53 7) 96-3416

**Complejo Autopista**

*Department store*

Autopista y 244. La Lisa.

Phone: (53 7) 33-7071

**Mini Super Las Terrazas**

*Market*

Ave. Las Terrazas e/ 8 y 10,

Playa Santa María del Mar.

La Habana del Este.

Phone: (53 7) 97-1268

**Complejo Brimart**

*Department store*

Calzada de 10 de Octubre

e/ Concepción y San Francisco.

Diez de Octubre. La Habana

Phone: (53 7) 41-3294

**Mini Super Santa María**

Ave. Las Terrazas e/ 6 y 8,

Playa Santa María del Mar.

Phone: (53 7) 97-1326

**Copacabana**

*Department store*

Hotel Copacabana. Playa.

Phone: (53 7) 204-1037

**Mini Super Villa Panamericana**

*Market*

Villa Panamericana.

La Habana del Este. La Habana

Phone: (53 7) 95-4241

**Coral Negro Albita**

*Jewelry*

Calle Infanta No. 204.

Centro Habana. La Habana

Phone: (53 7) 33-5907

**Miramar**

*Department store*

Hotel Miramar.

La Habana del Este. La Habana

Phone: (53 7) 96-2507

**Coral Negro Primor**

*Jewelry*

Calle Belascoaín esq. a San

Rafael. Centro Habana.

La Habana

Phone: (53 7) 66-6213

**Mónaco**

*Department store*

Calle Juan Delgado y Acosta,

Víbora. Diez de Octubre.

La Habana

**Coral Negro Volga**

*Jewelry*

Boulevar Santiago de las Vegas.

Boyeros. La Habana

Phone: (53 7) 33-8402

**Nacional**

*Commercial Center*

Hotel Nacional de Cuba.

Plaza de la Revolución. La Habana

Phone: (53 7) 33-5722

**Danubio**

*Department store*

Calle 26 esq. a 23, Vedado.

Plaza de la Revolución. La Habana

Phone: (53 7) 33-4565

**Náutico**

*Commercial Center*

5ta Ave. e/ 152 y 154, Reparto

Náutico. Playa. La Habana

Phone: (53 7) 33-6252

**DITA**

*Electronics and Hardware*

Ave. 84 e/ 7ma. y 9na,

Miramar. Playa. La Habana

Phone: (53 7) 204-5119

**Nautilius**

*Department store*

Ave. Las Terrazas e/ 9 y 10,

Playa Santa María del Mar.

Phone: (53 7) 97-1277

**DITA**

*Electronics and Hardware*

Calle 1ra. e/ Paseo y A, Vedado.

Plaza de la Revolución.

La Habana

Phone: (53 7) 55-3921

**Neptuno-Tritón**

*Commercial Center*

Hotel Neptuno-Tritón.

Playa. La Habana

Phone: (53 7) 204-0098

# WHERE TO SHOP
## (HAVANA CITY)

**DITA**
*Electronics and Hardware*
Calle 23 e/ L y M, Vedado. Plaza
de la Revolución. La Habana
Phone: (53 7) 55-3278

**Palco**
*Commercial Center*
Calle 188 e/ 5ta. Ave. y 1ra.,
Reparto Flores. Playa.
La Habana
Phone: (53 7) 33-2168

**DITA**
*Electronics and Hardware*
Calle Calzada No. 475 e/ E y F,
Plaza de la Revolución.
La Habana
Phone: (53 7) 33-4127

**Panorama**
*Department store*
Ave. 42 esq. a 23.
Playa. La Habana
Phone: (53 7) 204-9736

**DITA**
*Electronics and Hardware*
Calle 3ra. e/ 78 y 80, Miramar.
Playa. La Habana

**Photoservice 23 y O**
*Photography*
Calle 23 y O, Vedado.
Plaza de la Revolución.
Phone: (53 7) 33-5031

**El Balcón de la Lisa**
*Department store*
La Lisa. La Habana
Phone: (53 7) 267-1873

**Photoservice Articolor**
*Photography*
Calle Goss y Acosta.
Diez de Octubre. La Habana
Phone: (53 7) 41-6557

**El Batey**
*Department store*
Marina Hemingway,
Hotel y Villa. Playa. La Habana
Phone: (53 7) 204-6816

**Photoservice Capricornio**
*Photography*
Calle Aguila y Neptuno.
Centro Habana. La Habana

**El Compás**
*Department store*
Ave. 101 esq. a 18. Cotorro.
La Habana
Phone: (53 7) 66-9015

**Photoservice Cerro**
*Photography*
Calzada del Cerro No. 1322.
Cerro. La Habana
Phone: (53 7) 870-4557

**El Dandy**
*Department store*
Boulevar Santiago de las Vegas.
Boyeros. La Habana
Phone: (53 7) 33-5775

**Photoservice Colorama**
*Photography*
Calzada de Güines No. 805.
San Miguel del Padrón.
La Habana
Phone: (53 7) 91-1975

**El Diezmero**
*Department store*
Virgen del Camino. San Miguel
del Padrón. La Habana
Phone: (53 7) 55-8408

**Photoservice Comodoro**
*Photography*
Hotel Comodoro.
Playa. La Habana
Phone: (53 7) 204-1969

**El Faro**
*Cigar, Rum and Coffee store*
Complejo Morro-Cabaña.
La Habana del Este. La Habana
Phone: (53 7) 66-9766

**Photoservice Festival**
*Photography*
Calzada de 10 de Octubre
y Carmen. Diez de Octubre.
La Habana

**El Festival**
*Department store*
Ave. 28108 e/ 281 y 283.
Boyeros. La Habana

**Photoservice Focsa**
*Photography*
Calle 17 y M, Vedado.
Plaza de la Revolución.
La Habana
Phone: (53 7) 66-2112

**El Fierro**
*Boutique*
Villa Panamericana, Edif. 1ra.
La Habana del Este.
La Habana

# WHERE TO SHOP
## (HAVANA CITY)

**Photoservice Gala**

*Photography*

Calle L e/ 23 y 25. Plaza de
la Revolución. La Habana

Phone: (53 7) 832-2205

**El Palenque**

*Department store*

Calle Martí y Lama.
Guanabacoa. La Habana

Phone: (53 7) 97-9510

**Photoservice Galiano**

*Photography*

Calle Galiano No. 512.
Centro Habana. La Habana

Phone: (53 7) 33-8141

**El Progreso**

*Department store*

Alamar. La Habana del Este.
La Habana

Phone: (53 7) 55-9379

**Photoservice Gama**

*Photography*

Calle 23 e/ 12 y 14. Plaza de
la Revolución. La Habana

Phone: (53 7) 830-6833

**El Puente**

*Department store*

Ave. 51 s/n, Arroyo Arenas.
La Lisa. La Habana

Phone: (53 7) 271-9442

**Photoservice Guanabacoa**

*Photography*

Calle Martí No. 215.
Guanabacoa. La Habana

Phone: (53 7) 97-8588

**El Roble**

*Cigar, Rum and Coffee store*

Calzada del Cerro No. 1417,
Fábrica de ron Bocoy. Cerro.

Phone: (53 7) 870-5642

**Photoservice Guanabo**

*Photography*

Calle 5ta. No. 48009.
La Habana del Este. La Habana

**El Sol**

*Department store*

Calle 3ra. No. 340, Zona 1,
Alamar. La Habana del Este.
La Habana

Phone: (53 7) 33-8234

**Photoservice La Lisa**

*Photography*

Calle 51 y 180. La Lisa.
La Habana

Phone: (53 7) 267-1629

**El Taita**

*Department store*

Aparthotel Las Terrazas.
La Habana del Este. La Habana

Phone: (53 7) 97-1685

**Photoservice Marianao**

*Photography*

Calle 124 y 49. Marianao.
La Habana

Phone: (53 7) 260-5040

**Flores**

*Market*

Calle 176 e/ 1ra. y 3ra., Reparto
Flores. Playa. La Habana

Phone: (53 7) 33-6512

**Photoservice Regla**

*Photography*

Martí s/n e/ Agramonte y
Céspedes. Regla. La Habana

Phone: (53 7) 97-7553

**Flores**

*Department store*

Calle 178 No. 109 e/ 1ra. y 5ta.,
Rpto Flores. Playa. La Habana

Phone: (53 7) 33-6490

**Photoservice Riviera**

*Photography*

Hotel Habana Riviera. Plaza de
la Revolución. La Habana

Phone: (53 7) 33-3867

**Floriarte**

*Flowers y Ornamental Plants*

5ta. Ave. e/ 24 y 26, Miramar.
Playa. La Habana

Phone: (53 7) 204-1952

**Photoservice
Santiago de las Vegas**

*Photography*

Calle 17 esq. a 11. Boyeros.

Phone: (53 7) 66-6046

**Focsa**

*Department store*

Calle 17 esq. a M, Vedado. Plaza
de la Revolución. La Habana

Phone: (53 7) 33-3486

**Photoservice Tropicoco**

*Photography*

Hotel Tropicoco.
La Habana del Este. La Habana

Phone: (53 7) 97-1084

# WHERE TO SHOP
## (HAVANA CITY)

**Fondo Cubano**
**de Bienes Culturales**
*Handicrafts*
Ave. 47 No. 4702 esq. a 36,
Reparto Kohly. Playa.
La Habana
Phone: (53 7) 204-8005

**Photoservice Villa**
**Panamericana**
*Photography*
Edif. 28, Villa Panamericana.
La Habana del Este. La Habana
Phone: (53 7) 95-2106

**Foto Vídeo 17 y Paseo**
*Photography*
Calle 17 y Paseo, Vedado.
Plaza de la Revolución.

**Plaza Caracol Tropicoco**
*Department store*
Calle 5ta. e/ 464 y 466, Playa
Guanabo. La Habana del Este.

**Foto Vídeo 23 y H**
*Photography*
Calle 23 e/ G y H, Vedado.
Plaza de la Revolución.
Phone: (53 7) 66-2120

**Primavera**
*Department store*
Calle Martí y E. Hart, Campo
Florido. La Habana del Este.
La Habana

**Foto Vídeo 23 y L**
*Photography*
Calle 23 e/ L y M, Vedado.
Plaza de la Revolución.

**Puerto Santo**
*Cigar, Rum and Coffee store*
Hotel Tropicoco.
La Habana del Este. La Habana
Phone: (53 7) 97-1652

**Foto Vídeo 3ra. y 70**
*Photography*
Calle 3ra. y 70, Miramar.
Playa. La Habana

**Punta Brava**
*Department store*
Calle 251 No. 4419 e/ 44 y 46.
La Lisa. La Habana
Phone: (53 7) 208-9370

**Foto Vídeo 5ta. y 40**
*Photography*
Calle 5ta. A e/ 40 y 42,
Miramar. Playa. La Habana
Phone: (53 7) 204-6251

**Residencial Tarará**
*Department store*
Calle 23 No. 33714 e/ 6 y 6ta.,
Tarará. La Habana del Este.
Phone: (53 7) 97-1684

**Foto Vídeo Galerías Paseo**
*Photography*
Calle 1ra. e/ Paseo y A, Vedado.
Plaza de la Revolución.
La Habana
Phone: (53 7) 55-3170

**Riviera**
*Commercial Center*
Hotel Habana Riviera. Plaza
de la Revolución. La Habana
Phone: (53 7) 33-3828

**Galápago**
*Department store*
Vía Blanca y Tarará.
La Habana del Este. La Habana
Phone: (53 7) 97-1029

**Riviera**
*Department store*
Calle Galiano No. 456.
Centro Habana. La Habana
Phone: (53 7) 33-9601

**Galería Chateau Miramar**
*Department store*
Hotel Chateau Miramar. Playa.
Phone: (53 7) 204-1952

**Santa Fe**
*Department store*
Calle 1ra. y 298, Santa Fe.
Playa. La Habana
Phone: (53 7) 271-0877

**Galería Habana**
*Handicrafts*
Calle Línea e/ E y F, Vedado.
Plaza de la Revolución.
Phone: (53 7) 832-7101

**Santa Fe**
*Department store*
Ave. 7ma. y 294, Santa Fe.
Playa. La Habana
Phone: (53 7) 208-7239

**Galerías Amazonas**
*Department store*
Calle 12 e/ 23 y 25, Vedado.
Plaza de la Revolución.
La Habana
Phone: (53 7) 66-2437

# WHERE TO SHOP
## (HAVANA CITY)

**Sensación**

*Shoe stores*
Calle Belascoaín No. 204.
Centro Habana. La Habana
Phone: (53 7) 33-5766

**Galerías Cohiba**

*Commercial Center*
Calle 3ra. e/ Paseo y 2,
Plaza de la Revolución.
La Habana
Phone: (53 7) 33-3636

**Sierra Maestra**

*Department store*
Managua. Boyeros. La Habana
Phone: (53 7) 57-9338

**Galerías Comodoro**

*Commercial Center*
Hotel Comodoro.
Playa. La Habana
Phone: (53 7) 204-0308

**Sierra Maestra**

*Commercial Center*
Calle 1ra. y 0, Miramar.
Playa. La Habana
Phone: (53 7) 204-1484

**Galerías de Paseo**

*Commercial Center*
Calle 1ra. e/ Paseo y A,
Plaza de la Revolución.
La Habana
Phone: (53 7) 55-3921

**Supermercado 70**

*Market*
Calle 3ra. e/ 68 y 70,
Miramar. Playa. La Habana
Phone: (53 7) 204-2890

**Grocery Comodoro**

*Market*
Hotel Comodoro.
Playa. La Habana
Phone: (53 7) 204-0308

**Tángana**

*Boutique*
Línea y Malecón, Plaza de
la Revolución. La Habana
Phone: (53 7) 33-4692

**H´Upman**

*Department store*
Calle Infanta esq. a Zapata.
Plaza de la Revolución.
La Habana
Phone: (53 7) 33-5956

**Tarará**

*Department store*
Calle 7ma. y 2da.
La Habana del Este. La Habana
Phone: (53 7) 33-5510

**Habana Libre**

*Commercial Center*
Hotel Tryp Habana Libre.
Plaza de la Revolución.
Phone: (53 7) 33-4011

**Tienda Amelia Peláez**

*Souvenirs*
Hotel Tryp Habana Libre.
Plaza de la Revolución.

**Havana Golf Club**

*Department store*
Carretera de Vento km. 8.
Boyeros. La Habana
Phone: (53 7) 45-4578

**Tienda Artex**

*Music*
Hotel Habana Riviera. Plaza de
la Revolución. La Habana
Phone: (53 7) 33-4051

**Horizontes**

*Department store*
Calle Monte No. 115 e/ Antón
Recio y San Nicolás. Centro
Habana. La Habana
Phone: (53 7) 863-3766

**Tienda Artex L y 23**

*Music*
Calle L y 23, Vedado. Plaza de
la Revolución. La Habana
Phone: (53 7) 832-0632

**Indochina**

*Department store*
Calle N esq. a 23. Plaza de la
Revolución. La Habana
Phone: (53 7) 33-4363

**Tienda Artex Miramar**

*Music*
Calle 18 No. 509, Miramar.
Playa. La Habana
Phone: (53 7) 204-1212

**Jicarazo**

*Cigar, Rum and Coffee store*
Calle A y Ave. Central.
La Habana del Este. La Habana
Phone: (53 7) 97-3063

**Tienda Casa de la Música**

*Music*
Calle 20 No. 3308 esq. a 35,
Miramar. Playa. La Habana
Phone: (53 7) 204-0447

# WHERE TO SHOP
## (HAVANA CITY)

**Kiosko Cuatro Caminos**
*Clothes*
Calle 105 esq. a 100.
Cotorro. La Habana

**Tienda de Tabaco Bacará**
*Cigar, Rum and Coffee store*
Cabaret Tropicana. Marianao.
Phone: (53 7) 267-1365

**Kiosko Guaicanamar**
Calle Carlos M. Céspedes
esq. a Guaicanamar. Regla.

**Tienda de Tabaco
El Aljibe**
*Cigar, Rum and Coffee store*
Calle 7ma. esq. a 24, Miramar.
Phone: (53 7) 204-1012

**Kioskos Fontanar**
*Department store*
Entrada al Reparto Fontanar.
Boyeros. La Habana
Phone: (53 7) 33-5872

**Tienda de Tabaco
El Corojo**
*Cigar, Rum and Coffee store*
Hotel Meliá Cohiba. Vedado.
Phone: (53 7) 33-3636

**La Arcada**
*Department store*
Calle Martí No. 179.
Guanabacoa. La Habana
Phone: (53 7) 66-9351

**Tienda de Tabaco
La Ferminia**
*Cigar, Rum and Coffee store*
5ta. Ave. y 186, Reparto Flores.

**La Barrena**
*Department store*
Reparto Baluarte, Rancho
Boyeros. Boyeros. La Habana
Phone: (53 7) 45-2286

**Tienda de Tabaco La
Giraldilla**
*Cigar, Rum and Coffee store*
Calle 222 esq. a 37. La Lisa.
Phone: (53 7) 33-1155

**La Caribeña**
*Department store*
Concha y Luyanó. San Miguel
del Padrón. La Habana
Phone: (53 7) 55-7181

**Palacio de Convenciones**
*Department store*
Calle 146 e/ 11 y 13,
Cubanacán. Playa. La Habana
Phone: (53 7) 202-5511

**La Casa del Habano
Hotel Nacional**
Hotel Nacional de Cuba. Plaza
de la Revolución. La Habana

**Tropicoco**
*Department store*
Hotel Tropicoco.
La Habana del Este. La Habana
Phone: (53 7) 97-1662

**La Casa del Habano
La Vigía**
*Cigar, Rum and Coffee store*
5ta. Ave. y 248, Marina
Hemingway. Playa.
Phone: (53 7) 204-6772

**Tulipán**
*Department store*
Ave. Rancho Boyeros No. 909.
Plaza de la Revolución.
Phone: (53 7) 878-3573

**La Casa del Habano
Partagás**
*Cigar, Rum and Coffee store*
Calle Industria No. 520
e/ Dragones y Barcelona.
Centro Habana. La Habana
Phone: (53 7) 33-8060

**Variedades Bello Caribe**
*Department store*
Hotel Bello Caribe. Playa.
Phone: (53 7) 33-0576

**La Casa del Tabaco 23 y P**
*Cigar shop*
Calle 23 esq. a P, Vedado.
Plaza de la Revolución.

**Vedado**
*Department store*
Hotel Vedado. Plaza de la
Revolución. La Habana
Phone: (53 7) 33-4072

**La Casa del Tabaco
Hotel Tryp Habana Libre**
*Cigar shop*
Hotel Tryp Habana Libre.
Plaza de la Revolución.

**Viazul**
*Department store*
Ave. 26 y Zoológico, Nuevo
Vedado. Plaza de la Revolución.
Phone: (53 7) 881-1413

# WHERE TO SHOP
## (HAVANA CITY)

**La Casita de Piedra**
*Children´s Clothes*
5ta. Ave. y 248, Santa Fe.
Playa. La Habana
Phone: (53 7) 204-6816

**Victoria**
*Department store*
Hotel Victoria. Plaza de la
Revolución. La Habana
Phone: (53 7) 33-3510

**La Ceiba**
*Department store*
Abel Santamaría.
Boyeros. La Habana
Phone: (53 7) 55-8796

**Vídeo Centro**
*Music*
Calle 23 e/ L y M. Plaza de la
Revolución. La Habana
Phone: (53 7) 66-2334

**La Comercial**
*Department store*
Calzada de Vento s/n e/
Acosta y 4ta., Casino Deportivo.
Cerro. La Habana
Phone: (53 7) 40-8007

**Vídeo Centro**
*Music*
Calle 3ra. No. 1206 e/ 12 y 14,
Miramar. Playa. La Habana
Phone: (53 7) 204-1782

**Vídeo Centro Siboney**
*Music*
Autopista y 244. Playa.
La Habana

**Vídeo Centro**
*Music*
5ta. Ave. y 86, Miramar.
Playa. La Habana
Phone: (53 7) 204-2302

**La Cuevita**
*Department store*
Rpto. Monterrey. San Miguel
del Padrón. La Habana
Phone: (53 7) 91-4946

**Vídeo Centro**
*Music*
Calle Ayestarán y Boyeros.
Cerro. La Habana
Phone: (53 7) 66-6051

**La Estrella**
*Department store*
Vía Blanca y Durege.
Diez de Octubre. La Habana

**Vídeo Centro Max Music**
*Music*
Ave. 41 e/ 28 y 30. Playa.
La Habana
Phone: (53 7) 204-3376

**La Feria Caribeña**
*Department store*
Calle 101 s/n e/ 14 y 16.
Cotorro. La Habana
Phone: (53 7) 57-9581

**La Giraldilla**
*Market*
Rpto. La Coronela.
La Lisa. La Habana
Phone: (53 7) 33-6489

**Villa Panamericana**
*Commercial Center*
Villa Panamericana.
La Habana del Este. La Habana
Phone: (53 7) 95-3606

**La Habanera**
*Jewelry*
Calle 12 No. 505 e/ 5ta. y 7ma.
Playa. La Habana
Phone: (53 7) 204-2546

**Yumurí**
*Department store*
Calle Belascoaín No. 601.
Centro Habana. La Habana
Phone: (53 7) 33-8606

**La Iluminación**
*Department store*
Calzada del Cerro y Arzobispo.
Cerro. La Habana
Phone: (53 7) 40-9109

**La Cordial**
*Department store*
Santiago de las Vegas.
Boyeros. La Habana
Phone: (53 7) 57-9317

# WHERE TO SHOP
## (SANTIAGO DE CUBA)

**Albión**

*Handicrafts*

Calle Enramada e/ Calvario y Carnicería. Santiago de Cuba

**La Catedral**

*Department store*

Calle Heredia e/ Félix Pena y Lacret. Santiago de Cuba
Phone: (53 226) 65-1055

**Amistad**

*Department store*

Carretera Central y Donato Mármol (Edificio 27 de Diciembre). Palma Soriano. Santiago de Cuba
Phone: (53 225) 2402

**La Escuadra**

*Hardware*

Calle Félix Pena esq. a San Fernando. Santiago de Cuba
Phone: (53 226) 65-1395

**Artesanía**

*Department store*

Hotel Meliá Santiago de Cuba. Santiago de Cuba
Phone: (53 226) 64-2612

**La Granada**

*Shoe stores*

Calle Enramada No. 302. Santiago de Cuba
Phone: (53 226) 65-1055

**Balcón del Caribe**

*Department store*

Hotel Balcón del Caribe. Santiago de Cuba
Phone: (53 226) 69-1011

**La Importadora**

*Department store*

Palma Soriano. Santiago de Cuba
Phone: (53 225) 2402

**Barra del Ron Caney**

*Cigar, Rum and Coffee store*

Calle Peralejo No. 703, Fábrica de Ron Caney.
Phone: (53 226) 62-5576

**La Maison**

*Boutique*

Ave. Manduley No. 52 esq. a 1ra., Reparto Vista Alegre. Santiago de Cuba
Phone: (53 22) 64-1117

**Bucanero**

*Department store*

Hotel Bucanero. Santiago de Cuba

**Las Américas**

*Department store*

Hotel Las Américas. Santiago de Cuba.

**Casa de la Artesanía**

*Department store*

Calle Lacret No. 724 e/ San Basilio y Heredia. Santiago de Cuba
Phone: (53 226) 62-4027

**Las Brisas**

*Department store*

Carretera Central km. 2½, Alturas de Quintero. Santiago de Cuba.
Phone: (53 226) 63-2578

**Photoservice 4ta. y Garzón**

*Photography*

Calle 4ta. esq. a Garzón. Santiago de Cuba

**El Oasis**

*Department store*

Carretera de Baconao km. 5. Santiago de Cuba
Phone: (53 226) 63-9227

**Photoservice Catedral**

*Photography*

Calle San Pedro e/ San Basilio y Heredia. Santiago de Cuba
Phone: (53 226) 62-2226

**Ensueño**

*Boutique*

Calle Aguilera esq. a Reloj. Santiago de Cuba
Phone: (53 226) 62-4561

**Plaza de Marte**

*Commercial Center*

Calle Garzón No. 4. Santiago de Cuba
Phone: (53 226) 62-3442

**Fondo Cubano de Bienes Culturales**

*Handicrafts*

Calle Lacret No. 704 esq. a Heredia. Santiago de Cuba
Phone: (53 22) 652358

**Primor**

*Department store*

Calle Enramada No. 302. Santiago de Cuba
Phone: (53 226) 65-1055

# WHERE TO SHOP
## (SANTIAGO DE CUBA)

**Foto Express**
*Photography*
Calle San Pedro e/ José A. Saco
y Carmen. Santiago de Cuba

**San Juan**
*Department store*
Hotel San Juan.
Santiago de Cuba
Phone: (53 226) 64-2478

**Galería de Arte Universal**
*Handicrafts*
Calle C e/ M y Terrazas,
Reparto Vista Alegre.

**Santiago**
*Boutique*
Hotel Meliá Santiago de Cuba.
Santiago de Cuba
Phone: (53 226) 64-2612

**Galería Hermanos Tejeda**
*Handicrafts*
Hotel Meliá Santiago de Cuba.
Santiago de Cuba

**Tienda Artex**
*Handicrafts*
Calle Heredia No. 304
e/ Carnicería y Calvario.
Santiago de Cuba

**Galería La Confronta**
*Handicrafts*
Calle Heredia e/ Carnicería
y San Félix. Santiago de Cuba

**Tienda Artex La Catedral**
*Music*
Calle Heredia s/n e/ San Pedro
y Félix Pena. Santiago de Cuba

**Galería Oriente**
Calle Lacret No. 653 e/ Heredia
y Aguilera. Santiago de Cuba

**Tienda Artex La Punta**
*Music*
Carretera de Baconao.
Santiago de Cuba

**Galería Santiago**
*Handicrafts*
Calle San Pedro esq. a Heredia.
Santiago de Cuba

**Tienda Artex Valle de la Prehistoria**
*Music*
Carretera de Baconao.
Santiago de Cuba

**Gaviota**
*Department store*
Villa Santiago de Cuba.
Santiago de Cuba
Phone: (53 226) 68-7166

**Trayler El Morro**
*Department store*
Castillo del Morro.
Santiago de Cuba
Phone: (53 226) 69-1527

**Ilusión**
*Department store*
Calle 9 esq. a 6. Contramaestre.
Phone: (53 226) 68-9282

**Trayler Ferreiro**
*Department store*
Calle 6 No. 409 esq. a 17.
Santiago de Cuba
Phone: (53 226) 64-1901

**Internacional**
*Department store*
Hotel Meliá Santiago de Cuba.
Phone: (53 226) 64-2628

**Trayler Reloj**
*Department store*
Calle 6 No. 409 esq. a 17.
Santiago de Cuba
Phone: (53 226) 64-1901

**La Alameda**
*Commercial Center*
Ave. Lorraine e/ Heredia
y Aguilera. Santiago de Cuba
Phone: (53 226) 65-2078

**Versalles**
*Department store*
Hotel Versalles.
Santiago de Cuba
Phone: (53 226) 69-1016

**La Casa del Habano Santiago de Cuba**
*Cigar, Rum and Coffee store*
Ave. Jesús Menéndez No. 703.
Santiago de Cuba
Phone: (53 226) 62-2366

**Villa Trópico**
*Department store*
Reparto 30 de Noviembre.
Santiago de Cuba
Phone: (53 264) 4-2336

**Vista Alegre**
*Market*
Carretera del Caney e/ 13 y 15,
Reparto Vista Alegre.
Santiago de Cuba
Phone: (53 226) 64-1165

# WHERE TO SHOP
## (HOLGUÍN)

**Baybrama**
*Department store*
Hotel Atlántico-Guardalavaca.
Banes. Holguín
Phone: (53 24) 3-0207

**La Casa del Tabaco**
*Guardalavaca*
Cigar shop
Playa Guardalavaca.
Banes. Holguín

**El Paraíso**
*Department store*
Hotel Brisas Guardalavaca.
Banes. Holguín
Phone: (53 24) 3-0391

**La Golondrina**
*Department store*
Hotel Brisas Guardalavaca.
Banes. Holguín
Phone: (53 24) 3-0206

**La Casa del Habano
El Cuje**
*Department store*
Bungalows Hotel Atlántico-
Guardalavaca. Banes. Holguín
Phone: (53 24) 3-0431

**Las Arenas**
*Department store*
Bungalows Hotel Atlántico-
Guardalavaca. Banes. Holguín
Phone: (53 24) 3-0207

**Framboyán**
*Department store*
Playa Guardalavaca.
Banes. Holguín

**Photoservice
Guardalavaca**
*Photography*
Boulevard Hotel Atlántico-
Guardalavaca. Banes. Holguín
Phone: (53 24) 30382

**La Aromática**
*Department store*
Hotel Brisas Guardalavaca.
Banes. Holguín
Phone: (53 24) 3-0391

**Trayler No. 1**
*Department store*
La Rotonda, Playa
Guardalavaca. Banes. Holguín

**Especialidades**
*Boutique*
Hotel Atlántico-Guardalavaca.
Banes. Holguín
Phone: (53 24) 3-0309

**La Orquídea**
*Department store*
Hotel Atlántico-Guardalavaca.
Banes. Holguín
Phone: (53 24) 3-0190

**Facilidades**
*Department store*
Calle 10 e/ 1ra. y 3ra. Rafael
Freyre. Holguín

**Venus**
*Department store*
Hotel Brisas Guardalavaca.
Banes. Holguín
Phone: (53 24) 3-0188

# WHERE TO SHOP
## (CAYO LARGO DEL SUR)

**Aeropuerto Cayo Largo**
*Department store*
Cayo Largo del Sur.
Isla de la Juventud
Phone: (53 45) 248125

**La Casa del Tabaco Hotel
Sol Pelícano**
*Cigar shop*
Hotel Sol Pelícano.
Isla de la Juventud

**Bucanero**
*Department store*
Playa del Pirata, Cayo Largo
del Sur. Isla de la Juventud
Phone: (53 45) 248131

**Lindamar**
*Department store*
Villa Lindamar, Cayo Largo
del Sur. Isla de la Juventud
Phone: (53 45) 248023

**Capricho**
*Department store*
Villa Capricho, Cayo Largo
del Sur. Isla de la Juventud
Phone: (53 45) 248122

**Pelícano**
*Department store*
Hotel Sol Pelícano.
Isla de la Juventud
Phone: (53 45) 248124

**Iguana**
*Department store*
Villa Iguana, Cayo Largo
del Sur. Isla de la Juventud
Phone: (53 45) 248121

**Photoservice Cayo Largo**
*Photography*
Cayo Largo del Sur.
Isla de la Juventud
Phone: (53 45) 248209

**Isla del Sur**
*Department store*
Hotel Isla del Sur, Cayo Largo
del Sur. Isla de la Juventud
Phone: (53 45) 248123

# WHERE TO SHOP
## (SOROA & VIÑALES)

**Soroa**
*Department store*
Villa Soroa.
Candelaria. Artemisa
Phone: (53 85) 2122

**El Mogote**
*Department store*
Calle Salvador Cisneros
No. 57 e/ Ceferino Fernández
y J. Pérez. Viñales. Pinar del Río

**Los Jazmines**
*Department store*
Hotel Los Jazmines.
Viñales. Pinar del Río
Phone: (53 8) 9-3265

**La Ermita**
*Department store*
Hotel La Ermita.
Viñales. Pinar del Río
Phone: (53 8) 9-3204

# WHERE TO SHOP
## (TRINIDAD)

**Aeropuerto Trinidad**
*Department store*
Carretera de Casilda.
Trinidad. Sancti Spiritus
Phone: (53 419) 2547

**La Canchánchara**
*Department store*
Calle Rubén Martínez Villena
No. 74. Trinidad. Sancti Spiritus

**Ancón**
*Department store*
Hotel Ancón. Trinidad.
Sancti Spiritus
Phone: (53 419) 6120

**Casa del Tabaco Trinidad**
*Cigar shop*
Calle Francisco J. Zerquera No.
304 esq. a Maceo.
Trinidad. Sancti Spiritus

**Casa del Tabaco Trinidad**
*Cigar, Rum and Coffee store*
Calle José Martí No. 296 esq. a
Parque Trinidad.
Trinidad. Sancti Spiritus
Phone: (53 419) 6149

**Las Cuevas**
*Department store*
Hotel Las Cuevas.
Trinidad. Sancti Spiritus
Phone: (53 419) 4013

**Casilda**
*Department store*
Calle Real, Casilda.
Trinidad. Sancti Spiritus

**Manacas-Iznaga**
*Department store*
Carretera de Sancti Spíritus km.
12, Valle de los Ingenios.
Trinidad. Sancti Spiritus
Phone: (53 419) 7241

**Cochera Brunet**
*Department store*
Calle Simón Bolívar No. 501.
Trinidad. Sancti Spiritus
Phone: (53 419) 2139

**Mesón del Regidor**
*Department store*
Calle Simón Bolívar No. 312.
Trinidad. Sancti Spiritus

**Costasur**
*Department store*
Hotel Costasur. Trinidad.
Sancti Spiritus
Phone: (53 419) 6174

**Mini Super La Delicia**
*Market*
Calle Francisco J. Zerquera
No. 7. Trinidad. Sancti Spiritus

**El Campesino**
*Department store*
Carretera a Cienfuegos
km. 1½, Finca El Campesino.
Trinidad. Sancti Spiritus
Phone: (53 419) 3581

**Photoservice Trinidad**
*Photography*
Hotel Ancón. Trinidad.
Sancti Spiritus

**Fondo Cubano de Bienes**
*Culturales*
Handicrafts
Calle Simón Bolívar e/ Ernesto
Valdés y Francisco Gómez Toro.
Trinidad. Sancti Spiritus

**Santa Ana**
*Department store*
Calle Camilo Cienfuegos s/n
y J. M. García. Trinidad.
Sancti Spiritus
Phone: (53 419) 3523

**Galería de Arte**
*Handicrafts*
Calle Simón Bolívar esq. a Ruben
Martínez Villena. Trinidad.
Sancti Spiritus

**Tienda Artex Playa Ancón**
*Music*
Hotel Ancón. Trinidad.
Sancti Spiritus
Phone: (53 419) 6120

**Galerías Trinidad**
*Commercial Center*
Calle José Martí s/n e/ Rosario
y Colón. Trinidad. Sancti Spiritus
Phone: (53 419) 2581

**Trinidad**
*Department store*
Calle Antonio Maceo No. 442.
Trinidad. Sancti Spiritus

# WHERE TO DINE
## (VARADERO)

**Albacora**
*Fish and seafood*
Calle 59 y Mar.
Cárdenas. Matanzas
Phone: (53 45) 61-3650

**La Habana**
*Buffet restaurant*
Hotel Meliá Varadero.
Cárdenas. Matanzas
Phone: (53 45) 66-7013

**Antigüedades**
*Fish and seafood*
Calle 1ra. e/ 56 y 58, Parque
Josone. Cárdenas. Matanzas
Phone: (53 45) 66-7329

**La Hacienda**
*Mexican cuisine*
Hotel Bella Costa.
Cárdenas. Matanzas
Phone: (53 45) 66-7210

**Antillano**
*Buffet restaurant*
Hotel Varadero Internacional.
Cárdenas. Matanzas
Phone: (53 45) 66-7038

**La Hacienda**
*Buffet restaurant*
Hotel Iberostar Barlovento.
Cárdenas. Matanzas
Phone: (53 45) 66-7140

**Ara**
*Buffet restaurant*
Hotel Paradisus Varadero.
Cárdenas. Matanzas
Phone: (53 45) 66-8700

**La Isabelica**
*Buffet restaurant*
Hotel Iberostar Taínos.
Cárdenas. Matanzas
Phone: (53 45) 66-8656

**Atenas de Cuba**
*Cuban cuisine*
Hotel Club Amigo Varadero.
Cárdenas. Matanzas
Phone: (53 45) 66-8243

**La Isleta**
*International cuisine*
Marina Dársena de Varadero.
Cárdenas. Matanzas
Phone: (53 45) 61-3730

**Atlántico**
*International cuisine*
Aparthotel Mar del Sur.
Cárdenas. Matanzas
Phone: (53 45) 61-2246

**La Laguna**
*Cuban cuisine*
Hotel Tryp Península
Varadero. Cárdenas. Matanzas
Phone: (53 45) 66-8800

**Bacunayagua**
*Cuban cuisine*
Hotel Barceló Marina Palace.
Cárdenas. Matanzas
Phone: (53 45) 66-9966

**La Marina**
*Buffet restaurant*
Hotel Barceló Marina Palace.
Cárdenas. Matanzas
Phone: (53 45) 66-9966

**Barbecue**
*Grill*
Hotel Playa Alameda
Varadero. Cárdenas. Matanzas
Phone: (53 45) 66-8822

**La Panchita**
*Buffet restaurant*
Hotel Sol Palmeras.
Cárdenas. Matanzas
Phone: (53 45) 66-7009

**Beach Club
"Ranchón Bucanero"**
*Light Meals*
Hotel Playa Alameda
Varadero. Cárdenas. Matanzas
Phone: (53 45) 66-8822

**La Piazza**
*Italian cuisine*
Hotel Palma Real.
Cárdenas. Matanzas
Phone: (53 45) 61-4555

**Bello Mar**
*Light Meals*
Hotel Arenas Blancas.
Cárdenas. Matanzas
Phone: (53 45) 61-4450

**La Polymita**
*International cuisine*
Hotel & Villas Tortuga.
Cárdenas. Matanzas
Phone: (53 45) 61-4747

**Biergarten Prost**
*Cuban cuisine*
Hotel Sol Sirenas-Coral.
Cárdenas. Matanzas
Phone: (53 45) 66-8070

# WHERE TO DINE
## (VARADERO)

**La Robleza**
*Cuban cuisine*
Hotel Meliá Las Américas.
Cárdenas. Matanzas
Phone: (53 45) 66-7600

**Bodegón Criollo**
*Cuban cuisine*
Ave. Playa y 40.
Cárdenas. Matanzas
Phone: (53 45) 66-7784

**La Sangría**
*International cuisine*
Calle 1ra. e/ 8 y 9.
Cárdenas. Matanzas

**Buffet**
*Buffet restaurant*
Hotel Tuxpan.
Cárdenas. Matanzas
Phone: (53 45) 66-7560

**La Sirena**
*Buffet restaurant*
Hotel Los Delfines.
Cárdenas. Matanzas
Phone: (53 45) 66-7720

**Burgui Varadero**
*Light Meals*
Ave. 1ra. y 43.
Cárdenas. Matanzas
Phone: (53 45) 66-7578

**La Taberna**
*Cuban cuisine*
Camino del Mar e/ 13 y 14.
Cárdenas. Matanzas
Phone: (53 45) 61-2223

**Café Carnaval**
*Italian cuisine*
Hotel Meliá Las Antillas.
Cárdenas. Matanzas
Phone: (53 45) 66-8470

**La Tasca**
*Buffet restaurant*
Hotel Kawama.
Cárdenas. Matanzas
Phone: (53 45) 61-4416

**Caguairan**
*Grill*
Hotel Playa Caleta.
Cárdenas. Matanzas
Phone: (53 45) 66-7120

**La Terraza**
*Buffet restaurant*
Hotel Meliá Las Américas.
Cárdenas. Matanzas
Phone: (53 45) 66-7600

**Capri**
*Italian cuisine*
Calle 42 e/ Ave. y Playa.
Cárdenas. Matanzas
Phone: (53 45) 61-2117

**La Terraza**
*Light Meals*
Autopista Sur km. 11, Plaza
América. Cárdenas. Matanzas
Phone: (53 45) 66-8181

**Casa de Al**
*Spanish cuisine*
Villa Punta Blanca.
Cárdenas. Matanzas
Phone: (53 45) 66-8050

**La Trovatta**
*Italian cuisine*
Hotel Varadero Internacional.
Cárdenas. Matanzas
Phone: (53 45) 66-7038

**Casablanca**
*International cuisine*
Hotel Playa Caleta.
Cárdenas. Matanzas
Phone: (53 45) 66-7120

**La Vicaria**
*Cuban cuisine*
Ave. 1ra. y 38.
Cárdenas. Matanzas
Phone: (53 45) 61-4721

**Castell Nuovo**
*Italian cuisine*
Calle 1ra. y 11.
Cárdenas. Matanzas
Phone: (53 45) 66-7786

**La Zarzuela**
*Spanish cuisine*
Hotel Barceló Marina Palace.
Cárdenas. Matanzas
Phone: (53 45) 66-9966

**Cayo Libertad**
*International cuisine*
Marina Dársena de Varadero.
Cárdenas. Matanzas
Phone: (53 45) 61-3730

**Laguna Azul**
*Light Meals*
Hotel Playa Alameda
Varadero. Cárdenas. Matanzas
Phone: (53 45) 66-8822

# WHERE TO DINE
## (VARADERO)

**Chez Plaza**
*International cuisine*
Autopista Sur km. 11, Plaza
América. Cárdenas. Matanzas
Phone: (53 45) 66-8181

**Lai Lai**
*Asian cuisine*
Calle 1ra. y 18.
Cárdenas. Matanzas
Phone: (53 45) 61-3297

**Chiringuito**
*Grill*
Hotel Paradisus Varadero.
Cárdenas. Matanzas
Phone: (53 45) 66-8700

**Las Américas**
*International cuisine*
Carretera Las Américas
km. 8 ½, Mansión Xanadu.
Cárdenas. Matanzas
Phone: (53 45) 66-7388

**Continental**
*International cuisine*
Hotel Varadero Internacional.
Cárdenas. Matanzas
Phone: (53 45) 66-7038

**Las Brasas**
*International cuisine*
Camino del Mar y 12.
Cárdenas. Matanzas
Phone: (53 45) 61-2407

**Continental**
*Buffet restaurant*
Aparthotel Mar del Sur.
Cárdenas. Matanzas
Phone: (53 45) 61-2246

**Las Brisas**
*International cuisine*
Hotel Brisas del Caribe.
Cárdenas. Matanzas
Phone: (53 45) 66-8030

**Coral**
*Buffet restaurant*
Hotel Las Morlas.
Cárdenas. Matanzas
Phone: (53 45) 66-7230

**Las Dalias**
*Buffet restaurant*
Villa Cuba Resort.
Cárdenas. Matanzas
Phone: (53 45) 66-8280

**Coral Negro**
*Fish and seafood*
Calle 1ra. y Punta Blanca.
Cárdenas. Matanzas

**Las Olas**
*Grill*
Hotel Las Morlas.
Cárdenas. Matanzas
Phone: (53 45) 66-7230

**Crucero**
*Buffet restaurant*
Aparthotel Mar del Sur.
Cárdenas. Matanzas
Phone: (53 45) 61-2246

**Las Palmas**
*Buffet restaurant*
Hotel Cuatro Palmas.
Cárdenas. Matanzas
Phone: (53 45) 66-7040

**Dante**
*Italian cuisine*
Calle 1ra. e/ 56 y 58, Parque
Josone. Cárdenas. Matanzas
Phone: (53 45) 66-7738

**Las Perlas**
*International cuisine*
Hotel & Villas Tortuga.
Cárdenas. Matanzas
Phone: (53 45) 61-4747

**Dolce Vita**
*Italian cuisine*
Hotel Arenas Doradas.
Cárdenas. Matanzas
Phone: (53 45) 66-8150

**Lindamar**
*Buffet restaurant*
Hotel Barceló Solymar Beach
Resort. Cárdenas. Matanzas
Phone: (53 45) 61-4499

**Don Alfredo**
*Italian cuisine*
Hotel Bella Costa.
Cárdenas. Matanzas
Phone: (53 45) 66-7210

**Los Bohíos**
*Grill*
Hotel Breezes Varadero.
Cárdenas. Matanzas
Phone: (53 45) 66-7030

**Don Alfredo**
*Italian cuisine*
Hotel Playa Alameda Varadero.
Cárdenas. Matanzas
Phone: (53 45) 66-8822

# WHERE TO DINE
## (VARADERO)

**Los Corales**
*Italian cuisine*
Hotel Barceló Solymar Beach
Resort. Cárdenas. Matanzas
Phone: (53 45) 61-4499

**El Brocal**
*Buffet restaurant*
Villas Punta Blanca.
Cárdenas. Matanzas
Phone: (53 45) 66-8050

**Mesón del Quijote**
*International cuisine*
Carretera de Las Américas
km. 1, Cárdenas. Matanzas
Phone: (53 45) 66-7796

**Doñaneli**
*Baking-Pastry*
Calle 1ra. y 43.
Cárdenas. Matanzas
Phone: (53 45) 66-7578

**Marina Chapelín**
*Fish and seafood*
Carretera Las Morlas
km. 12 ½ Cárdenas. Matanzas
Phone: (53 45) 66-7550

**El Caribeño**
*Grill*
Hotel Sol Palmeras.
Cárdenas. Matanzas
Phone: (53 45) 66-7009

**Los Corales**
*Italian cuisine*
Hotel Los Delfines.
Cárdenas. Matanzas
Phone: (53 45) 66-7720

**El Buho**
*Buffet restaurant*
Hotel Acuazul.
Cárdenas. Matanzas
Phone: (53 45) 66-7132

**Mi Casita**
*International cuisine*
Camino del Mar e/ 11 y 12.
Cárdenas. Matanzas
Phone: (53 45) 61-3787

**El Arlequino**
*Italian cuisine*
Hotel Barceló Marina Palace.
Cárdenas. Matanzas
Phone: (53 45) 66-9966

**Martino´s**
*Italian cuisine*
Hotel Breezes Varadero.
Cárdenas. Matanzas
Phone: (53 45) 66-7030

**El Colibrí**
*International cuisine*
Hotel Tuxpan.
Cárdenas. Matanzas
Phone: (53 45) 66-7560

**Los Jardines**
*Buffet restaurant*
Hotel Arenas Blancas.
Cárdenas. Matanzas
Phone: (53 45) 61-4450

**El Cactus**
*Mexican cuisine*
Hotel Iberostar Barlovento.
Cárdenas. Matanzas
Phone: (53 45) 66-7140

**Mirador**
*International cuisine*
Hotel Bella Costa.
Cárdenas. Matanzas
Phone: (53 45) 66-7210

**El Arrecife**
*Fish and seafood*
Calle 13 y Camino del Mar.
Cárdenas. Matanzas
Phone: (53 45) 61-3787

**Mediterráneo**
*International cuisine*
Calle 54 y 1ra.
Cárdenas. Matanzas
Phone: (53 45) 61-2460

**El Criollo**
*Cuban cuisine*
Villa Cuba Resort.
Cárdenas. Matanzas
Phone: (53 45) 66-8280

**Mallorca**
*International cuisine*
Calle 1ra. e/ 61 y 62.
Cárdenas. Matanzas
Phone: (53 45) 66-7746

**El Candil**
*Cuban cuisine*
Hotel Kawama.
Cárdenas. Matanzas
Phone: (53 45) 61-4416

**Mistral**
*Buffet restaurant*
Hotel Sol Sirenas-Coral.
Cárdenas. Matanzas
Phone: (53 45) 66-8070

# WHERE TO DINE
## (VARADERO)

**El Criollo**
*Cuban cuisine*
Calle 1ra. y 18.
Cárdenas. Matanzas
Phone: (53 45) 61-4794

**Natura**
*International cuisine*
Hotel Arenas Doradas.
Cárdenas. Matanzas
Phone: (53 45) 66-8150

**El Dorado**
*Buffet restaurant*
Hotel Playa de Oro.
Cárdenas. Matanzas
Phone: (53 45) 66-8566

**Nautilus**
*Buffet restaurant*
Hotel Sun Beach.
Cárdenas. Matanzas
Phone: (53 45) 66-7490

**El Dorado**
*Buffet restaurant*
Villa La Mar.
Cárdenas. Matanzas
Phone: (53 45) 61-3910

**O Sole Mio**
*Italian cuisine*
Hotel Sol Palmeras.
Cárdenas. Matanzas
Phone: (53 45) 66-7009

**El Dujo**
*International cuisine*
Hotel Sun Beach.
Cárdenas. Matanzas
Phone: (53 45) 66-7490

**Oshin**
*Asian cuisine*
Hotel Sol Palmeras.
Cárdenas. Matanzas
Phone: (53 45) 66-7009

**El Escarpe**
*Buffet restaurant*
Hotel Arenas Doradas.
Cárdenas. Matanzas
Phone: (53 45) 66-8150

**Palma Real**
*Buffet restaurant*
Hotel Tryp Península Varadero.
Cárdenas. Matanzas
Phone: (53 45) 66-8800

**El Faro**
*Fish and seafood*
Hotel Barceló Marina Palace.
Cárdenas. Matanzas
Phone: (53 45) 66-9966

**Panorama**
*Light Meals*
Hotel Varadero Internacional.
Cárdenas. Matanzas
Phone: (53 45) 66-7038

**El Flamboyan**
*International cuisine*
Hotel Palma Real.
Cárdenas. Matanzas
Phone: (53 45) 61-4555

**Papa Fundo**
*Light Meals*
Hotel Acuazul.
Cárdenas. Matanzas
Phone: (53 45) 66-7132

**El Framboyán**
*Light Meals*
Hotel Barlovento.
Cárdenas. Matanzas
Phone: (53 45) 66-7140

**Pizza Nova**
*Italian cuisine*
Autopista Sur km. 11, Plaza
América. Cárdenas. Matanzas
Phone: (53 45) 66-8181

**El Fuerte**
*Buffet restaurant*
Hotel Club Tropical.
Cárdenas. Matanzas
Phone: (53 45) 61-3915

**Pizzería**
*Italian cuisine*
Oasis Tennis Centre.
Cárdenas. Matanzas
Phone: (53 45) 66-7380

**El Galeón**
*Buffet restaurant*
Aparthotel Mar del Sur.
Cárdenas. Matanzas
Phone: (53 45) 61-2246

**Playa Caleta**
*Cuban cuisine*
Hotel Playa de Oro.
Cárdenas. Matanzas
Phone: (53 45) 66-8566

**El Galeón**
*Grill*
Hotel Arenas Doradas.
Cárdenas. Matanzas
Phone: (53 45) 66-8150

# WHERE TO DINE
## (VARADERO)

**Puesta de Sol**
*Cuban cuisine*
Villas Punta Blanca.
Cárdenas. Matanzas
Phone: (53 45) 66-8050

**El Galeón**
*Fish and seafood*
Marina Gaviota Varadero.
Cárdenas. Matanzas
Phone: (53 45) 61-6296

**Pullman**
*International cuisine*
Hotel Pullman.
Cárdenas. Matanzas
Phone: (53 45) 66-7161

**El Habanero**
*Buffet restaurant*
Hotel Varadero 1920.
Cárdenas. Matanzas
Phone: (53 45) 66-8288

**Quianmen**
*Asian cuisine*
Hotel Sol Sirenas-Coral.
Cárdenas. Matanzas
Phone: (53 45) 66-8070

**El Istmo**
*International cuisine*
Hotel Dos Mares.
Cárdenas. Matanzas
Phone: (53 45) 61-2702

**Rancho "El Caney"**
*International cuisine*
Calle 1ra. y 40.
Cárdenas. Matanzas

**El Marino**
*Fish and seafood*
Hotel Arenas Blancas.
Cárdenas. Matanzas
Phone: (53 45) 61-4450

**Ranchón Arizona**
*International cuisine*
Hotel Meliá Las Antillas.
Cárdenas. Matanzas
Phone: (53 45) 66-8470

**El Melaíto**
*Cuban cuisine*
Calle 38 y 1ra. Ave.
Cárdenas. Matanzas

**Ranchón del Caribe**
*Cuban cuisine*
Villa La Mar.
Cárdenas. Matanzas
Phone: (53 45) 61-3910

**El Mojito**
*Cuban cuisine*
Hotel Breezes Varadero.
Cárdenas. Matanzas
Phone: (53 45) 66-7030

**Ranchón El Compay**
*Cuban cuisine*
Calle 54 e/ 1ra. y Playa.
Cárdenas. Matanzas
Phone: (53 45) 61-2460

**El Nilo**
*Buffet restaurant*
Oasis Tennis Centre.
Cárdenas. Matanzas
Phone: (53 45) 66-7380

**Ranchón El Criollito**
*Cuban cuisine*
Calle 1ra y 40.
Cárdenas. Matanzas
Phone: (53 45) 61-2180

**El Paso**
*Light Meals*
Hotel & Villas Tortuga.
Cárdenas. Matanzas
Phone: (53 45) 61-4747

**Ranchón Playa Grill**
*Grill*
Hotel Barceló Marina Palace.
Cárdenas. Matanzas
Phone: (53 45) 66-9966

**El Paso**
*Light Meals*
Ave. 1ra. y 7, Reparto Kawama.
Cárdenas. Matanzas

**Ranchón Tropimar**
*Buffet restaurant*
Hotel Barceló Solymar Beach
Resort. Cárdenas. Matanzas
Phone: (53 45) 61-4499

**El Picante**
*Grill*
Hotel Varadero Internacional.
Cárdenas. Matanzas
Phone: (53 45) 66-7038

**Reflexión**
*Buffet restaurant*
Hotel Meliá Las Antillas.
Cárdenas. Matanzas
Phone: (53 45) 668470

# WHERE TO DINE
## (VARADERO)

**El Potro**
*International cuisine*
Hotel Herradura.
Cárdenas. Matanzas
Phone: (53 45) 61-3703

**Restaurante Buffet**
*Buffet restaurant*
Hotel Breezes Varadero.
Cárdenas. Matanzas
Phone: (53 45) 66-7030

**El Proel**
*Grill*
Hotel Sol Sirenas-Coral.
Cárdenas. Matanzas
Phone: (53 45) 66-8070

**Restaurante Chino**
*Asian cuisine*
Calle 54 y 1ra.
Cárdenas. Matanzas
Phone: (53 45) 61-2460

**El Rancho**
*Mexican cuisine*
Hotel Tuxpan.
Cárdenas. Matanzas
Phone: (53 45) 66-7560

**Restaurante Especial
A la Carte**
*International cuisine*
Hotel Arenas Blancas.
Cárdenas. Matanzas
Phone: (53 45) 61-4450

**El Ranchón**
*Light Meals*
Hotel Taínos.
Cárdenas. Matanzas
Phone: (53 45) 66-8656

**Restaurantes de Pizzas
y Pastas**
*Italian cuisine*
Hotel Arenas Blancas.
Cárdenas. Matanzas
Phone: (53 45) 61-4450

**El Ranchón**
*Grill*
Hotel Cuatro Palmas.
Cárdenas. Matanzas
Phone: (53 45) 66-7040

**Rizzolino**
*Italian cuisine*
Hotel Kawama.
Cárdenas. Matanzas
Phone: (53 45) 61-4416

**El Retiro**
*International cuisine*
Calle 1ra. e/ 56 y 58, Parque
Josone. Cárdenas. Matanzas
Phone: (53 45) 66-7228

**Salón de la Reina**
*International cuisine*
Calle 1ra. e/ 25 y 26.
Cárdenas. Matanzas
Phone: (53 45) 66-7736

**El Rodizio**
*International cuisine*
Hotel Taínos.
Cárdenas. Matanzas
Phone: (53 45) 66-8656

**Salón Violeta**
*Italian cuisine*
Calle 44 y 1ra.
Cárdenas. Matanzas
Phone: (53 45) 61-2866

**El Timonel**
*Buffet restaurant*
Hotel Sol Sirenas-Coral.
Cárdenas. Matanzas
Phone: (53 45) 66-8070

**Santa Clara**
*French cuisine*
Hotel Varadero 1920.
Cárdenas. Matanzas
Phone: (53 45) 66-8288

**El Toro**
*Red meat*
Hotel Club Tropical.
Cárdenas. Matanzas
Phone: (53 45) 61-3915

**Schooners**
*Fish and seafood*
Hotel Meliá Las Antillas.
Cárdenas. Matanzas
Phone: (53 45) 668470

**Fantasía**
*International cuisine*
Hotel Brisas del Caribe.
Cárdenas. Matanzas
Phone: (53 45) 66-8030

**Semi**
*Buffet restaurant*
Hotel Club Puntarena.
Cárdenas. Matanzas
Phone: (53 45) 66-7125

**Fuerteventura**
*International cuisine*
Hotel Meliá Varadero.
Cárdenas. Matanzas
Phone: (53 45) 66-7013

# WHERE TO DINE
## (VARADERO)

**Sirena**
*Light Meals*
Villa La Mar.
Cárdenas. Matanzas
Phone: (53 45) 61-3910

**Guaimaré**
*International cuisine*
Ave. 1ra. e/ 26 y 27.
Cárdenas. Matanzas
Phone: (53 45) 61-1893

**Taíno**
*Light Meals*
Hotel Brisas del Caribe.
Cárdenas. Matanzas
Phone: (53 45) 66-8030

**Gran Canal**
*International cuisine*
Hotel Kawama.
Cárdenas. Matanzas
Phone: (53 45) 61-4416

**Splash**
*Grill*
Villas Punta Blanca.
Cárdenas. Matanzas
Phone: (53 45) 66-8050

**Islas**
*Buffet restaurant*
Hotel Club Amigo Varadero.
Cárdenas. Matanzas
Phone: (53 45) 66-8243

**Sirocco**
*International cuisine*
Hotel Sol Sirenas-Coral.
Cárdenas. Matanzas
Phone: (53 45) 66-8070

**Guantanamera**
*Light Meals*
Hotel Meliá Varadero.
Cárdenas. Matanzas
Phone: (53 45) 66-7013

**Tihulam**
*Asian cuisine*
Hotel Palma Real.
Cárdenas. Matanzas
Phone: (53 45) 61-4555

**Grill**
*Grill*
Hotel Brisas del Caribe.
Cárdenas. Matanzas
Phone: (53 45) 66-8030

**Stella Di Mare**
*Italian cuisine*
Hotel Paradisus Varadero.
Cárdenas. Matanzas
Phone: (53 45) 66-8700

**Kiki´s Club**
*Italian cuisine*
Ave. 1ra. y 6.
Cárdenas. Matanzas
Phone: (53 45) 61-4115

**Sol Cubano**
*Cuban cuisine*
Hotel Sol Palmeras.
Cárdenas. Matanzas
Phone: (53 45) 66-7009

**Halong**
*Asian cuisine*
Camino del Mar y 12.
Cárdenas. Matanzas
Phone: (53 45) 61-3787

**Tocororo**
*Cuban cuisine*
Hotel Tryp Península Varadero.
Cárdenas. Matanzas
Phone: (53 45) 66-8800

**Grill Los Loritos**
*Grill*
Hotel Arenas Doradas.
Cárdenas. Matanzas
Phone: (53 45) 66-8150

**Taberna Dortmurder Kneipe**
*German cuisine*
Camino del Mar e/ 13 y 14.
Cárdenas. Matanzas

**La Alhambra**
*Spanish cuisine*
Hotel Paradisus Varadero.
Cárdenas. Matanzas
Phone: (53 45) 66-8700

**Sol y Arena**
*Cuban cuisine*
Hotel Barceló Solymar Beach Resort. Cárdenas. Matanzas
Phone: (53 45) 61-4499

**Imperial**
*International cuisine*
Hotel Los Delfines.
Cárdenas. Matanzas
Phone: (53 45) 66-7720

**Tortuga Grill**
*International cuisine*
Hotel & Villas Tortuga.
Cárdenas. Matanzas
Phone: (53 45) 61-4747

# WHERE TO DINE
## (VARADERO)

**La Arcada**
*International cuisine*
Hotel Meliá Las Américas.
Cárdenas. Matanzas
Phone: (53 45) 66-7600

**Turey**
*International cuisine*
Hotel Paradisus Varadero.
Cárdenas. Matanzas
Phone: (53 45) 66-8700

**La Esquina**
*Cuban cuisine*
Calle 36 esq. a 1ra.
Cárdenas. Matanzas
Phone: (53 45) 61-4021

**Trinidad**
*Grill*
Hotel Meliá Varadero.
Cárdenas. Matanzas
Phone: (53 45) 66-7013

**La Caleta**
*Italian cuisine*
Hotel Meliá Las Américas.
Cárdenas. Matanzas
Phone: (53 45) 66-7600

**Varadero**
*Buffet restaurant*
Hotel Bella Costa.
Cárdenas. Matanzas
Phone: (53 45) 66-7210

**La Arcada**
*Buffet restaurant*
Villas Punta Blanca.
Cárdenas. Matanzas
Phone: (53 45) 66-8050

**Universal**
*International cuisine*
Hotel Varadero Internacional.
Cárdenas. Matanzas
Phone: (53 45) 66-7038

**La Floresta**
*Light Meals*
Hotel Playa Caleta.
Cárdenas. Matanzas
Phone: (53 45) 66-7120

**Trinidad**
*Italian cuisine*
Hotel Varadero 1920.
Cárdenas. Matanzas
Phone: (53 45) 66-8288

**La Campana**
*Cuban cuisine*
Calle 1ra. e/ 56 y 58, Parque
Josone. Cárdenas. Matanzas
Phone: (53 45) 66-7228

**Varadero**
*Buffet restaurant*
Hotel Brisas del Caribe.
Cárdenas. Matanzas
Phone: (53 45) 66-8030

**La Barbacoa**
*Red meat*
Calle 1ra. y 64.
Cárdenas. Matanzas
Phone: (53 45) 66-7795

**Varadero**
*Buffet restaurant*
Hotel Playa Alameda Varadero.
Cárdenas. Matanzas
Phone: (53 45) 66-8822

**La Fondue**
**Casa del Queso Cubano**
*International cuisine*
Ave. 1ra. e/ 62 y 63.
Cárdenas. Matanzas
Phone: (53 45) 66-7747

**Tropimar**
*Fish and seafood*
Hotel Barceló Solymar Beach
Resort. Cárdenas. Matanzas
Phone: (53 45) 61-4499

**La Colina**
*International cuisine*
Hotel Turquesa.
Cárdenas. Matanzas
Phone: (53 45) 66-8471

**Varazul**
*Grill*
Hotel Acuazul.
Cárdenas. Matanzas
Phone: (53 45) 66-7132

**La Cabañita**
*International cuisine*
Camino del Mar y 10.
Cárdenas. Matanzas
Phone: (53 45) 61-3787

**Varadero**
*Grill*
Hotel Meliá Varadero.
Cárdenas. Matanzas
Phone: (53 45) 66-7013

**La Fontana**
*Italian cuisine*
Villa Cuba Resort.
Cárdenas. Matanzas
Phone: (53 45) 66-8280

# WHERE TO DINE
## (HAVANA COLONIAL)

**La Bodeguita del Medio**
*Cuban cuisine*
Calle Empedrado No. 206 e/
San Ignacio y Cuba. La Habana
Vieja. La Habana
Phone: (53 7) 867-1374

**A Prado y Neptuno**
*Italian cuisine*
Paseo del Prado esq. a Neptuno.
La Habana Vieja. La Habana
Phone: (53 7) 860-9636

**Al Medina**
*Arab cuisine*
Calle Oficios No. 12 e/ Obispo
y Obrapía. La Habana Vieja.
Phone: (53 7) 867-1041

**La Casa del Sandwich**
*Light Meals*
Calle Empedrado e/ Tacón
y Ave. del Puerto. La Habana
Vieja. La Habana

**Anacaona**
*International cuisine*
Hotel Saratoga.
La Habana Vieja. La Habana
Phone: (53 7) 866-4317

**La Casablanca**
*Light Meals*
Calle Empedrado esq. a Tacón.
La Habana Vieja. La Habana
Phone: (53 7) 867-1027

**Bar Cabaña**
*White meat*
Calle Cuba No. 12.
La Habana Vieja. La Habana
Phone: (53 7) 860-5670

**La Dichosa**
*Light Meals*
Calle Obispo esq. a Compostela.
La Habana Vieja. La Habana

**Bodegón "Onda"**
*Spanish cuisine*
Hotel El Comendador.
La Habana Vieja. La Habana
Phone: (53 7) 867-1037

**La Dominica**
*Italian cuisine*
Calle O'Reilly No. 108
esquina a Mercaderes.
La Habana Vieja. La Habana
Phone: (53 7) 860-2918

**Café del Oriente**
*International cuisine*
Calle Oficios esq. a Amargura.
La Habana Vieja. La Habana
Phone: (53 7) 860-6686

**La Eminencia**
*Baking-Pastry*
Calle Jesús María esq. a
Compostela. La Habana Vieja.
La Habana

**Café del Prado**
*Light Meals*
Hotel Caribbean.
Centro Habana. La Habana
Phone: (53 7) 860-8233

**La Floridana**
*International cuisine*
Hotel Florida.
La Habana Vieja. La Habana
Phone: (53 7) 862-4127

**Café La Logia**
*Light Meals*
Capitolio de La Habana.
La Habana Vieja. La Habana

**La Marina**
*International cuisine*
Calle Teniente Rey esq. a Oficios.
La Habana Vieja. La Habana
Phone: (53 7) 862-9510

**Café Taberna "Benny Moré"**
*International cuisine*
Calle Mercaderes esq. a
Teniente Rey. La Habana Vieja.
La Habana
Phone: (53 7) 861-1637

**La Mina**
*Cuban cuisine*
Calle Obispo No. 106 esq. a
Oficios. La Habana Vieja.
La Habana
Phone: (53 7) 862-0216

**Cantabria**
*International cuisine*
Hotel Armadores de Santander.
La Habana Vieja. La Habana
Phone: (53 7) 862-8000

**La Paella**
*Paellas*
Hostal Valencia.
La Habana Vieja. La Habana
Phone: (53 7) 867-1037

**Casa de las Infusiones**
*Light Meals*
Calle Mercaderes e/ Obispo y
Obrapía. La Habana Vieja.
La Habana

# WHERE TO DINE
## (HAVANA COLONIAL)

**Don Ricardo**
*International cuisine*
Hotel Palacio O'Farrill.
La Habana Vieja. La Habana
Phone: (53 7) 860-5080

**La Zaragozana**
*Spanish cuisine*
Calle Monserrate No. 352.
La Habana Vieja. La Habana
Phone: (53 7) 867-1033

**Doña Isabel**
*Light Meals*
Calle Tacón No. 4.
La Habana Vieja. La Habana
Phone: (53 7) 867-1027

**Las Columnas**
*Light Meals*
Hotel Florida.
La Habana Vieja. La Habana
Phone: (53 7) 862-4127

**El Baturro**
*Spanish cuisine*
Calle Egido No. 661 e/ Jesús
María y Merced.
La Habana Vieja. La Habana
Phone: (53 7) 860-9078

**Las Palmeras de
Tallapiedra**
*Cuban cuisine*
Calle Tallapiedra e/ Alambique
y Diaria. La Habana Vieja.
Phone: (53 7) 862-8349

**El Bosquecito**
Calle O'Reilly esq. a San Ignacio
La Habana Vieja. La Habana
Phone: (53 7) 33-5670

**Las Terrazas de Prado**
*Light Meals*
Paseo del Prado esq. a Genios.
La Habana Vieja. La Habana
Phone: (53 7) 863-2814

**El Colonial**
*International cuisine*
Hotel Inglaterra.
La Habana Vieja. La Habana
Phone: (53 7) 860-8594

**Los Cañones**
*Light Meals*
Calle Cuba esq. a Peña Pobre.
La Habana Vieja. La Habana
Phone: (53 7) 860-5670

**El Condado**
*International cuisine*
Hotel Santa Isabel.
La Habana Vieja. La Habana
Phone: (53 7) 860-8201

**Los Marinos**
*Light Meals*
Calle Egido esq. a Merced.
La Habana Vieja. La Habana
Phone: (53 7) 862-1773

**El Corojo**
*Light Meals*
Hotel Conde de Villanueva.
La Habana Vieja. La Habana
Phone: (53 7) 862-9293

**Los Marinos**
*Fish and seafood*
Ave. del Puerto e/ Justiz y
Obrapía. La Habana Vieja.
La Habana
Phone: (53 7) 867-1402

**El Floridita**
*Fish and seafood*
Calle Obispo No. 557 esq. a
Moserrate. La Habana Vieja.
La Habana
Phone: (53 7) 867-1300

**Los Portales**
*Cuban cuisine*
Hotel Plaza. La Habana Vieja.
La Habana
Phone: (53 7) 860-8591

**El Globo**
*Light Meals*
Hotel Santa Isabel.
La Habana Vieja. La Habana
Phone: (53 7) 860-8201

**Mediterráneo**
*International cuisine*
Hotel Parque Central.
La Habana Vieja. La Habana
Phone: (53 7) 860-6627

**El Laurel**
*Light Meals*
Calle Obispo esq. a Compostela.
La Habana Vieja. La Habana

**Park View**
*International cuisine*
Hotel Park View.
La Habana Vieja. La Habana
Phone: (53 7) 861-3293

**El Louvre**
*Light Meals*
Hotel Inglaterra.
La Habana Vieja. La Habana
Phone: (53 7) 860-8594

# WHERE TO DINE
## (HAVANA COLONIAL)

**Pastelería Francesa**
*Baking-Pastry*
Paseo del Prado e/ San Rafael
y Neptuno. La Habana Vieja.
Phone: (53 7) 862-0739

**El Mercurio**
*Diet-Vegetarian Cuisine*
Lonja del Comercio, Plaza de
San Francisco de Asís.
La Habana Vieja. La Habana
Phone: (53 7) 860-6168

**Plaza de Armas**
*International cuisine*
Hotel Ambos Mundos.
La Habana Vieja. La Habana
Phone: (53 7) 860-9530

**El Mesón de la Flota**
*Spanish cuisine*
Calle Mercaderes No. 257 e/
Teniente Rey y Amargura.
La Habana Vieja. La Habana
Phone: (53 7) 863-3838

**Prado y Animas**
*Light Meals*
Prado y Animas.
La Habana Vieja. La Habana

**El Naranjal**
*Ice Creams*
Calle Obispo esq. a Cuba.
La Habana Vieja. La Habana
Phone: (53 7) 862-4127

**Puerto de Sagua**
*Fish and seafood*
Calle Egido No. 603 esq. a
Acosta. La Habana Vieja.
Phone: (53 7) 867-1026

**La Dichosa**
*Light Meals*
Calle Obispo esq. a Compostela.
La Habana Vieja. La Habana

**Bodegón "Onda"**
*Spanish cuisine*
Hotel El Comendador.
La Habana Vieja. La Habana
Phone: (53 7) 867-1037

**La Dominica**
*Italian cuisine*
Calle O'Reilly No. 108 esq. a
Mercaderes. La Habana Vieja.
La Habana
Phone: (53 7) 860-2918

**Café del Oriente**
*International cuisine*
Calle Oficios esq. a Amargura.
La Habana Vieja. La Habana
Phone: (53 7) 860-6686

**La Eminencia**
*Baking-Pastry*
Calle Jesús María esq. a
Compostela. La Habana Vieja.
La Habana

**Café del Prado**
*Light Meals*
Hotel Caribbean. Centro
Habana. La Habana
Phone: (53 7) 860-8233

**La Floridana**
*International cuisine*
Hotel Florida.
La Habana Vieja. La Habana
Phone: (53 7) 862-4127

**Café La Logia**
*Light Meals*
Capitolio de La Habana.
La Habana Vieja. La Habana

**La Marina**
*International cuisine*
Calle Teniente Rey esq. a Oficios.
La Habana Vieja. La Habana
Phone: (53 7) 862-9510

**Café Taberna "Benny Moré"**
*International cuisine*
Calle Mercaderes esq. a Teniente
Rey. La Habana Vieja.
La Habana
Phone: (53 7) 861-1637

**La Mina**
*Cuban cuisine*
Calle Obispo No. 106 esq. a
Oficios. La Habana Vieja.
La Habana
Phone: (53 7) 862-0216

**Cantabria**
*International cuisine*
Hotel Armadores de Santander.
La Habana Vieja. La Habana
Phone: (53 7) 862-8000

**La Paella**
*Paellas*
Hostal Valencia.
La Habana Vieja. La Habana
Phone: (53 7) 867-1037

**Casa de las Infusiones**
*Light Meals*
Calle Mercaderes e/ Obispo y
Obrapía. La Habana Vieja.
La Habana

# WHERE TO DINE
## (HAVANA COLONIAL)

**El Paseo**

*International cuisine*
Hotel Parque Central.
La Habana Vieja. La Habana
Phone: (53 7) 860-6627

**Real Plaza**

*International cuisine*
Hotel Plaza. La Habana Vieja.
La Habana
Phone: (53 7) 860-8591

**El Patio**

*International cuisine*
Calle San Ignacio No. 54,
Plaza de la Catedral.
La Habana Vieja. La Habana
Phone: (53 7) 867-1034

**Roof Garden**

*International cuisine*
Hotel Ambos Mundos.
La Habana Vieja. La Habana
Phone: (53 7) 860-9530

**Entresuelo**

*Light Meals*
Hostal Valencia. La Habana
Vieja. La Habana
Phone: (53 7) 867-1027

**Salón Catedral**

*International cuisine*
Hotel del Tejadillo.
La Habana Vieja. La Habana
Phone: (53 7) 863-7283

**Fausto**

*Buffet restaurant*
Hotel Plaza. La Habana Vieja.
La Habana
Phone: (53 7) 860-8591

**San Carlos**

*Light Meals*
Hotel del Tejadillo.
La Habana Vieja. La Habana
Phone: (53 7) 863-7283

**Fornos Chá**

*Cuban cuisine*
Calle Neptuno e/ Prado y
Consulado. La Habana Vieja.
La Habana
Phone: (53 7) 867-1032

**San José**

*Light Meals*
Calle Obispo e/ Mercaderes y
San Ignacio. La Habana Vieja.
Phone: (53 7) 860-9326

**Fundación Havana Club**

*Light Meals*
Ave. del Puerto No. 162.
La Habana Vieja. La Habana
Phone: (53 7) 861-1900

**Santo Angel**

*International cuisine*
Calle Teniente Rey esq. a San
Ignacio. La Habana Vieja.
Phone: (53 7) 861-1626

**Gentiluomo**

*Italian cuisine*
Calle Obispo esq. a Bernaza.
La Habana Vieja. La Habana
Phone: (53 7) 867-1300

**Telégrafo**

*International cuisine*
Hotel Telégrafo.
La Habana Vieja. La Habana
Phone: (53 7) 861-1010

**Hanoi**

*Cuban cuisine*
Calle Teniente Rey No. 507
esq. a Bernaza. La Habana Vieja.
La Habana
Phone: (53 7) 867-1029

**Torrelavega**

*Light Meals*
Calle Obrapía e/ Oficios y
Mercaderes. La Habana Vieja.
La Habana

**Isamán**

*Light Meals*
Ave. del Puerto y Empedrado.
La Habana Vieja. La Habana
Phone: (53 7) 867-1027

**Vuelta Abajo**

*Cuban cuisine*
Hotel Conde de Villanueva.
La Habana Vieja. La Habana
Phone: (53 7) 862-9293

**La Azucena China**

*Asian cuisine*
Calle Cienfuegos esq. a Monte.
La Habana Vieja. La Habana
Phone: (53 7) 860-9181

# WHERE TO DINE
## (HAVANA CITY)

**1830**
*Cuban cuisine*
Calle Calzada esq. a 20,
Plaza de la Revolución.
La Habana
Phone: (53 7) 55-3090

**Habana Café**
*International cuisine*
Hotel Meliá Cohiba. Plaza de
la Revolución. La Habana
Phone: (53 7) 33-3636

**3ra. y 62**
*Light Meals*
Calle 3ra. e/ 62 y 64,
Miramar. Playa. La Habana
Phone: (53 7) 204-0369

**Habana Dentro**
*International cuisine*
Hotel Lido. Centro Habana.
La Habana
Phone: (53 7) 867-1102

**Acqua Marina**
*Light Meals*
Hotel Deauville.
Centro Habana. La Habana
Phone: (53 7) 33-8812

**Itapoa**
*International cuisine*
Hotel Copacabana. Playa.
La Habana
Phone: (53 7) 204-1037

**Al Fresco**
*Light Meals*
Hotel Habana Riviera. Plaza de
la Revolución. La Habana
Phone: (53 7) 33-4051

**Jardín de la Terraza**
*Grill*
Hotel Lincoln.
Centro Habana. La Habana
Phone: (53 7) 33-8209

**Allegro**
*Italian cuisine*
Hotel Panamericano Resort.
La Habana del Este.
Phone: (53 7) 95-1010

**Kasalta Sport Café**
*Italian cuisine*
5ta. Ave. y 2, Miramar.
Playa. La Habana
Phone: (53 7) 204-0434

**Amelia**
*International cuisine*
Calle 3ra. e/ 78 y 80,
Miramar. Playa. La Habana

**Kilimanjaro**
*International cuisine*
Marina Hemingway Hotel y
Villas. Playa. La Habana
Phone: (53 7) 204-7628

**Anacapri**
*Buffet restaurant*
Hotel Capri. Plaza de la
Revolución. La Habana
Phone: (53 7) 33-3747

**Kiosko Atlántico**
*Light Meals*
Aparthotel Atlántico.
La Habana del Este.
La Habana
Phone: (53 7) 97-1203

**Arcoiris**
*International cuisine*
Hotel Bello Caribe. Playa.
La Habana
Phone: (53 7) 33-9906

**L´Aiglon**
*International cuisine*
Hotel Habana Riviera. Plaza de
la Revolución. La Habana
Phone: (53 7) 33-4051

**Asador el Manantial**
*International cuisine*
Calle 28 e/ 5ta. y 7ma.,
Miramar. Playa. La Habana
Phone: (53 7) 204-7410

**La Arboleda**
*Light Meals*
Hotel Nacional de Cuba. Plaza
de la Revolución. La Habana
Phone: (53 7) 33-3564

**Atlántico**
*Italian cuisine*
Hotel Atlántico.
La Habana del Este. La Habana
Phone: (53 7) 97-1085

**La Bella Cubana**
*International cuisine*
Hotel Meliá Habana. Playa.
La Habana
Phone: (53 7) 204-8500

**Bazar 43**
*Light Meals*
Calle 43 y 22. Playa.
La Habana
Phone: (53 7) 202-1872

# WHERE TO DINE
## (HAVANA CITY)

**La Bonanza**
*International cuisine*
Villa Los Pinos.
La Habana del Este. La Habana
Phone: (53 7) 97-1361

**Bim Bom**
*Ice Creams*
5ta. Ave. y 118, Miramar.
Playa. La Habana
Phone: (53 7) 33-9597

**La Brasa**
*Grill*
Hotel Meliá Cohiba. Plaza de
la Revolución. La Habana
Phone: (53 7) 33-3636

**Bim Bom**
*Ice Creams*
Calle 23 y Infanta, Vedado.
Plaza de la Revolución.
Phone: (53 7) 879-2892

**La Casa del Pescador**
*Fish and seafood*
Calle 5ta. e/ 440 y 442, Playa
Boca Ciega. La Habana del Este
Phone: (53 7) 96-3653

**Bodegón Criollo**
*Cuban cuisine*
Ave Monumental, La Cabaña.
La Habana del Este. La Habana
Phone: (53 7) 862-0617

**La Casa del Tequila**
*Mexican cuisine*
Hotel Neptuno-Tritón.
Playa. La Habana
Phone: (53 7) 204-1606

**Boise**
*Light Meals*
Comunidad Turística Marina
Hemingway. Playa. La Habana
Phone: (53 7) 204-7628

**La Cascada**
*Buffet restaurant*
Hotel Comodoro.
Playa. La Habana
Phone: (53 7) 204-5551

**Bosque de La Habana**
*Ice Creams*
Hotel Meliá Habana.
Playa. La Habana
Phone: (53 7) 204-8500

**La Casona de 17**
*Cuban cuisine*
Calle 17 No. 60, Vedado. Plaza
de la Revolución. La Habana
Phone: (53 7) 33-4529

**Bugambil**
*Buffet restaurant*
Hotel Mégano.
La Habana del Este. La Habana
Phone: (53 7) 97-1610

**La Cecilia**
*Cuban cuisine*
5ta. Ave. e/ 110 y 112,
Miramar. Playa. La Habana
Phone: (53 7) 204-1562

**Burgui 23 y H**
*Light Meals*
Calle 23 y H, Vedado.
Plaza de la Revolución.
Phone: (53 7) 33-4500

**La Central**
*Light Meals*
Calle Monte esq. a Belascoaín.
La Habana Vieja. La Habana

**Burgui 26**
*Light Meals*
Calle 26 e/ Kohly y 35, Nuevo
Vedado. Plaza de la Revolución.

**La Divina Pastora**
*Fish and seafood*
Ave Monumental, La Cabaña.
La Habana del Este. La Habana
Phone: (53 7) 860-8341

**Burgui 5ta y 118**
*Light Meals*
5ta. Ave. y 118, Miramar.
Playa. La Habana
Phone: (53 7) 33-9597

**La Estancia**
*Cuban cuisine*
Carretera de Vento km. 8,
Reparto Capdevila. Boyeros.
La Habana
Phone: (53 7) 33-8918

**Burgui 5ta. y 98**
*Light Meals*
5ta. Ave. y 98, Miramar.
Playa. La Habana
Phone: (53 7) 204-0788

**La Estancia**
*International cuisine*
Hotel Bello Caribe.
Playa. La Habana
Phone: (53 7) 33-9906

# WHERE TO DINE
## (HAVANA CITY)

**Burgui América**
*Light Meals*
Calle Galiano y Neptuno.
Centro Habana. La Habana
Phone: (53 7) 33-8430

**La Ferminia**
*International cuisine*
5ta. Ave. No. 18207, Reparto
Flores. Playa. La Habana
Phone: (53 7) 33-6786

**Burgui Línea**
*Light Meals*
Calle Línea y Paseo, Vedado.
Plaza de la Revolución.
La Habana

**La Florentina**
*Italian cuisine*
Hotel Capri. Plaza de la
Revolución. La Habana
Phone: (53 7) 33-3747

**Café 42**
*Light Meals*
Calle 5ta. A e/ 40 y 42,
Miramar. Playa. La Habana

**La Floresta**
*International cuisine*
Hotel Mariposa. La Lisa.
La Habana
Phone: (53 7) 204-9137

**Café D'Porto**
*Italian cuisine*
Hotel Copacabana. Playa.
La Habana
Phone: (53 7) 204-1037

**La Fuente**
*Cuban cuisine*
Calle 72 e/ 41 y 45.
Marianao. La Habana
Phone: (53 7) 267-1584

**Casa Club Horizontes Atlántico**
*International cuisine*
Aparthotel Atlántico.
La Habana del Este.
Phone: (53 7) 97-1494

**La Fuente**
*International cuisine*
Calle 5ta. A e/ 40 y 42,
Miramar. Playa. La Habana
Phone: (53 7) 204-2372

**Chef D'Oeuvre**
*French cuisine*
Club Le Select, 5ta. Ave. y 30,
Miramar. Playa. La Habana
Phone: (53 7) 204-7410

**La Giraldilla**
*International cuisine*
Calle 222 e/ 37 y Autopista,
Reparto La Coronela. La Lisa.
Phone: (53 7) 33-6390

**Chef Vedado**
*Buffet restaurant*
Hotel Vedado. Plaza de la
Revolución. La Habana
Phone: (53 7) 33-4072

**La Maison**
*International cuisine*
Calle 16 e/ 7ma. y 9na.,
Miramar. Playa. La Habana
Phone: (53 7) 204-1543

**Cojímar**
*Fish and seafood*
Marina Tarará.
La Habana del Este.
Phone: (53 7) 97-1159

**La Parrillada**
*Red meat*
Hotel Neptuno-Tritón.
Playa. La Habana
Phone: (53 7) 204-1606

**Colonial**
*International cuisine*
Hotel Lincoln.
Centro Habana. La Habana
Phone: (53 7) 33-8209

**La Pérgola**
*Italian cuisine*
Calle 49-C y 28-A, Reparto
Kohly. Playa. La Habana
Phone: (53 7) 204-4990

**Comedor de Aguiar**
*International cuisine*
Hotel Nacional de Cuba.
Plaza de la Revolución.
La Habana
Phone: (53 7) 33-3564

**La Piazza**
*Italian cuisine*
Hotel Meliá Cohiba.
Plaza de la Revolución.
Phone: (53 7) 33-3636

**Comodoro**
*International cuisine*
Hotel Comodoro.
Playa. La Habana
Phone: (53 7) 204-5551

# WHERE TO DINE
## (HAVANA CITY)

**La Picola Italia**

*Italian cuisine*

Hotel Blau Club Arenal.
La Habana del Este.
Phone: (53 7) 97-1272

**Concha y Cristina**

*Light Meals*

Concha esq. a Cristina.
La Habana Vieja. La Habana

**La Pradera**

*International cuisine*

Hotel La Pradera. Playa.
Phone: (53 7) 33-7467

**Coppelia**

*Ice Creams*

Calle 23 esq. a L, Vedado.
Plaza de la Revolución.

**La Rampa**

*Light Meals*

Hotel Habana Libre Tryp.
Plaza de la Revolución.
Phone: (53 7) 33-4011

**Coral Negro**

*International cuisine*

Hotel Neptuno-Tritón. Playa.
Phone: (53 7) 204-1606

**La Roca**

*International cuisine*

Calle 21 esq. a M, Vedado.
Plaza de la Revolución.
Phone: (53 7) 33-4501

**Costa Norte**

*International cuisine*

Hotel Deauville. Centro Habana
Phone: (53 7) 33-8812

**La Rueda**

*Cuban cuisine*

Calle 294 e/ 181 y 187, Rpto.
El Chico. Boyeros. La Habana
Phone: (53 7) 45-3246

**Cuatro Caminos**

*Light Meals*

Calle Monte e/ Matadero y
Arroyo. La Habana Vieja.
Phone: (53 7) 860-9608

**La Scala**

*Italian cuisine*

Hotel Meliá Habana. Playa.
Phone: (53 7) 204-8500

**Cubanitas 3ra. y 70**

*Light Meals*

Calle 3ra. y 70, Miramar.
Playa. La Habana
Phone: (53 7) 204-2890

**La Taberna del 1830**

*International cuisine*

Calle Calzada esq. a 20, Vedado.
Plaza de la Revolución.
Phone: (53 7) 833-9907

**Cubanitas Focsa**

*Light Meals*

Calle 17 esq. a N, Bajos Edificio
Focsa, Vedado. Plaza de la
Revolución. La Habana
Phone: (53 7) 33-4499

**La Tasca**

*Fish and seafood*

Ave Monumental, La Cabaña.
La Habana del Este. La Habana
Phone: (53 7) 860-8341

**Cubanitas Pavo Real**

*Light Meals*

Calle 7ma. e/ 2 y 4, Miramar.
Playa. La Habana
Phone: (53 7) 204-2315

**La Terraza**

*Grill*

Hotel Meliá Habana.
Playa. La Habana
Phone: (53 7) 204-8500

**Don Cangrejo**

*Fish and seafood*

Calle 1ra. No. 1606,
Miramar. Playa. La Habana
Phone: (53 7) 204-4169

**La Terraza de Cojímar**

*Fish and seafood*

Calle Real No. 161, Cojímar.
La Habana del Este. La Habana
Phone: (53 7) 55-9232

**Dona-Dona**

*Light Meals*

5ta Ave. y 118, Miramar.
Playa. La Habana
Phone: (53 7) 33-9597

**La Terraza di Roma**

*Italian cuisine*

Hotel Comodoro.
Playa. La Habana
Phone: (53 7) 204-5551

**Doñaneli**

*Baking-Pastry*

Galerías de Paseo, Calle 1ra.
e/ Paseo y A, Vedado.
Plaza de la Revolución.
Phone: (53 7) 55-3170

# WHERE TO DINE
## (HAVANA CITY)

**La Torre**

*International cuisine*
Calle 17 No. 55, Edificio Focsa
piso 36, Vedado. Plaza de la
Revolución. La Habana
Phone: (53 7) 55-3088

**Doñaneli**

*Baking-Pastry*
Calle 182 e/ 13 y 15, Reparto
Siboney. Playa. La Habana
Phone: (53 7) 33-6452

**La Veranda**

*Buffet restaurant*
Hotel Nacional de Cuba. Plaza
de la Revolución. La Habana
Phone: (53 7) 33-3564

**Doñaneli**

*Baking-Pastry*
Calle 5ta.A y 42, Miramar.
Playa. La Habana

**La Vicaria**

*International cuisine*
5ta Ave. esq. a 180, Reparto
Flores. Playa. La Habana
Phone: (53 7) 33-9100

**Dos Lunas**

*Buffet restaurant*
Hotel Atlántico.
La Habana del Este.
La Habana
Phone: (53 7) 97-1085

**La Yagruma**

*Light Meals*
Hotel El Bosque.
Playa. La Habana
Phone: (53 7) 204-9232

**El Abanico de Cristal**

*International cuisine*
Hotel Meliá Cohíba.
Plaza de la Revolución.
Phone: (53 7) 33-3636

**Las Antillas**

*Buffet restaurant*
Hotel Habana Libre Tryp.
Plaza de la Revolución.
Phone: (53 7) 33-4011

**El Acana**

*Light Meals*
Hotel Bello Caribe.
Playa. La Habana
Phone: (53 7) 33-9906

**Las Arenas**

*International cuisine*
Villa Armonía Tarará.
La Habana del Este.
Phone: (53 7) 97-1616

**El Aljibe**

*Cuban cuisine*
Calle 7ma. e/ 24 y 26,
Miramar. Playa. La Habana
Phone: (53 7) 204-1583

**Las Bulerías**

*Spanish cuisine*
Calle L e/ 23 y 25, Vedado.
Plaza de la Revolución.
La Habana
Phone: (53 7) 832-3283

**El Ancora**

*Grill*
Hotel Atlántico.
La Habana del Este.
Phone: (53 7) 97-1085

**Las Palmas**

*Buffet restaurant*
Hotel Tropicoco.
La Habana del Este.
Phone: (53 7) 97-1371

**El Bambú**

*Diet-Vegetarian Cuisine*
Jardín Botánico Nacional.
Arroyo Naranjo. La Habana
Phone: (53 7) 44-8743

**Las Ruinas**

*International cuisine*
Calle 100 y Cortina de la Presa,
Parque Lenin. Arroyo Naranjo.
Phone: (53 7) 57-8286

**El Barracón**

*Cuban cuisine*
Hotel Habana Libre Tryp.
Plaza de la Revolución.
Phone: (53 7) 33-4011

**Las Terrasitas**

*Light Meals*
Villa Armonía Tarará.
La Habana del Este.
Phone: (53 7) 97-1616

**El Bodegón del Este**

*Cuban cuisine*
Calle 1ra. y 2da., Playa Boca
Ciega. La Habana del Este.
Phone: (53 7) 96-3089

**Las Terrazas**

*International cuisine*
Aparthotel Las Terrazas.
La Habana del Este.
Phone: (53 7) 97-1344

# WHERE TO DINE
## (HAVANA CITY)

**El Brocal**

*Mexican cuisine*
Calle 5ta. esq. a 500, Playa
Guanabo. La Habana del Este.
Phone: (53 7) 96-2892

**Las Vistas**

*International cuisine*
Villas Mirador del Mar.
La Habana del Este.
Phone: (53 7) 97-1354

**El Chino**

*Asian cuisine*
Vía Blanca km 18.
La Habana del Este.
Phone: (53 7) 97-1097

**Le Roi**

*International cuisine*
Hotel Chateau Miramar.
Playa. La Habana
Phone: (53 7) 204-1952

**El Conejito**

*White meat*
Calle M y 17, Vedado.
Plaza de la Revolución.
La Habana
Phone: (53 7) 832-4671

**Los Doce Apóstoles**

*Cuban cuisine*
Ave Monumental, La Cabaña.
La Habana del Este
Phone: (53 7) 860-8341

**El Cortijo**

*Spanish cuisine*
Hotel Vedado. Plaza de la
Revolución. La Habana
Phone: (53 7) 33-4072

**Los Jardines de Tropicana**

*International cuisine*
Calle 72 e/ 41 y 45.
Marianao. La Habana
Phone: (53 7) 267-1717

**El Cotilo**

*Light Meals*
Hotel Meliá Cohiba.
Plaza de la Revolución.
Phone: (53 7) 33-3636

**Los Nísperos**

*Grill*
Hotel Bello Caribe.
Playa. La Habana
Phone: (53 7) 33-9906

**El Criollo**

*Cuban cuisine*
Hotel Lincoln.
Centro Habana. La Habana
Phone: (53 7) 33-8209

**Los Orishas**

*International cuisine*
Calle Martí e/ Cruz Verde y
Lamas. Guanabacoa.
Phone: (53 7) 97-9510

**El Dorado**

*International cuisine*
Villa Bacuranao.
La Habana del Este.
Phone: (53 7) 65-7645

**Mamá Inés**

*Cuban cuisine*
Hotel Saint John's.
Plaza de la Revolución.
Phone: (53 7) 33-3740

**El Emperador**

*International cuisine*
Calle 17 e/ M y N, Edificio Focsa,
Vedado. Plaza de la Revolución.
Phone: (53 7) 832-4998

**Marakas**

*Light Meals*
Calle O No. 206 e/ 23 y
Humboldt, Vedado. Plaza de
la Revolución. La Habana
Phone: (53 7) 33-3740

**El Galeón**

*International cuisine*
Aparthotel Atlántico.
La Habana del Este.
Phone: (53 7) 97-1203

**Mi Casita de Coral**

*International cuisine*
Ave. Las Terrazas Sur y Ave.
Las Banderas. La Habana del
Este. La Habana
Phone: (53 7) 97-1602

**El Jardín**

*Light Meals*
Hotel Kohly. Playa. La Habana
Phone: (53 7) 204-0240

**Mi Cayito**

*Cuban cuisine*
Laguna Itabo, Playa Santa María
del Mar. La Habana del Este.
Phone: (53 7) 97-1339

**El Juvenil**

*Light Meals*
Calle Monte No. 107.
La Habana Vieja. La Habana
Phone: (53 7) 860-9181

# WHERE TO DINE
## (HAVANA CITY)

**Mi Patio**
*Italian cuisine*
Hotel Kohly. Playa. La Habana
Phone: (53 7) 204-0240

**El Lugar**
*International cuisine*
Calle 49-C y 28-A, Reparto
Kohly. Playa. La Habana
Phone: (53 7) 204-4990

**Mi Rinconcito**
*Italian cuisine*
Villa Los Pinos.
La Habana del Este. La Habana
Phone: (53 7) 97-1361

**El Mandarín**
*Asian cuisine*
Calle 23 y M, Vedado. Plaza de
la Revolución. La Habana
Phone: (53 7) 832-0677

**Mirador Habana**
*Grill*
Hotel Habana Riviera. Plaza de
la Revolución. La Habana
Phone: (53 7) 33-4051

**El Mesón de La Chorrera**
*Spanish cuisine*
Malecón e/ 18 y 20, Vedado.
Plaza de la Revolución.
La Habana
Phone: (53 7) 833-4504

**Miramar**
*Buffet restaurant*
Hotel Meliá Habana.
Playa. La Habana
Phone: (53 7) 204-8500

**El Mirador**
*International cuisine*
Villas Mirador del Mar.
La Habana del Este. La Habana
Phone: (53 7) 97-1354

**Monseigneur**
*International cuisine*
Calle 21 esq. a 0, Vedado. Plaza
de la Revolución. La Habana
Phone: (53 7) 832-9884

**El Náutico**
*Grill*
Villas Mirador del Mar.
La Habana del Este. La Habana
Phone: (53 7) 97-1354

**Montaña de Oro**
*Asian cuisine*
Hotel Lincoln.
Centro Habana. La Habana
Phone: (53 7) 33-8209

**El Nautilius**
*Light Meals*
5ta Ave. y 152, Rpto.
Náutico. Playa. La Habana
Phone: (53 7) 33-05005

**Náutico**
*Light Meals*
Centro Comercial Náutico.
Playa. La Habana
Phone: (53 7) 33-6252

**El Oasis**
*Light Meals*
Paseo del Prado e/ Animas y
Trocadero. Centro Habana.
Phone: (53 7) 863-2122

**Olímpico**
*International cuisine*
Hotel Panamericano Resort.
La Habana del Este. La Habana
Phone: (53 7) 95-1010

**El Palenque**
*Cuban cuisine*
Ave. 17 e/ 174 y 190, Reparto
Siboney. Playa. La Habana

**Pabellón del Tesoro**
*Asian cuisine*
Comunidad Turística Marina
Hemingway. Playa. La Habana

**El Patio**
*Light Meals*
Calle 17 esq. M, Edificio Focsa,
Vedado. Plaza de la Revolución.
La Habana
Phone: (53 7) 33-4499

**Panorama**
*International cuisine*
Hotel Panorama.
Playa. La Habana
Phone: (53 7) 204-0100

**El Patio de Quinta**
*International cuisine*
Hotel Miramar.
Playa. La Habana
Phone: (53 7) 204-3584

**Papa-Sam**
*Asian cuisine*
Hotel Tropicoco.
La Habana del Este. La Habana
Phone: (53 7) 97-1371

# WHERE TO DINE
## (HAVANA CITY)

**El Pedregal**
*International cuisine*
Ave. 23 y 198. La Lisa.
La Habana
Phone: (53 7) 33-7832

**Papa´s**
*Fish and seafood*
Marina Hemingway.
Playa. La Habana
Phone: (53 7) 209-7920

**El Polinesio**
*Asian cuisine*
Hotel Habana Libre Tryp.
Plaza de la Revolución.
Phone: (53 7) 33-4011

**Parrillada**
*Grill*
Hotel La Pradera.
Playa. La Habana
Phone: (53 7) 33-7467

**El Rancho**
*Cuban cuisine*
Calle 140 y 19, Reparto
Cubanacán. Playa. La Habana
Phone: (53 7) 208-9346

**Parrillada**
*Grill*
Hotel Mariposa. La Lisa.
La Habana
Phone: (53 7) 204-9137

**El Ranchón**
*Grill*
Hotel Blau Club Arenal.
La Habana del Este.
Phone: (53 7) 97-1272

**Parrillada**
*Grill*
Hotel Comodoro.
Playa. La Habana
Phone: (53 7) 204-5551

**El Ranchón**
*Cuban cuisine*
5ta. Ave. esq. a 16,
Miramar. Playa. La Habana
Phone: (53 7) 204-1185

**Parrillada La Caribeña**
*Cuban cuisine*
Calle 7ma. esq. a 26,
Miramar. Playa. La Habana
Phone: (53 7) 204-2353

**El Rápido "100 y 51"**
*Light Meals*
Ave. 100 y 51.
Marianao. La Habana
Phone: (53 7) 267-1362

**Pavo Real**
*Asian cuisine*
Calle 7ma. No. 205 e/ 2 y 4,
Miramar. Playa. La Habana
Phone: (53 7) 204-2315

**El Rápido "11 y 4"**
*Light Meals*
Calle 4 e/ 11 y 13, Vedado.
Plaza de la Revolución.
Phone: (53 7) 33-4492

**Pico Blanco**
*Grill*
Hotel Saint John´s. Plaza de
la Revolución. La Habana
Phone: (53 7) 33-3740

**El Rápido "114 y 39"**
*Light Meals*
Calle 114 e/ 37 y 39.
Marianao. La Habana
Phone: (53 7) 267-1452

**Pinomar**
*Light Meals*
Villa Los Pinos.
La Habana del Este. La Habana
Phone: (53 7) 97-1361

**El Rápido "15 y L"**
*Light Meals*
Calle 15 e/ L y M, Vedado. Plaza
de la Revolución. La Habana
Phone: (53 7) 33-4497

**Pizza Nova**
*Italian cuisine*
Calle 17 esq. a 10, Vedado. Plaza
de la Revolución. La Habana

**El Rápido "23 y 14"**
*Light Meals*
Calle 23 esq. a 14, Vedado. Plaza
de la Revolución. La Habana
Phone: (53 7) 33-3992

**Pizza Nova**
*Italian cuisine*
Calle 3ra. esq. a 46,
Miramar. Playa. La Habana

**El Rápido "3ra. y 10"**
*Light Meals*
Calle 3ra. esq. a 10, Vedado.
Plaza de la Revolución.
La Habana
Phone: (53 7) 33-4716

# WHERE TO DINE
## (HAVANA CITY)

**Pizza Nova La Cova**
*Italian cuisine*
Marina Hemingway.
Playa. La Habana
Phone: (53 7) 204-6969

**El Rápido "Camagüey"**
*Light Meals*
Calle Galiano e/ Virtudes y
Concordia. Centro Habana.
La Habana
Phone: (53 7) 33-5622

**Plaza Habana**
*Buffet restaurant*
Hotel Meliá Cohiba. Plaza de
la Revolución. La Habana
Phone: (53 7) 33-3636

**El Rápido "Casablanca"**
*Light Meals*
Ave. 1ra. y 36,
Miramar. Playa. La Habana

**Primavera**
*Buffet restaurant*
Hotel Habana Riviera. Plaza de
la Revolución. La Habana
Phone: (53 7) 33-4051

**El Rápido "Cibeles"**
*Light Meals*
Calle N e/ 23 y 25, Vedado.
Plaza de la Revolución.
Phone: (53 7) 66-2368

**Rancho Mi Hacienda**
*Cuban cuisine*
Calzada de Justiz Km. 4 ½,
Campo Florido.
La Habana del Este. La Habana
Phone: (53 7) 96-4711

**El Rápido "Dominica"**
*Light Meals*
Vía Blanca Km. 13.
La Habana del Este.

**Ranchón Caney**
*Grill*
Hotel Tropicoco.
La Habana del Este.
Phone: (53 7) 97-1371

**El Rápido "El Sol"**
*Light Meals*
Calle 3ra. No. 340, Zona 1,
Alamar. La Habana del Este.
La Habana

**Ranchón El Bajareque**
*Cuban cuisine*
5ta. Ave. e/ 110 y 112,
Miramar. Playa. La Habana
Phone: (53 7) 204-1562

**El Rápido "Faro de Guanabo"**
*Light Meals*
Vía Blanca Km. 26.
La Habana del Este.
Phone: (53 7) 96- 2770

**Ranchón Hatuey**
*Cuban cuisine*
Carretera de Vento km. 8,
Reparto Capdevila. Boyeros.
La Habana
Phone: (53 7) 33-8918

**El Rápido "Faro Infanta"**
*Light Meals*
Calle Infanta esq. a San Rafael.
Centro Habana. La Habana
Phone: (53 7) 33-5951

**Rincón Criollo**
*Cuban cuisine*
Hotel Panamericano Resort.
La Habana del Este. La Habana
Phone: (53 7) 95-1010

**El Rápido "Havana in Bond"**
*Light Meals*
Valle de Berroa.
La Habana del Este. La Habana
Phone: (53 7) 66-9859

**Rossini**
*Italian cuisine*
Calle 5ta. A e/ 40 y 42,
Miramar. Playa. La Habana
Phone: (53 7) 204-2450

**El Rápido "La Estrella"**
*Light Meals*
Vía Blanca y Durege, Rpto.
Santos Suárez. Diez de Octubre.
La Habana

**Salón Cristal**
*Buffet restaurant*
Hotel Neptuno-Tritón.
Playa. La Habana
Phone: (53 7) 204-1606

**El Rápido "La Palma"**
*Light Meals*
Calle Porvenir y Georgia.
Arroyo Naranjo. La Habana

**San Remo**
*Grill*
Ave. 6ta. y 1ra., Playa Boca
Ciega. La Habana del Este.
La Habana
Phone: (53 7) 96-3068

# WHERE TO DINE
## (HAVANA CITY)

### El Rápido
**"La Primera del Cerro"**
*Light Meals*
Calle Santa Catalina y Vento.
Cerro. La Habana
Phone: (53 7) 880-3192

### Shanghai
*Asian cuisine*
Calle 7ma. esq. a 26,
Miramar. Playa. La Habana
Phone: (53 7) 204-2353

### El Rápido "Mantilla"
*Light Meals*
Calzada Managua y Progreso.
Arroyo Naranjo. La Habana

### Snack bar Grill
*Light Meals*
Hotel Miramar.
Playa. La Habana
Phone: (53 7) 204-3584

### El Rápido
**"Rincón Español"**
*Light Meals*
Calle Ayestarán y Requena.
Plaza de la Revolución.
La Habana

### Sylvain
*Baking-Pastry*
Calle Línea No. 951, Vedado.
Plaza de la Revolución.
La Habana

### El Rápido "Sevillana"
*Light Meals*
Calle Zapata esq. a 26. Plaza de
la Revolución. La Habana
Phone: (53 7) 33-4495

### Sylvain
*Baking-Pastry*
Calle 19 No. 3605, Miramar.
Playa. La Habana

### El Rápido "Sierra Maestra"
*Light Meals*
Calle 1ra. e/ 0 y 2, Miramar.
Playa. La Habana
Phone: (53 7) 204-2268

### Tapatío
*Mexican cuisine*
Hotel Panamericano Resort.
La Habana del Este. La Habana
Phone: (53 7) 95-1010

### El Rápido "Ultra"
*Light Meals*
Calle Reina Nro. 109.
Centro Habana. La Habana
Phone: (53 7) 66-9222

### Taramar
*Fish and seafood*
Vía Blanca km 18.
La Habana del Este. La Habana
Phone: (53 7) 97-1097

### El Roble
*International cuisine*
Villa Armonía Tarará.
La Habana del Este. La Habana
Phone: (53 7) 97-1616

### Terracita
*Grill*
Hotel Blau Club Arenal.
La Habana del Este. La Habana
Phone: (53 7) 97-1272

### El Toro
*Red meat*
Hotel Panamericano Resort.
La Habana del Este. La Habana
Phone: (53 7) 95-2866

### Terraza Habana
*Light Meals*
Ave. 47, Rpto. Kohly.
Playa. La Habana
Phone: (53 7) 203-6523

### El Toro
*Red meat*
Hotel Saint John´s.
Plaza de la Revolución.
Phone: (53 7) 33-3740

### Tocororo
*International cuisine*
Calle 18 y 3ra., Miramar.
Playa. La Habana
Phone: (53 7) 204-2209

### Fiat
*Light Meals*
Malecón e/ Marina y Príncipe.
Centro Habana. La Habana
Phone: (53 7) 33-5827

### Tropical
*International cuisine*
Hotel Colina. Plaza de la
Revolución. La Habana
Phone: (53 7) 33-4071

### Fiesta
*Spanish cuisine*
Residencial Marina Hemingway.
Playa. La Habana
Phone: (53 7) 209-7917

# WHERE TO DINE
## (HAVANA CITY)

**Tropical**

*International cuisine*
Hotel Panamericano Resort.
La Habana del Este.
Phone: (53 7) 95-1010

**Finca Guanabito**

*Cuban cuisine*
Carretera de Jústiz km. 4,
Campo Florido.
La Habana del Este.
Phone: (53 7) 96-4610

**Trópico**

*International cuisine*
Hotel Kohly. Playa. La Habana
Phone: (53 7) 204-0240

**Flores**

*Light Meals*
Calle 176 e/ 1ra. y 5ta., Reparto
Flores. Playa. La Habana
Phone: (53 7) 33-6512

**Tucán**

*Buffet restaurant*
Hotel Copacabana.
Playa. La Habana
Phone: (53 7) 204-1037

**Gambina**

*Italian cuisine*
Calle 7ma. esq. a 26,
Miramar. Playa. La Habana
Phone: (53 7) 204-9662

**Gato Tuerto**

*International cuisine*
Calle O e/ 17 y 19, Vedado.
Plaza de la Revolución.
La Habana
Phone: (53 7) 66-2224

**Victoria**

*International cuisine*
Hotel Victoria. Plaza de la
Revolución. La Habana
Phone: (53 7) 33-3510

**Gaviota**

*International cuisine*
Aparthotel Atlántico.
La Habana del Este.
Phone: (53 7) 97-1203

**Villa Diana**

*International cuisine*
Calle 49 y 28-A, Reparto
Kohly. Playa. La Habana
Phone: (53 7) 202-7670

**Gaviota**

*International cuisine*
Hotel Blau Club Arenal.
La Habana del Este.
Phone: (53 7) 97-1272

**Vuelta al Mundo**

*International cuisine*
Hotel Miramar. Playa.
Phone: (53 7) 204-3584

**Wakamba**

*International cuisine*
Calle O e/ 23 y 25, Vedado.
Plaza de la Revolución.
Phone: (53 7) 878-4526

**Habana**

*Light Meals*
Hotel Vedado. Plaza de la
Revolución. La Habana
Phone: (53 7) 33-4072

**Yara**

*Italian cuisine*
Aparthotel Las Terrazas.
La Habana del Este.
Phone: (53 7) 97-1344

**Turquino**

*International cuisine*
Hotel Saint John's. Plaza de
la Revolución. La Habana
Phone: (53 7) 33-3740

**Guanabo Club**

*Cuban cuisine*
Calle 468 e/ 13 y 15, Playa
Guanabo. La Habana del Este.
La Habana
Phone: (53 7) 96-2884

# WHERE TO DINE
## (SANTIAGO DE CUBA)

**Alondra**

*Ice Creams*

Ave. Garzón No. 398 e/ 5ta. y
6ta., Reparto Santa Bárbara.
Santiago de Cuba

**La Fontana**

*Italian cuisine*

Hotel Meliá Santiago de Cuba.
Santiago de Cuba
Phone: (53 22) 687-070

**Baconao**

*Buffet restaurant*

Hotel Bucanero.
Santiago de Cuba
Phone: (53 22) 68-6363

**La Isabelica**

*International cuisine*

Hotel Meliá Santiago de Cuba.
Santiago de Cuba
Phone: (53 22) 687-070

**Balcón de Santiago**

*International cuisine*

Motel Rancho Club.
Santiago de Cuba
Phone: (53 22) 63-3202

**La Punta**

*Cuban cuisine*

Carretera Baconao km. 22 ½,
La Punta. Santiago de Cuba

**Barbecue**

*Grill*

Hotel Carisol-Los Corales.
Santiago de Cuba
Phone: (53 22) 635-6150

**La Teressina**

*Italian cuisine*

Calle Aguilera e/ Calvario
y Reloj. Santiago de Cuba
Phone: (53 22) 65-2205

**Costa Sol**

*Light Meals*

Hotel Balcón del Caribe.
Santiago de Cuba
Phone: (53 22) 691-506

**La Terraza**

*Light Meals*

Hotel Casa Granda.
Santiago de Cuba
Phone: (53 22) 68-6600

**Cupey**

*Buffet restaurant*

Hotel Sierra Mar. Guamá.
Santiago de Cuba
Phone: (53 22) 62-6319

**Lambada**

*Buffet restaurant*

Hotel Carisol-Los Corales.
Santiago de Cuba
Phone: (53 22) 635-6150

**Don Antonio**

*Cuban cuisine*

Calle Aguilera e/ Calvario
y Reloj. Santiago de Cuba
Phone: (53 22) 65-2205

**Las Acacias**

*International cuisine*

Villa Santiago de Cuba.
Santiago de Cuba
Phone: (53 22) 64 1368

**Doñaneli**

*Baking-Pastry*

Calle 15 y 4, Reparto Vista
Alegre. Santiago de Cuba
Phone: (53 22) 64-1869

**Las Américas**

*Light Meals*

Hotel Las Américas.
Santiago de Cuba
Phone: (53 22) 64-2011

**El Caney**

*International cuisine*

Hacienda El Caney.
Santiago de Cuba
Phone: (53 22) 68-7134

**Las Américas**

*Buffet restaurant*

Hotel Las Américas.
Santiago de Cuba
Phone: (53 22) 64-2011

**El Cayo**

*Fish and seafood*

Cayo Granma, Bahía de Santiago
de Cuba. Santiago de Cuba
Phone: (53 22) 69-0109

**Las Caletas**

*International cuisine*

Hotel Balcón del Caribe.
Santiago de Cuba
Phone: (53 22) 691-506

**El Colmadito**

*Light Meals*

Hotel Meliá Santiago de Cuba.
Santiago de Cuba
Phone: (53 22) 687-070

# WHERE TO DINE
## (SANTIAGO DE CUBA)

**Las Columnitas**

*Light Meals*

Calle San Félix y Callejón del
Carmen. Santiago de Cuba
Phone: (53 22) 68-6028

**El Criollo**

*Grill*

Hotel Meliá Santiago de Cuba.
Santiago de Cuba
Phone: (53 22) 687-070

**Leningrado**

*Buffet restaurant*

Hotel San Juan.
Santiago de Cuba
Phone: (53 22) 68-7200

**El Mirador**

*Light Meals*

Carretera de Baconao,
Sigua. Santiago de Cuba

**Los Galeones**

*Buffet restaurant*

Hotel Sierra Mar. Guamá.
Santiago de Cuba
Phone: (53 22) 62-6160

**El Morro**

*Cuban cuisine*

Carretera del Morro Km. 8½.
Santiago de Cuba
Phone: (53 22) 68-7151

**Los Vitrales**

*International cuisine*

Hotel Versalles.
Santiago de Cuba
Phone: (53 22) 69-1016

**El Panalito**

*International cuisine*

Calle Manduley esq. a General
Cebreco, Reparto Vista Alegre.
Santiago de Cuba
Phone: (53 22) 64-1651

**Marinero**

*Fish and seafood*

Hotel Carisol-Los Corales.
Santiago de Cuba
Phone: (53 22) 635-6150

**El Ranchón**

*Light Meals*

Hotel Costa Morena.
Santiago de Cuba
Phone: (53 22) 635- 6126

**Matamoros**

*Cuban cuisine*

Calle Calvario e/ Enramada
y Aguilera. Santiago de Cuba

**El Ranchón**

*Cuban cuisine*

Hotel El Saltón. Tercer Frente.
Santiago de Cuba
Phone: (53 225) 6492

**Orquídea**

*International cuisine*

Hotel Costa Morena.
Santiago de Cuba
Phone: (53 22) 635- 6126

**El Rodeo**

*Cuban cuisine*

Carretera de Baconao, Barrio
Oasis. Santiago de Cuba

**Parrillada**

*Grill*

Hotel Bucanero.
Santiago de Cuba
Phone: (53 22) 68-6363

**El Toro**

*Red meat*

Hotel Las Américas.
Santiago de Cuba
Phone: (53 22) 642-011

**Paso Doble**

*Buffet restaurant*

Hotel Carisol-Los Corales.
Santiago de Cuba
Phone: (53 22) 635-6150

**Finca El Porvenir**

*Cuban cuisine*

Carretera de Baconao km. 18,
Alturas del río Juraguá.
Santiago de Cuba

**Pavo Real**

*International cuisine*

Autopista km. 1 ½.
Santiago de Cuba
Phone: (53 22) 64-1071

**Gran Piedra**

*International cuisine*

Motel Gran Piedra.
Santiago de Cuba
Phone: (53 22) 686147

**Roof Garden**

*Buffet restaurant*

Hotel Casa Granda.
Santiago de Cuba
Phone: (53 22) 68-6600

# WHERE TO DINE
## (SANTIAGO DE CUBA)

**Joturo**
*International cuisine*
Hotel Sierra Mar. Guamá.
Santiago de Cuba
Phone: (53 22) 629110

**San Juan**
*Light Meals*
Hotel San Juan.
Santiago de Cuba
Phone: (53 22) 68-7200

**Kiam Sand**
*Asian cuisine*
Carretera de Ciudamar km. 4 ½
y Entronque de Punta Gorda.
Santiago de Cuba
Phone: (53 22) 69-1889

**Sitio de Compay Segundo**
*Cuban cuisine*
Calle Montenegro s/n,
Siboney. Santiago de Cuba

**La Casa de Rolando**
*Cuban cuisine*
Carrtera Baconao km. 53.
Santiago de Cuba

**Tratoria**
*Italian cuisine*
Hotel Carisol-Los Corales.
Santiago de Cuba
Phone: (53 22) 635-6150

**La Casona**
*Buffet restaurant*
Hotel Meliá Santiago de Cuba.
Santiago de Cuba
Phone: (53 22) 687-070

**Tropicana Santiago**
*International cuisine*
Autopista Nacional km. 1 ½.
Santiago de Cuba
Phone: (53 22) 64-3036

**La Cecilia**
*Cuban cuisine*
Carretera a Ciudamar km. 4.
Santiago de Cuba
Phone: (53 22) 69-1889

**Versalles**
*Grill*
Hotel Versalles.
Santiago de Cuba
Phone: (53 22) 691-016

**Tocororo**
*International cuisine*
Ave. Manduley No. 159, Reparto
Vista Alegre. Santiago de Cuba
Phone: (53 22) 64-1369

**La Cascada**
*Light Meals*
Hotel El Saltón. Tercer Frente.
Santiago de Cuba
Phone: (53 225) 6492

**La Ceiba**
*Cuban cuisine*
Hotel San Juan.
Santiago de Cuba
Phone: (53 22) 68-7200

**Zunzún**
*International cuisine*
Ave. Manduley No. 159 e/ 5ta.
y 7ma., Reparto Vista Alegre.
Santiago de Cuba
Phone: (53 22) 641-528

# WHERE TO DINE
## (HOLGUÍN)

**Acuario Cayo Naranjo**
*Fish and seafood*
Carretera Guardalavaca km. 54.
Rafael Freyre. Holguín
Phone: (53 24) 30-132

**La Ceiba**
*Buffet restaurant*
Hotel Paradisus Río de Oro.
Rafael Freyre. Holguín
Phone: (53 24) 3-0090

**Arenas Nuevas**
*Light Meals*
Villa Don Lino.
Rafael Freyre. Holguín
Phone: (53 24) 3-0259

**La Floresta**
*International cuisine*
Villa El Cocal. Holguín
Phone: (53 24) 46-1902

**Atabey**
*Buffet restaurant*
Hotel Atlántico-Guardalavaca.
Banes. Holguín
Phone: (53 24) 3-0195

**La Foresta**
*Italian cuisine*
Hotel Occidental Grand Playa
Turquesa. Rafael Freyre.
Holguín

**Bucanero**
*Mediterranean cuisine*
Hotel Occidental Grand Playa
Turquesa. Rafael Freyre.
Holguín

**La Guira**
*International cuisine*
Villa Cayo Saetía.
Mayarí. Holguín
Phone: (53 24) 96900

**Carabela**
*International cuisine*
Hotel Sol Río de Luna y Mares.
Rafael Freyre. Holguín
Phone: (53 24) 3-0030

**La Hacienda**
*Buffet restaurant*
Hotel Occidental Grand Playa
Turquesa. Rafael Freyre.
Holguín

**Casa Criolla**
*Cuban cuisine*
Playa Guardalavaca.
Banes. Holguín

**La Higuana**
*Buffet restaurant*
Villa Cayo Saetía.
Mayarí. Holguín
Phone: (53 24) 96900

**Colombo**
*Cuban cuisine*
Parque Nacional Cristóbal
Colón, Cayo Bariay. Rafael
Freyre. Holguín

**La Laguna**
*Grill*
Hotel Paradisus Río de Oro.
Rafael Freyre. Holguín
Phone: (53 24) 30090

**Colón**
*Buffet restaurant*
Hotel Sol Río de Luna y Mares.
Rafael Freyre. Holguín
Phone: (53 24) 3-0030

**La Niña**
*Light Meals*
Hotel Sol Río de Luna y Mares.
Rafael Freyre. Holguín
Phone: (53 24) 3-0030

**Compaygallo**
*Cuban cuisine*
Carretera Guardalavaca km. 3.
Banes. Holguín
Phone: (53 24) 3-0132

**La Pinta**
*Diet-Vegetarian Cuisine*
Hotel Sol Río de Luna y Mares.
Rafael Freyre. Holguín
Phone: (53 24) 3-0030

**Conuco de Mongo Viña**
*Cuban cuisine*
Bahía de Naranjo.
Rafael Freyre. Holguín
Phone: (53 24) 30-915

**La Terraza**
*International cuisine*
Hotel Atlántico-Guardalavaca.
Banes. Holguín
Phone: (53 24) 3-0180

**Conuco´s**
*Grill*
Hotel Playa Costa Verde.
Rafael Freyre. Holguín
Phone: (53 24) 3-0520

# WHERE TO DINE
## (HOLGUÍN)

**La Trattoria**
*Italian cuisine*
Hotel Guardalavaca. Banes.
Phone: (53 24) 3-0218

**El Ancla**
*Fish and seafood*
Cayo Bariay. Rafael Freyre.
Phone: (53 24) 30-237

**La Turquesa**
*Buffet restaurant*
Hotel Guardalavaca. Banes.
Phone: (53 24) 3-0218

**El Bohío**
*Cuban cuisine*
Hotel Paradisus Río de Oro.
Rafael Freyre. Holguín
Phone: (53 24) 3-0090

**El Cayuelo**
*Fish and seafood*
Playa Guardalavaca. Banes.
Phone: (53 24) 30-422

**Las Arcadas**
*Buffet restaurant*
Hotel Atlántico-Guardalavaca.
Banes. Holguín
Phone: (53 24) 3-0180

**Galileo**
*Cuban cuisine*
Hotel Sol Río de Luna y Mares.
Rafael Freyre. Holguín
Phone: (53 24) 3-0030

**Il Ponticello**
Hotel Blau Costa Verde.
Rafael Freyre. Holguín
Phone: (53 24) 3-0510

**El Delfín**
*Fish and seafood*
Playa Guardalavaca.
Banes. Holguín

**Las Carabelas de Colón**
*Fish and seafood*
Cayo Bariay. Rafael Freyre.
Holguín

**El Framboyan**
*Fish and seafood*
Playa Guardalavaca.
Banes. Holguín

**Lucy´s**
*Light Meals*
Hotel Playa Costa Verde.
Rafael Freyre. Holguín
Phone: (53 24) 3-0520

**El Jagüey**
*White meat*
Playa Guardalavaca.
Banes. Holguín

**Mar Azul**
*Buffet restaurant*
Villa Don Lino. Rafael Freyre.
Phone: (53 24) 3-0259

**El Patio**
*International cuisine*
Hotel Paradisus Río de Oro.
Rafael Freyre. Holguín
Phone: (53 24) 3-0090

**Mar y Sol**
*International cuisine*
Hotel Blau Costa Verde.
Rafael Freyre. Holguín
Phone: (53 24) 3-0510

**El Patio**
*Fish and seafood*
Hotel Guardalavaca. Banes.
Phone: (53 24) 30-218

**Martino´s**
*Italian cuisine*
Hotel Playa Costa Verde.
Rafael Freyre. Holguín
Phone: (53 24) 3-0520

**El Toto**
*Light Meals*
Playa Guardalavaca.
Banes. Holguín

**Munahana**
*Asian cuisine*
Hotel Playa Costa Verde.
Rafael Freyre. Holguín
Phone: (53 24) 3-0520

**El Uvero**
*International cuisine*
Playa Guardalavaca.
Banes. Holguín

**Pizza Nova**
*Italian cuisine*
Playa Guardalavaca. Banes.
Phone: (53 24) 30-137

**El Zaguán**
*Buffet restaurant*
Hotel Guardalavaca. Banes.
Phone: (53 24) 30-218

**Restaurante Buffet**
*Buffet restaurant*
Hotel Playa Costa Verde.
Rafael Freyre. Holguín
Phone: (53 24) 3-0520

# WHERE TO DINE
## (CAYO LARGO DEL SUR)

**El Espigón**

*Fish and seafood*

Villa Lindamar.

Isla de la Juventud

Phone: (53 45) 248 111

**Los Quelonios**

*Cuban cuisine*

Hotel Sol Pelícano.

Isla de la Juventud

Phone: (53 45) 248-333

**El Gavilán**

*Italian cuisine*

Villa Iguana.

Isla de la Juventud

Phone: (53 45) 248-111

**Merlin Azul**

*Buffet restaurant*

Villa Capricho.

Isla de la Juventud

Phone: (53 45) 248-111

**Entre Mares**

*International cuisine*

Hotel Sol Pelícano.

Isla de la Juventud

Phone: (53 45) 248-333

**Olazul**

*Buffet restaurant*

Hotel Barceló Cayo Largo Beach

Resort. Isla de la Juventud

Phone: (53 45) 248-080

**La Piazzoletta**

*Italian cuisine*

Villa Coral. Isla de la Juventud

Phone: (53 45) 248-111

**Opalino**

*International cuisine*

Hotel Barceló Cayo Largo Beach

Resort. Isla de la Juventud

Phone: (53 45) 248-080

**La Yana**

*Italian cuisine*

Hotel Sol Pelícano.

Isla de la Juventud

Phone: (53 45) 248-333

**Ranchón Cayo Rico**

*International cuisine*

Marina Cayo Largo del Sur.

Isla de la Juventud

**Las Dunas**

*Buffet restaurant*

Hotel Sol Cayo Largo.

Isla de la Juventud

Phone: (53 45) 248-260

**Ranchón Sirena**

*International cuisine*

Marina Cayo Largo del Sur.

Isla de la Juventud

**Las Trinas**

*International cuisine*

Hotel Sol Cayo Largo.

Isla de la Juventud

Phone: (53 45) 248-260

**Solazul**

*Light Meals*

Hotel Sol Cayo Largo.

Isla de la Juventud

Phone: (53 45) 248-260

**Lindamar**

*Buffet restaurant*

Villa Lindamar.

Isla de la Juventud

Phone: (53 45) 248-111

**Taberna del Pirata**

*International cuisine*

Marina Cayo Largo del Sur.

Isla de la Juventud

**Lindarena**

*Cuban cuisine*

Hotel Sol Cayo Largo.

Isla de la Juventud

Phone: (53 45) 248-260

**Velamar**

*Cuban cuisine*

Hotel Barceló Cayo Largo Beach

Resort. Isla de la Juventud

Phone: (53 45) 248-080

**Los Canarreos**

*International cuisine*

Hotel Isla del Sur.

Isla de la Juventud

Phone: (53 45) 248-111

**Zun Zun**

*Light Meals*

Hotel Sol Pelícano.

Isla de la Juventud

Phone: (53 45) 248-333

# WHERE TO DINE
## (TRINIDAD)

**1514**
*Buffet restaurant*
Hotel Trinidad del Mar.
Trinidad. Sancti Spiritus
Phone: (53 41) 96234

**Los Cobos**
*Grill*
Hotel Trinidad del Mar.
Trinidad. Sancti Spiritus
Phone: (53 41) 96234

**Arrecife**
*Buffet restaurant*
Hotel Costasur.
Trinidad. Sancti Spiritus
Phone: (53 419) 6174

**Ma´ Dolores**
*Cuban cuisine*
Finca Ma´ Dolores.
Trinidad. Sancti Spiritus
Phone: (53 419) 6481

**Bahía de Casilda**
*Buffet restaurant*
Hotel Ancón.
Trinidad. Sancti Spiritus
Phone: (53 419) 6120

**Manacas-Iznaga**
*Cuban cuisine*
Carretera de Sancti Spíritus Km.
12, Valle de Los Ingenios.
Trinidad. Sancti Spiritus
Phone: (53 419) 7241

**El Pescador**
*Grill*
Hotel Ancón. Trinidad.
Sancti Spiritus
Phone: (53 419) 6120

**Caucobú**
*International cuisine*
Hotel Las Cuevas.
Trinidad. Sancti Spiritus
Phone: (53 419) 6133

**Olaya**
*Italian cuisine*
Hotel Ancón. Trinidad.
Sancti Spiritus
Phone: (53 419) 6120

**Don Antonio**
*International cuisine*
Calle Gustavo Izquierdo
No. 118. Trinidad.
Sancti Spiritus
Phone: (53 419) 3198

**Plaza Mayor**
*International cuisine*
Calle Ruben Martínez Villena
esq. a Francisco J. Zerquera.
Trinidad. Sancti Spiritus
Phone: (53 419) 3180

**El Jigüe**
*White meat*
Calle Rubén Martínez Villena
No. 70. Trinidad. Sancti Spiritus
Phone: (53 419) 4315

**Plaza Santa Ana**
*International cuisine*
Calle Santo Domingo y Santa
Ana. Trinidad. Sancti Spiritus
Phone: (53 419) 3523

**Ranchón La Boca**
*Fish and seafood*
Playa La Boca. Trinidad.
Sancti Spiritus

**Hacienda Los Molinos**
*Cuban cuisine*
Carretera Sancti Spíritus km. 35.
Trinidad. Sancti Spiritus

**Ruinas de Lleonci**
*International cuisine*
Calle Gustavo Izquierdo No. 114.
Trinidad. Sancti Spiritus
Phone: (53 419) 3198

**Las Conchas**
*Light Meals*
Hotel Ancón. Trinidad.
Sancti Spiritus
Phone: (53 419) 6120

**Trinidad Colonial**
*International cuisine*
Calle Maceo No. 402.
Trinidad. Sancti Spiritus
Phone: (53 419) 3873

**Lina**
*Italian cuisine*
Hotel Costasur.
Trinidad. Sancti Spiritus
Phone: (53 419) 6174

**Yara**
*International cuisine*
Hotel La Ronda.
Trinidad. Sancti Spiritus
Phone: (53 419) 4011

# WHERE TO DINE
## (SOROA, LAS TERRAZAS & VIÑALES)

**Buenavista**

*Cuban cuisine*
Complejo Las Terrazas.
Candelaria. Artemisa

**Moka**

*Cuban cuisine*
Hotel Moka.
Candelaria. Artemisa
Phone: (53 82) 778600

**Casa del Campesino**

*Cuban cuisine*
Complejo Las Terrazas.
Candelaria. Artemisa

**Parrillada**

*Grill*
Hotel Moka.
Candelaria. Artemisa
Phone: (53 82) 778600

**Castillo**

*Cuban cuisine*
Villa Soroa.
Candelaria. Artemisa
Phone: (53 85) 2122

**Rancho Curujey**

*Cuban cuisine*
Complejo Las Terrazas.
Candelaria. Artemisa

**Centro**

*International cuisine*
Villa Soroa. Candelaria.
Phone: (53 85) 2122

**La Terraza**

*Buffet restaurant*
Hotel La Ermita. Viñales.
Phone: (53 8) 93-6071

**Salto**

*Cuban cuisine*
Villa Soroa. Candelaria.
Phone: (53 85) 2122

**Fonda de Mercedes**

*Cuban cuisine*
Complejo Las Terrazas.
Candelaria. Artemisa

**Casa de Don Tomás**

*Cuban cuisine*
Valle de Viñales. Viñales.
Pinar del Río
Phone: (53 8) 79-3114

**Las Arcadas**

*Cuban cuisine*
Hotel Rancho San Vicente.
Viñales. Pinar del Río
Phone: (53 8) 93-6201

**Casa del Marisco**

*Fish and seafood*
Carretera a Puerto Esperanza
km. 38. Viñales. Pinar del Río

**Mirador Valle de Viñales**

Carretera a Viñales km. 25.
Viñales. Pinar del Río
Phone: (53 8) 79-3205

**Cueva del Indio**

*Cuban cuisine*
Carretera a Puerto Esperanza
km. 38. Viñales. Pinar del Río
Phone: (53 8) 79-3202

**Vitral**

*International cuisine*
Hotel Los Jazmines. Viñales.
Phone: (53 8) 93-6205

**Mural de la Prehistoria**

*Cuban cuisine*
Valle de Viñales. Viñales.
Pinar del Río
Phone: (53 8) 79-3394

**Cuevas de Viñales**

*Cuban cuisine*
Carretera a Puerto Esperanza
km. 36. Viñales. Pinar del Río
Phone: (53 8) 79-3203

**Ranchón San Vicente**

*Cuban cuisine*
Carretera a Puerto Esperanza
km. 38. Viñales. Pinar del Río
Phone: (53 82) 79-3200

**Fausto Azul**

*Grill*
Hotel La Ermita.
Viñales. Pinar del Río
Phone: (53 8) 93-6071

**Restaurante a la carta**

*Cuban cuisine*
Villa Aguas Claras.
Viñales. Pinar del Río
Phone: (53 8) 27-8426

**Jurásico**

*International cuisine*
Villa Dos Hermanas.
Viñales. Pinar del Río
Phone: (53 8) 793223

**Vera**

*International cuisine*
Hotel Los Jazmines.
Viñales. Pinar del Río
Phone: (53 8) 93-6205

# NIGHTLIFE
## (VARADERO)

**Acuabar Los Cocos**
*Pool bar*
Hotel Arenas Doradas.
Cárdenas. Matanzas
Phone: (53 45) 66-8150

**Gran Canal**
*Bar*
Hotel Kawama.
Cárdenas. Matanzas
Phone: (53 45) 61-4416

**Aguja**
*Piano bar*
Hotel Las Morlas.
Cárdenas. Matanzas
Phone: (53 45) 66-7230

**Grumete**
*Snack bar*
Hotel Sol Sirenas-Coral.
Cárdenas. Matanzas
Phone: (53 45) 66-8070

**Alisio**
*Lobby bar*
Hotel Sol Sirenas-Coral.
Cárdenas. Matanzas
Phone: (53 45) 66-8070

**Habana Café**
*Nightclub*
Hotel Sol Sirenas-Coral.
Cárdenas. Matanzas
Phone: (53 45) 66-8070

**Amelia**
*Bar*
Hotel Club Amigo Varadero.
Cárdenas. Matanzas
Phone: (53 45) 66-8243

**Havana Club**
*Disco*
Calle 62 y 3ra.
Cárdenas. Matanzas
Phone: (53 45) 61-4555

**Anaida**
*Pool bar*
Hotel Brisas del Caribe.
Cárdenas. Matanzas
Phone: (53 45) 66-8030

**Havana Club**
*Beach bar*
Hotel Meliá Las Américas.
Cárdenas. Matanzas
Phone: (53 45) 66-7600

**Aquabar**
*Pool bar*
Hotel Meliá Las Américas.
Cárdenas. Matanzas
Phone: (53 45) 66-7600

**Hicacos**
*Bar*
Hotel Playa de Oro.
Cárdenas. Matanzas
Phone: (53 45) 66-8566

**Arábica**
*Lobby bar*
Hotel Brisas del Caribe.
Cárdenas. Matanzas
Phone: (53 45) 66-8030

**Horizontes**
*Snack bar*
Hotel Barceló Solymar Beach
Resort. Cárdenas. Matanzas
Phone: (53 45) 61-4499

**Arcoiris**
*Bar*
Hotel Club Puntarena.
Cárdenas. Matanzas
Phone: (53 45) 66-7125

**Hoyo 19**
*Snack bar*
Carretera Las Américas km. 8 ½,
Mansión Xanadu.
Cárdenas. Matanzas
Phone: (53 45) 66-7388

**Areíto**
*Disco*
Hotel Paradisus Varadero.
Cárdenas. Matanzas
Phone: (53 45) 66-8700

**Isleta**
*Bar*
Marina Dársena de Varadero.
Cárdenas. Matanzas
Phone: (53 45) 61-3730

**Arrecife**
*Pool bar*
Hotel Sol Sirenas-Coral.
Cárdenas. Matanzas
Phone: (53 45) 66-8070

**Jardines Mediterráneo**
*Cabaret*
Calle 1ra. y 54.
Cárdenas. Matanzas
Phone: (53 45) 61-2460

**Arrecife**
*Pool bar*
Hotel Tryp Península Varadero.
Cárdenas. Matanzas
Phone: (53 45) 66-8800

# NIGHTLIFE
## (VARADERO)

**Karaoke 440**
*Nightclub*
Camino del Mar e/ 14 y 15.
Cárdenas. Matanzas

**Atabey**
*Snack bar*
Hotel Turquesa.
Cárdenas. Matanzas
Phone: (53 45) 66-8471

**Kiki´s**
*Snack bar*
Calle 6 y Ave. 1ra.
Cárdenas. Matanzas

**Bar Grill**
*Bar*
Villas Punta Blanca.
Cárdenas. Matanzas
Phone: (53 45) 66-8050

**La Bamba**
*Disco*
Hotel Tuxpan.
Cárdenas. Matanzas
Phone: (53 45) 66-7560

**Bar Karaoke**
*Nightclub*
Autopista Sur km. 11 ½, Plaza
América. Cárdenas. Matanzas

**La Barrica**
*Bar*
Hotel Varadero Internacional.
Phone: (53 45) 66-7038

**La Bomba**
*Disco*
Hotel Playa de Oro. Cárdenas.
Phone: (53 45) 66-8566

**Bar Karaoke**
*Karaoke*
Hotel Arenas Blancas.
Cárdenas. Matanzas
Phone: (53 45) 61-4450

**Bar Marino**
*Bar*
Autopista Sur km. 11 ½, Plaza
América. Cárdenas. Matanzas
Phone: (53 45) 66-8181

**La Boya**
*Pool bar*
Hotel Barceló Marina Palace.
Cárdenas. Matanzas
Phone: (53 45) 66-9966

**Bar Piscina**
*Bar*
Calle 1ra. y 56, Parque Josone.
Cárdenas. Matanzas
Phone: (53 45) 66-7228

**La Caleta**
*Beach bar*
Hotel Brisas del Caribe.
Cárdenas. Matanzas
Phone: (53 45) 66-8030

**Bar Piscina**
*Pool bar*
Hotel Barceló Marina Palace.
Cárdenas. Matanzas
Phone: (53 45) 66-9966

**La Carpa**
*Bar*
Hotel Palma Real.
Cárdenas. Matanzas
Phone: (53 45) 61-4555

**Bar Piscina**
*Pool bar*
Hotel Breezes Varadero.
Cárdenas. Matanzas
Phone: (53 45) 66-7030

**La Cascada**
*Lobby bar*
Hotel Bella Costa.
Cárdenas. Matanzas
Phone: (53 45) 66-7210

**Bar Piscina**
*Pool bar*
Villas Punta Blanca.
Cárdenas. Matanzas
Phone: (53 45) 66-8050

**La Colmena**
*Snack bar*
Calle 1ra. e/ 25 y 26.
Cárdenas. Matanzas
Phone: (53 45) 66-7736

**Bar Piscina**
*Pool bar*
Hotel Meliá Las Américas.
Cárdenas. Matanzas
Phone: (53 45) 66-7600

**La Flor de Asia**
*Bar*
Calle 8 No. 228 e/ Camino del
Mar y Ave. Kawama.
Cárdenas. Matanzas

**Bar Playa**
*Beach bar*
Hotel Meliá Las Antillas.
Cárdenas. Matanzas
Phone: (53 45) 668470

# NIGHTLIFE
## (VARADERO)

**La Gruta**
*Bar*
Calle 1ra. y 56, Parque Josone.
Cárdenas. Matanzas
Phone: (53 45) 66-7228

**Bar Playa**
*Beach bar*
Hotel Taínos.
Cárdenas. Matanzas
Phone: (53 45) 66-8656

**La Guarapera**
*Bar*
Calle 1ra. y 56, Parque Josone.
Cárdenas. Matanzas
Phone: (53 45) 66-7228

**Bar Playa**
*Beach bar*
Hotel Las Morlas.
Cárdenas. Matanzas
Phone: (53 45) 66-7230

**La Hacienda**
*Bar*
Hotel Bella Costa.
Cárdenas. Matanzas
Phone: (53 45) 66-7210

**Bar Playa**
*Bar*
Hotel Cuatro Palmas.
Cárdenas. Matanzas
Phone: (53 45) 66-7040

**La Oliva**
*Disco*
Hotel Playa Alameda Varadero.
Cárdenas. Matanzas
Phone: (53 45) 66-8822

**Bar Playa Fritada Criolla**
*Beach bar*
Hotel Club Amigo Varadero.
Cárdenas. Matanzas
Phone: (53 45) 66-8243

**La Orquídea**
*Lobby bar*
Villa La Mar.
Cárdenas. Matanzas
Phone: (53 45) 61-3910

**Bar Playa Saoco**
*Beach bar*
Hotel Playa de Oro.
Cárdenas. Matanzas
Phone: (53 45) 66-8566

**La Pachanga**
*Disco*
Hotel Acuazul.
Cárdenas. Matanzas
Phone: (53 45) 66-7132

**Bar Sala de Fiestas**
*Bar*
Hotel Barceló Marina Palace.
Cárdenas. Matanzas
Phone: (53 45) 66-9966

**La Palma**
*Lobby bar*
Hotel Taínos.
Cárdenas. Matanzas
Phone: (53 45) 66-8656

**Bar Teatro**
*Bar*
Hotel Barceló Marina Palace.
Cárdenas. Matanzas
Phone: (53 45) 66-9966

**La Patana**
*Nightclub*
Vía Blanca. Cárdenas. Matanzas
Phone: (53 45) 61-9971

**Baracoa**
*Pool bar*
Hotel Meliá Varadero.
Cárdenas. Matanzas
Phone: (53 45) 66-7013

**La Red**
*Disco*
Villa La Mar.
Cárdenas. Matanzas
Phone: (53 45) 61-3910

**Beach Club "Ranchón Bucanero"**
*Beach bar*
Hotel Playa Alameda Varadero.
Cárdenas. Matanzas
Phone: (53 45) 66-8822

**La Sangría**
*Snack bar*
Calle 8 y Ave. 1ra.
Cárdenas. Matanzas
Phone: (53 45) 61-2025

**Benny Bar**
*Bar*
Camino del Mar e/ 12 y 13.
Cárdenas. Matanzas
Phone: (53 45) 61-3787

**La Sirenita**
*Pool bar*
Hotel Bella Costa.
Cárdenas. Matanzas
Phone: (53 45) 66-7210

# NIGHTLIFE
## (VARADERO)

**Bergantín**

*Lobby bar*

Hotel Sol Sirenas-Coral.

Cárdenas. Matanzas

Phone: (53 45) 66-8070

**La Taberna**

*Snack bar*

Camino del Mar e/ 13 y 14.

Cárdenas. Matanzas

**Blue Star**

*Bar*

Hotel Acuazul.

Cárdenas. Matanzas

Phone: (53 45) 66-7132

**La Taberna**

*Bar*

Hotel Breezes Varadero.

Cárdenas. Matanzas

Phone: (53 45) 66-7030

**Bodegoncito**

*Snack bar*

Ave. 1ra. y 40.

Cárdenas. Matanzas

**La Tinaja**

*Lobby bar*

Hotel Playa Alameda Varadero.

Cárdenas. Matanzas

Phone: (53 45) 66-8822

**Bohío Mar**

*Bar*

Camino del Mar e/ 10 y 11.

Cárdenas. Matanzas

Phone: (53 45) 61-2407

**Laguna Azul**

*Snack bar*

Hotel Playa Alameda Varadero.

Cárdenas. Matanzas

Phone: (53 45) 66-8822

**Brisote**

*Pool bar*

Hotel Sol Sirenas-Coral.

Cárdenas. Matanzas

Phone: (53 45) 66-8070

**Las Américas**

*Lobby bar*

Hotel Meliá Las Américas.

Cárdenas. Matanzas

Phone: (53 45) 66-7600

**Buona Sera**

*Bar*

Calle 1ra. y 11.

Cárdenas. Matanzas

Phone: (53 45) 61-2428

**Las Brisas**

*Disco*

Hotel Brisas del Caribe.

Cárdenas. Matanzas

Phone: (53 45) 66-8030

**Calle 62**

*Snack bar*

Ave. 1ra. y 22.

Cárdenas. Matanzas

**Las Dunas**

*Snack bar*

Hotel Barceló Solymar Beach
Resort. Cárdenas. Matanzas

Phone: (53 45) 61-4499

**Camaguey**

*Bar*

Hotel Club Amigo Varadero.

Cárdenas. Matanzas

Phone: (53 45) 66-8243

**Las Olas**

*Snack bar*

Hotel Cuatro Palmas.

Cárdenas. Matanzas

Phone: (53 45) 66-7040

**Carabo**

*Beach bar*

Hotel Paradisus Varadero.

Cárdenas. Matanzas

Phone: (53 45) 66-8700

**Las Palmas**

*Piano bar*

Hotel Meliá Varadero.

Cárdenas. Matanzas

Phone: (53 45) 66-7013

**Caribe**

*Lobby bar*

Hotel Brisas del Caribe.

Cárdenas. Matanzas

Phone: (53 45) 66-8030

**Las Redes**

*Beach bar*

Hotel Barceló Solymar Beach
Resort. Cárdenas. Matanzas

Phone: (53 45) 61-4499

**Casa Blanca**

*Bar*

Autopista Sur km. 8½, Mansión
Xanadú. Cárdenas. Matanzas

Phone: (53 45) 66-7388

# NIGHTLIFE
## (VARADERO)

**Las Sirenas**
*Lobby bar*
Hotel Las Morlas.
Cárdenas. Matanzas
Phone: (53 45) 66-7230

**Chequere**
*Disco*
Villa Cuba Resort.
Cárdenas. Matanzas
Phone: (53 45) 66-8280

**Los Corales**
*Snack bar*
Hotel Los Delfines.
Cárdenas. Matanzas
Phone: (53 45) 66-7720

**Casa de Al**
*Bar*
Villas Punta Blanca.
Cárdenas. Matanzas
Phone: (53 45) 66-8050

**Lobby Bar**
*Lobby bar*
Hotel Club Tropical.
Cárdenas. Matanzas
Phone: (53 45) 61-3915

**Coralia**
*Lobby bar*
Hotel Cuatro Palmas.
Cárdenas. Matanzas
Phone: (53 45) 66-7040

**Las Tejas**
*Lobby bar*
Villas Punta Blanca.
Cárdenas. Matanzas
Phone: (53 45) 66-8050

**Club Hemingway**
*Lobby bar*
Hotel Barceló Marina Palace.
Cárdenas. Matanzas
Phone: (53 45) 66-9966

**Los Delfines**
*Bar*
Hotel Barceló Solymar Beach
Resort. Cárdenas. Matanzas
Phone: (53 45) 61-4499

**Cascada**
*Bar*
Hotel Club Puntarena.
Cárdenas. Matanzas
Phone: (53 45) 66-7125

**Lobby Bar**
*Lobby bar*
Hotel Tuxpan.
Cárdenas. Matanzas
Phone: (53 45) 66-7560

**Cuba**
*Bar*
Hotel Club Amigo Varadero.
Cárdenas. Matanzas
Phone: (53 45) 66-8243

**Latino**
*Lobby bar*
Hotel Varadero Internacional.
Cárdenas. Matanzas
Phone: (53 45) 66-7038

**Coco Mar**
*Beach bar*
Hotel Dos Mares.
Cárdenas. Matanzas
Phone: (53 45) 61-2702

**Los Grumetes**
*Piano bar*
Hotel Barceló Solymar Beach
Resort. Cárdenas. Matanzas
Phone: (53 45) 61-4499

**Cayo Libertad**
*Bar*
Marina Dársena de Varadero.
Cárdenas. Matanzas
Phone: (53 45) 61-3730

**Lobby Piano Bar**
*Bar*
Hotel Meliá Las Antillas.
Cárdenas. Matanzas
Phone: (53 45) 668470

**Cubitas**
*Lobby bar*
Hotel Sol Palmeras.
Cárdenas. Matanzas
Phone: (53 45) 66-7009

**Lecuona**
*Lobby bar*
Hotel Tryp Península Varadero.
Cárdenas. Matanzas
Phone: (53 45) 66-8800

**Continental**
*Cabaret*
Hotel Varadero Internacional.
Cárdenas. Matanzas
Phone: (53 45) 66-7038

**Los Pelícanos**
*Beach bar*
Hotel Arenas Doradas.
Cárdenas. Matanzas
Phone: (53 45) 66-8150

# NIGHTLIFE
## (VARADERO)

**Cueva del Pirata**
*Cabaret*
Autopista Sur km. 11.
Cárdenas. Matanzas
Phone: (53 45) 66-7751

**Mediterráneo**
*Lobby bar*
Hotel Sol Sirenas-Coral.
Cárdenas. Matanzas
Phone: (53 45) 66-8070

**Duna**
*Bar*
Hotel Breezes Varadero.
Cárdenas. Matanzas
Phone: (53 45) 66-7030

**Mambo Club**
*Nightclub*
Carretera Las Morlas km. 14.
Cárdenas. Matanzas
Phone: (53 45) 66-8565

**Disco Bar**
*Disco*
Hotel Breezes Varadero.
Cárdenas. Matanzas
Phone: (53 45) 66-7030

**Mojito**
*Bar*
Hotel Barlovento.
Cárdenas. Matanzas
Phone: (53 45) 66-7140

**Cusubi**
*Lobby bar*
Hotel Paradisus Varadero.
Cárdenas. Matanzas
Phone: (53 45) 66-8700

**Memories**
*Disco*
Hotel Arenas Doradas.
Cárdenas. Matanzas
Phone: (53 45) 66-8150

**Eclipse**
*Disco*
Hotel Sun Beach.
Cárdenas. Matanzas
Phone: (53 45) 66-7490

**Marengo**
*Beach bar*
Hotel Playa Caleta.
Cárdenas. Matanzas
Phone: (53 45) 66-7120

**Don Café**
*Bar*
Hotel Taínos.
Cárdenas. Matanzas
Phone: (53 45) 66-8656

**Náutico**
*Bar*
Hotel Club Puntarena.
Cárdenas. Matanzas
Phone: (53 45) 66-7125

**Daikiri**
*Bar*
Hotel Palma Real.
Cárdenas. Matanzas
Phone: (53 45) 61-4555

**Mirador**
*Bar*
Villa Cuba Resort.
Cárdenas. Matanzas
Phone: (53 45) 66-8280

**El Brocal**
*Beach bar*
Villa Punta Blanca.
Cárdenas. Matanzas
Phone: (53 7) 66-8050

**Martino´s**
*Bar*
Hotel Breezes Varadero.
Cárdenas. Matanzas
Phone: (53 45) 66-7030

**Dos Mares**
*Snack bar*
Hotel Dos Mares.
Cárdenas. Matanzas
Phone: (53 45) 61-2702

**Noche Azul**
*Nightclub*
Calle 60 e/ 2da. y 3ra.
Cárdenas. Matanzas
Phone: (53 45) 66-7415

**Disco Bar**
*Disco*
Hotel Meliá Las Antillas.
Cárdenas. Matanzas
Phone: (53 45) 668470

**Mirador**
*Snack bar*
Vía Blanca km. 18.
Cárdenas. Matanzas
Phone: (53 45) 61-1085

**El Cactus**
*Pool bar*
Hotel Arenas Blancas.
Cárdenas. Matanzas
Phone: (53 45) 61-4450

# NIGHTLIFE
## (VARADERO)

**Oasis**
*Bar*
Hotel Oasis Tennis Centre.
Cárdenas. Matanzas
Phone: (53 45) 66-7380

**El Camino**
*Bar*
Camino del Mar y 11.
Cárdenas. Matanzas

**Palacio de La Rumba**
*Disco*
Ave. de Las Américas km. 4.
Cárdenas. Matanzas
Phone: (53 45) 66-8210

**El Candil**
*Beach bar*
Hotel Kawama.
Cárdenas. Matanzas
Phone: (53 45) 61-4416

**Paso de Carretera Playazul**
*Snack bar*
Vía Blanca km. 18.
Cárdenas. Matanzas
Phone: (53 45) 61-1085

**El Caribeño**
*Bar*
Villa Cuba Resort.
Cárdenas. Matanzas
Phone: (53 45) 66-8280

**Piano Bar**
*Piano bar*
Hotel Breezes Varadero.
Cárdenas. Matanzas
Phone: (53 45) 66-7030

**El Centralito**
*Bar*
Villas Punta Blanca.
Cárdenas. Matanzas
Phone: (53 45) 66-8050

**Piano Bar Delirio**
*Piano bar*
Hotel Brisas del Caribe.
Cárdenas. Matanzas
Phone: (53 45) 66-8030

**El Chiringuito**
*Beach bar*
Hotel Bella Costa.
Cárdenas. Matanzas
Phone: (53 45) 66-7210

**Playa y Arenas**
*Snack bar*
Hotel Arenas Blancas.
Cárdenas. Matanzas
Phone: (53 45) 61-4450

**El Cocotero**
*Pool bar*
Hotel Playa Caleta.
Cárdenas. Matanzas
Phone: (53 45) 66-7120

**Plaza**
*Lobby bar*
Hotel Barlovento.
Cárdenas. Matanzas
Phone: (53 45) 66-7140

**El Colibrí**
*Snack bar*
Hotel Tuxpan.
Cárdenas. Matanzas
Phone: (53 45) 66-7560

**Plaza El Escambray**
*Lobby bar*
Hotel Playa Caleta.
Cárdenas. Matanzas
Phone: (53 45) 66-7120

**El Colonial**
*Lobby bar*
Villa Cuba Resort.
Cárdenas. Matanzas
Phone: (53 45) 66-8280

**Popeye´s Bar**
*Bar*
Hotel & Villas Tortuga.
Cárdenas. Matanzas
Phone: (53 45) 61-2622

**El Coral**
*Bar*
Hotel Playa de Oro.
Cárdenas. Matanzas
Phone: (53 45) 66-8566

**Puesta de Sol**
*Bar*
Villas Punta Blanca.
Cárdenas. Matanzas
Phone: (53 45) 66-8050

**El Coral**
*Bar*
Aparthotel Mar del Sur.
Cárdenas. Matanzas
Phone: (53 45) 61-2246

**Ranchón**
*Bar*
Aparthotel Mar del Sur.
Cárdenas. Matanzas
Phone: (53 45) 61-2246

# NIGHTLIFE
## (VARADERO)

**El Coral**
*Snack bar*
Villa La Mar.
Cárdenas. Matanzas
Phone: (53 45) 61-3910

**Ranchón Bar**
*Bar*
Ave. Playa e/ 52 y 53.
Cárdenas. Matanzas

**El Delfín**
*Bar*
Autopista Sur km. 12.
Cárdenas. Matanzas
Phone: (53 45) 66-8031

**Ranchón Bar**
*Bar*
Hotel Meliá Las Antillas.
Matanzas
Phone: (53 45) 668470

**El Delfín**
*Beach bar*
Hotel Tuxpan.
Cárdenas. Matanzas
Phone: (53 45) 66-7560

**Ranchón Playa**
*Bar*
Hotel Palma Real.
Cárdenas. Matanzas
Phone: (53 45) 61-4555

**El Dorado**
*Snack bar*
Hotel Kawama.
Cárdenas. Matanzas
Phone: (53 45) 61-4416

**Ranchón Playa**
*Bar*
Villa Cuba Resort.
Cárdenas. Matanzas
Phone: (53 45) 66-8280

**El Emperador**
*Lobby bar*
Hotel Los Delfines.
Cárdenas. Matanzas
Phone: (53 45) 66-7720

**Rincón Cubano**
*Cabaret*
Hotel Meliá Las Américas.
Cárdenas. Matanzas
Phone: (53 45) 66-7600

**El Framboyán**
*Pool bar*
Hotel Barlovento.
Cárdenas. Matanzas
Phone: (53 45) 66-7140

**Rincón Latino**
*Bar*
Hotel Bella Costa.
Cárdenas. Matanzas
Phone: (53 45) 66-7210

**El Galeón**
*Lobby bar*
Hotel Dos Mares.
Cárdenas. Matanzas
Phone: (53 45) 61-2702

**Ron Coco**
*Snack bar*
Hotel Sol Palmeras.
Cárdenas. Matanzas
Phone: (53 45) 66-7009

**El Golfito**
*Bar*
Calle 1ra. y 42.
Cárdenas. Matanzas

**Ron Coco**
*Beach bar*
Hotel Meliá Varadero.
Cárdenas. Matanzas
Phone: (53 45) 66-7013

**El Kastillito**
*Nightclub*
Ave. Playa e/ 48 y 49.
Cárdenas. Matanzas
Phone: (53 45) 61-3888

**Santiago**
*Cabaret*
Hotel Meliá Varadero.
Cárdenas. Matanzas
Phone: (53 45) 66-7013

**El Mirador**
*Bar*
Hotel Bella Costa.
Cárdenas. Matanzas
Phone: (53 45) 66-7210

**Saoco**
*Snack bar*
Hotel Tryp Península Varadero.
Cárdenas. Matanzas
Phone: (53 45) 66-8800

**El Mojito**
*Pool bar*
Hotel Sol Palmeras.
Cárdenas. Matanzas
Phone: (53 45) 66-7009

# NIGHTLIFE
## (VARADERO)

**Saoko**
*Bar*
Hotel Palma Real.
Cárdenas. Matanzas
Phone: (53 45) 61-4555

**El Mojito**
*Bar*
Hotel Palma Real.
Cárdenas. Matanzas
Phone: (53 45) 61-4555

**Siboney**
*Bar*
Hotel Turquesa.
Cárdenas. Matanzas
Phone: (53 45) 66-8471

**El Mojito**
*Lobby bar*
Hotel Turquesa.
Cárdenas. Matanzas
Phone: (53 45) 66-8471

**Sol Cubano**
*Beach bar*
Hotel Sol Palmeras.
Cárdenas. Matanzas
Phone: (53 45) 66-7009

**El Náutico**
*Bar*
Aparthotel Mar del Sur.
Cárdenas. Matanzas
Phone: (53 45) 61-2246

**Solymar**
*Lobby bar*
Hotel Barceló Solymar Beach
Resort. Cárdenas. Matanzas
Phone: (53 45) 61-4499

**El Patio**
*Lobby bar*
Hotel Arenas Doradas.
Cárdenas. Matanzas
Phone: (53 45) 66-8150

**Splash**
*Disco*
Villa Punta Blanca.
Cárdenas. Matanzas
Phone: (53 45) 66-7090

**El Peñón**
*Bar*
Hotel Club Amigo Varadero.
Cárdenas. Matanzas
Phone: (53 45) 66-8243

**Taíno**
*Bar*
Hotel Brisas del Caribe.
Cárdenas. Matanzas
Phone: (53 45) 66-8030

**El Picante**
*Bar*
Hotel Varadero Internacional.
Cárdenas. Matanzas
Phone: (53 45) 66-7038

**Tea Corner**
*Lobby bar*
Hotel Sol Sirenas-Coral.
Cárdenas. Matanzas
Phone: (53 45) 66-8070

**El Pony**
*Lobby bar*
Hotel Herradura.
Cárdenas. Matanzas
Phone: (53 45) 61-3703

**Teclado**
*Lobby bar*
Hotel Arenas Blancas.
Cárdenas. Matanzas
Phone: (53 45) 61-4450

**El Ranchón**
*Pool bar*
Hotel Taínos.
Cárdenas. Matanzas
Phone: (53 45) 66-8656

**Tenerife**
*Karaoke*
Hotel Meliá Varadero.
Cárdenas. Matanzas
Phone: (53 45) 66-7013

**El Ranchoncito**
*Bar*
Calle 1ra. y 40.
Cárdenas. Matanzas

**Tennis Bar**
*Bar*
Hotel Breezes Varadero.
Cárdenas. Matanzas
Phone: (53 45) 66-7030

**El Rincón**
*Bar*
Camino del Mar e/ 11 y 12.
Cárdenas. Matanzas

**Toa**
*Pool bar*
Hotel Paradisus Varadero.
Cárdenas. Matanzas
Phone: (53 45) 66-8700

# NIGHTLIFE
## (VARADERO)

**El Taíno**
*Beach bar*
Hotel Turquesa.
Cárdenas. Matanzas
Phone: (53 45) 66-8471

**Tocororo**
*Bar*
Hotel Palma Real.
Cárdenas. Matanzas
Phone: (53 45) 61-4555

**El Trópico**
*Bar*
Aparthotel Mar del Sur.
Cárdenas. Matanzas
Phone: (53 45) 61-2246

**Tramontana**
*Beach bar*
Hotel Sol Sirenas-Coral.
Cárdenas. Matanzas
Phone: (53 45) 66-7240

**Espiral**
*Bar*
Hotel Club Puntarena.
Cárdenas. Matanzas
Phone: (53 45) 66-7125

**Trinidad**
*Bar*
Hotel Club Amigo Varadero.
Cárdenas. Matanzas
Phone: (53 45) 66-8243

**Esplanada Teatro**
*Bar*
Hotel Playa Alameda Varadero.
Cárdenas. Matanzas
Phone: (53 45) 66-8822

**Tropi Fruti**
*Bar*
Hotel Bella Costa.
Cárdenas. Matanzas
Phone: (53 45) 66-7210

**Extasis**
*Bar*
Villa Cuba Resort.
Cárdenas. Matanzas
Phone: (53 45) 66-8280

**Tropi Gala**
*Cabaret*
Hotel Tuxpan. Cárdenas.
Phone: (53 45) 66-7560

**FM-13**
*Snack bar*
Calle 1ra. y 13.
Cárdenas. Matanzas

**Tropical**
*Beach bar*
Hotel Club Puntarena. Cárdenas
Phone: (53 45) 66-7125

**Tropicuba**
*Nightclub*
Hotel Sol Palmeras. Cárdenas.
Phone: (53 45) 66-7009

**Varadero**
*Bar*
Hotel Brisas del Caribe.
Cárdenas. Matanzas
Phone: (53 45) 66-8030

**Fun Pub**
*Nightclub*
Hotel Sol Palmeras. Cárdenas.
Phone: (53 45) 66-7009

**FM-23**
*Snack bar*
Ave. 1ra. y 23.
Cárdenas. Matanzas

**Turquesa**
*Beach bar*
Hotel Sol Sirenas-Coral.
Cárdenas. Matanzas
Phone: (53 45) 66-8070

**FM-27**
*Snack bar*
Ave. 1ra. y 27.
Cárdenas. Matanzas

**Turquino**
*Bar*
Hotel Sol Palmeras.
Cárdenas. Matanzas
Phone: (53 45) 66-7009

**Fortuna**
*Lobby bar*
Hotel Kawama. Cárdenas.
Phone: (53 45) 61-4416

**Varadero**
*Cabaret*
Vía Blanca km. 31 y Carretera a
Cárdenas. Cárdenas. Matanzas
Phone: (53 45) 66-7130

**Fruti Tuxpan**
*Bar*
Hotel Tuxpan. Cárdenas.
Phone: (53 45) 66-7560

**Veraclub**
*Beach bar*
Villas Punta Blanca. Cárdenas.
Phone: (53 45) 66-8050

# NIGHTLIFE
## (HAVANA COLONIAL)

**Ambos Mundos**

*Bar*

Hotel Ambos Mundos.
La Habana Vieja. La Habana
Phone: (53 7) 860-9530

**La Dichosa**

*Bar*

Calle Obispo esq. a Compostela.
La Habana Vieja. La Habana
Phone: (53 7) 861-5292

**Anacaona**

*Bar*

Hotel Saratoga.
La Habana Vieja. La Habana
Phone: (53 7) 868-1000

**La Lluvia de Oro**

*Bar*

Calle Obispo esq. a Habana.
La Habana Vieja. La Habana
Phone: (53 7) 862-9870

**Bar Café Maragato**

*Bar*

Hotel Florida.
La Habana Vieja. La Habana
Phone: (53 7) 862-4127

**La Marina**

*Lobby bar*

Hotel Armadores de Santander.
La Habana Vieja. La Habana
Phone: (53 7) 862-8000

**Bar Mezanine**

*Bar*

Hotel Saratoga.
La Habana Vieja. La Habana
Phone: (53 7) 868-1000

**La Mina**

*Bar*

Calle Obispo No. 106 esq. a
Oficios. La Habana Vieja.
Phone: (53 7) 862-0216

**Bar Monserrate**

*Bar*

Calle Monserrate esq. a Obrapía
La Habana Vieja. La Habana
Phone: (53 7) 860-9751

**La Sevillana**

*Lobby bar*

Hotel Inglaterra. La Habana
Vieja. La Habana
Phone: (53 7) 860-8594

**Bosque de Boloña**

*Bar*

Calle Obispo No. 464 e/ Villegas
y Aguacate. La Habana Vieja.
Phone: (53 7) 866-4139

**La Terraza**

*Bar*

Hotel Inglaterra. La Habana
Vieja. La Habana
Phone: (53 7) 860-8594

**Café O´Reilly**

*Bar*

Calle O´Reilly e/ San Ignacio y
Cuba. La Habana Vieja.
La Habana

**Lobby Bar**

*Lobby bar*

Hotel Palacio San Miguel.
La Habana Vieja. La Habana
Phone: (53 7) 862-7656

**Café París**

*Bar*

Calle San Ignacio esq. a Obispo.
La Habana Vieja. La Habana

**Lobby Bar**

*Lobby bar*

Hotel Caribbean. Centro
Habana. La Habana
Phone: (53 7) 860-8233

**Chico O´Farrill**

*Snack bar*

Hotel Palacio O´Farrill.
La Habana Vieja. La Habana
Phone: (53 7) 860-5080

**Lobby Bar**

*Lobby bar*

Hotel Los Frailes.
La Habana Vieja. La Habana
Phone: (53 7) 862-9383

**Disco Karaoke**

*Disco*

Hotel Plaza.
La Habana Vieja. La Habana
Phone: (53 7) 860-8583

**Los Marinos**

*Snack bar*

Ave. del Puerto e/ Justiz y
Obrapía. La Habana Vieja.
La Habana
Phone: (53 7) 33-8808

**Dos Hermanos**

*Bar*

Ave. del Puerto esq. a Santa
Clara. La Habana Vieja.
Phone: (53 7) 861-3514

# NIGHTLIFE
## (HAVANA COLONIAL)

**Lounge Alameda**
*Bar*
Hotel Parque Central.
La Habana Vieja. La Habana
Phone: (53 7) 860-6627

**El Floridita**
*Bar*
Calle Obispo No. 557.
La Habana Vieja. La Habana
Phone: (53 7) 867-1300

**Mirador Saratoga**
*Snack bar*
Hotel Saratoga.
La Habana Vieja. La Habana
Phone: (53 7) 868-1000

**El Louvre**
*Snack bar*
Hotel Inglaterra. La Habana
Vieja. La Habana
Phone: (53 7) 860-8594

**Nostalgia**
*Bar*
Hostal Valencia. La Habana
Vieja. La Habana
Phone: (53 7) 867-1037

**El Patio**
*Bar*
Calle San Ignacio No. 54,
Plaza de la Catedral.
La Habana Vieja. La Habana
Phone: (53 7) 867-1035

**El Pórtico**
*Lobby bar*
Hotel Parque Central.
La Habana Vieja. La Habana
Phone: (53 7) 860-6627

**Santovenia**
*Lobby bar*
Hotel Santa Isabel.
La Habana Vieja. La Habana
Phone: (53 7) 860-8201

**Fausto**
*Bar*
Hotel Plaza.
La Habana Vieja. La Habana
Phone: (53 7) 860-8583

**Solarium**
*Bar*
Hotel Plaza.
La Habana Vieja. La Habana
Phone: (53 7) 860-8583

**Florida**
*Lobby bar*
Hotel Florida.
La Habana Vieja. La Habana
Phone: (53 7) 862-4127

**Terraza Mirador**
*Snack bar*
Hotel Palacio San Miguel.
La Habana Vieja. La Habana
Phone: (53 7) 862-7656

**Vitral**
*Lobby bar*
Hotel Plaza.
La Habana Vieja. La Habana
Phone: (53 7) 860-8583

**La Bodeguita del Medio**
*Bar*
Calle Empedrado No. 206.
La Habana Vieja. La Habana
Phone: (53 7) 867-1374

**Nuevo Mundo**
*Bar*
Hotel Parque Central.
La Habana Vieja. La Habana
Phone: (53 7) 860-6627

**Fundación Ron Havana Club**
*Bar*
Calle San Pedro No. 262 e/
Sol y Muralla. La Habana Vieja.
Phone: (53 7) 861-1900

# NIGHTLIFE
## (HAVANA CITY)

**70`s Café**
*Disco*
Hotel Deauville.
Centro Habana. La Habana
Phone: (53 7) 866-8812

**La Cecilia**
*Cabaret*
5ta. Ave. e/ 110 y 112,
Miramar. Playa. La Habana
Phone: (53 7) 204-1562

**Aire Mar**
*Bar*
Hotel Nacional de Cuba. Plaza
de la Revolución. La Habana
Phone: (53 7) 836-3564

**La Conga**
*Bar*
Hotel Tropicoco.
La Habana del Este. La Habana
Phone: (53 7) 797-1371

**Arrecifes**
*Snack bar*
Hotel Mariposa.
La Lisa. La Habana
Phone: (53 7) 204-9137

**La Fuente**
*Bar*
5ta. Ave. e/ 110 y 112,
Miramar. Playa. La Habana
Phone: (53 7) 204-1562

**Arrecifes**
*Snack bar*
Hotel Chateau Miramar.
Playa. La Habana
Phone: (53 7) 204-1957

**La Maison**
*Bar*
Calle 16 e/ 7ma. y 9na.,
Miramar. Playa. La Habana
Phone: (53 7) 204-1543

**Atardecer**
*Bar*
Hotel Lincoln. Centro Habana.
Phone: (53 7) 862-8061

**La Pérgola**
*Disco*
Hotel Comodoro.
Playa. La Habana
Phone: (53 7) 204-5551

**Atlántico**
*Cabaret*
Hotel Atlántico.
La Habana del Este.
Phone: (53 7) 797-1085

**La Zorra y el Cuervo**
**Jazz Club**
*Nightclub*
Calle 23 e/ N y O, Vedado. Plaza
de la Revolución. La Habana
Phone: (53 7) 833-2402

**Atlántico**
*Snack bar*
Aparthotel Atlántico.
La Habana del Este.
Phone: (53 7) 797-1494

**Las Bulerías**
*Nightclub*
Calle L e/ 23 y 25, Vedado. Plaza
de la Revolución. La Habana
Phone: (53 7) 832-3283

**Atlántico**
*Pool bar*
Aparthotel Atlántico.
La Habana del Este.
Phone: (53 7) 797-1494

**Las Terrazas**
*Bar*
Aparthotel Las Terrazas.
La Habana del Este.
Phone: (53 7) 797-1315

**Bar Arenas**
*Bar*
Villa Armonía Tarará. La
Habana del Este. La Habana
Phone: (53 7) 796-1616

**Las Terrazas**
*Pool bar*
Aparthotel Las Terrazas.
La Habana del Este.
Phone: (53 7) 797-1315

**Bar Azul**
*Bar*
Hotel Capri. Plaza de la
Revolución. La Habana
Phone: (53 7) 833-3747

**Las Vistas**
*Pool bar*
Villas Mirador del Mar.
La Habana del Este.
Phone: (53 7) 797-1362

**Bar Longina**
*Bar*
Calle 20 No. 3308 esq. a 35,
Miramar. Playa. La Habana
Phone: (53 7) 204-0447

# NIGHTLIFE
## (HAVANA CITY)

**Lido**
*Lobby bar*
Hotel Lido. Centro Habana.
La Habana
Phone: (53 7) 862-0653

**Bar Piscina**
*Bar*
Hotel Tropicoco.
La Habana del Este. La Habana
Phone: (53 7) 797-1371

**Lirio**
*Bar*
Hotel Kohly. Playa. La Habana
Phone: (53 7) 204-0240

**Bar piscina**
*Pool bar*
Hotel Bello Caribe.
Playa. La Habana
Phone: (53 7) 273-9906

**Lobby Bar**
*Bar*
Hotel Comodoro. Playa.
Phone: (53 7) 204-5551

**Bar piscina**
*Pool bar*
Hotel El Viejo y El Mar. Playa.
Phone: (53 7) 204-6820

**Lobby Bar**
*Bar*
Hotel Kohly. Playa. La Habana
Phone: (53 7) 204-0240

**Bar piscina**
*Pool bar*
Hotel La Pradera. Playa.
Phone: (53 7) 273-7467

**Lobby Bar**
*Bar*
Hotel Occidental Miramar.
Playa. La Habana
Phone: (53 7) 204-3584

**Bar Playa**
*Beach bar*
Hotel Comodoro.
Playa. La Habana
Phone: (53 7) 204-5551

**Lobby Bar**
*Lobby bar*
Hotel Bello Caribe.
Playa. La Habana
Phone: (53 7) 273-9906

**Bodegón de los Vinos**
*Snack bar*
Parque Histórico Militar
Morro-Cabaña.
La Habana del Este. La Habana
Phone: (53 7) 866-6475

**Lobby Bar**
*Lobby bar*
Hotel Copacabana.
Playa. La Habana
Phone: (53 7) 204-1037

**Boleros**
*Bar*
Hotel Atlántico.
La Habana del Este. La Habana
Phone: (53 7) 797-1085

**Los Delfines**
*Snack bar*
Hotel Comodoro.
Playa. La Habana
Phone: (53 7) 204-5551

**Café Cantante "Mi Habana"**
*Nightclub*
Teatro Nacional de Cuba,
Calle Paseo y 39. Plaza de la
Revolución. La Habana
Phone: (53 7) 878-4273

**Los Marinos**
*Snack bar*
Villas Mirador del Mar.
La Habana del Este. La Habana
Phone: (53 7) 797-1362

**Café Rodney**
*Bar*
Calle 72 e/ 41 y 45.
Marianao. La Habana
Phone: (53 7) 267-1717

**Los Nísperos**
*Snack bar*
Hotel Bello Caribe.
Playa. La Habana
Phone: (53 7) 273-9906

**Caipirinha**
*Snack bar*
Hotel Copacabana.
Playa. La Habana
Phone: (53 7) 204-1037

**Los Perritos**
*Snack bar*
Hotel Colina. Plaza de la
Revolución. La Habana
Phone: (53 7) 836-4071

**Capri**
*Pool bar*
Hotel Capri. Plaza de la
Revolución. La Habana
Phone: (53 7) 833-3747

# NIGHTLIFE
## (HAVANA CITY)

**Los Tres Monitos**
*Bar*
Hotel Lincoln.
Centro Habana. La Habana
Phone: (53 7) 862-8061

**Capri**
*Lobby bar*
Hotel Capri. Plaza de la
Revolución. La Habana
Phone: (53 7) 833-3747

**Macumba Habana**
*Nightclub*
Calle 222 e/ 37 y Autopista,
Reparto La Coronela.
La Lisa. La Habana
Phone: (53 7) 273-0568

**Capri**
*Bar*
Hotel Capri. Plaza de la
Revolución. La Habana
Phone: (53 7) 833-3747

**Marea Baja**
*Cabaret*
Hotel Mégano.
La Habana del Este.
Phone: (53 7) 797-1610

**Casa de la Música**
*Nightclub*
Calle 20 No. 3308 esq. a 35,
Miramar. Playa. La Habana
Phone: (53 7) 202-6147

**Mégano**
*Snack bar*
Hotel Mégano.
La Habana del Este.
Phone: (53 7) 797-1610

**Casa de la Música**
*Nightclub*
Calle Galiano e/ Neptuno y
Concordia. Centro Habana.
Phone: (53 7) 862-4165

**Mi Rinconcito**
*Bar*
Ave. de las Terrazas y Ave. 5ª.
Sta. María del Mar.
La Habana del Este.
Phone: (53 7) 797-1361

**Chan Chan**
*Nightclub*
Marina Hemingway.
Playa. La Habana
Phone: (53 7) 204-4698

**Mirador**
*Bar*
Villas Mirador del Mar.
La Habana del Este.
Phone: (53 7) 797-1362

**Chévere**
*Snack bar*
Calle 49-C y 28-A, Reparto
Kohly. Playa. La Habana
Phone: (53 7) 204-4990

**Mirador de Bellomonte**
*Nightclub*
Vía Blanca, Alturas de Marbella.
La Habana del Este.
Phone: (53 7) 796-3431

**Club Arenal**
*Lobby bar*
Hotel Blau Club Arenal.
La Habana del Este.
Phone: (53 7) 797-1272

**Mom Petit Chateau**
*Lobby bar*
Hotel Mariposa.
La Lisa. La Habana
Phone: (53 7) 204-9137

**Club Hoyo 19**
*Bar*
Club de Golf Habana, Carretera
de Vento km. 8, Capdevila.
Boyeros. La Habana
Phone: (53 7) 649-8918

**Mon Petit Chateau**
*Lobby bar*
Hotel Chateau Miramar.
Playa. La Habana
Phone: (53 7) 204-1957

**Club Imágenes**
*Nightclub*
Calle Calzada y C, Vedado.
Plaza de la Revolución.
La Habana
Phone: (53 7) 833-3606

**Neptuno**
*Lobby bar*
Hotel Neptuno-Tritón. Playa
Phone: (53 7) 204-1606

**Cocktail Blue**
*Piano bar*
Hotel Meliá Cohiba.
Plaza de la Revolución.
Phone: (53 7) 833-3636

**Neptuno**
*Snack bar*
Marina Tarará.
La Habana del Este.
Phone: (53 7) 796-0240

# NIGHTLIFE
## (HAVANA CITY)

**Colina**

*Lobby bar*

Hotel Colina. Plaza de la
Revolución. La Habana
Phone: (53 7) 836-4071

**Obenque**

*Snack bar*

Marina Tarará.
La Habana del Este.
Phone: (53 7) 796-0240

**Copa Room**

*Cabaret*

Hotel Habana Riviera.
Plaza de la Revolución.
Phone: (53 7) 836-4051

**Opus**

*Bar*

Calle Calzada y D, Vedado,
Teatro "Amadeo Roldán".
Plaza de la Revolución.
Phone: (53 7) 832-4521

**Coral**

*Lobby bar*

Aparthotel Montehabana.
Playa. La Habana
Phone: (53 7) 206-9595

**Papa's**

*Disco*

Ave. 7ª y 26 Playa.
Playa. La Habana
Phone: (53 7) 209-7920

**Debba**

*Lobby bar*

Hotel Acuario , Marina
Hemingway. Playa. La Habana
Phone: (53 7) 204-7628

**Parisién**

*Cabaret*

Hotel Nacional de Cuba.
Plaza de la Revolución.
Phone: (53 7) 836-3564

**Delirio Habanero**

*Piano bar*

Teatro Nacional de Cuba, Paseo
y 39. Plaza de la Revolución.
Phone: (53 7) 878-4275

**Piano bar**

*Piano bar*

Hotel Acuario , Marina
Hemingway. Playa. La Habana
Phone: (53 7) 204-7628

**Discobar**

*Disco*

Hotel Panamericano Resort.
La Habana del Este.
Phone: (53 7) 766-1010

**Piano Mar**

*Bar*

Hotel Habana Riviera.
Plaza de la Revolución.
Phone: (53 7) 836-4051

**El Arpón**

*Bar*

Villas Mirador del Mar.
La Habana del Este.
Phone: (53 7) 797-1362

**Pico Blanco**
**Rincón del Feeling**

*Nightclub*

Hotel St. John's. Plaza de la
Revolución. La Habana
Phone: (53 7) 833-3740

**El Carey**

*Snack bar*

Villa Bacuranao.
La Habana del Este.
Phone: (53 7) 65-7645

**Piel Canela**

*Cabaret*

Calle 7ma. y 16,
Miramar. Playa. La Habana
Phone: (53 7) 204-1543

**El Cobijo Real**

*VIP bar*

Hotel Meliá Cohiba. Plaza de
la Revolución. La Habana
Phone: (53 7) 833-3636

**Piscina Bar Grill**

*Bar*

Hotel Tryp Habana Libre. Plaza
de la Revolución. La Habana
Phone: (53 7) 834-6100

**El Cobo**

*Pool bar*

Hotel Meliá Habana.
Playa. La Habana
Phone: (53 7) 204-8500

**Piscina Snack Bar**

*Pool bar*

Hotel Nacional de Cuba. Plaza
de la Revolución. La Habana
Phone: (53 7) 836-3564

**El Cortijo**

*Nightclub*

Hotel Vedado. Plaza de la
Revolución. La Habana
Phone: (53 7) 836-4072

# NIGHTLIFE
## (HAVANA CITY)

**El Mirador**

*Bar*

Hotel Deauville.
Centro Habana. La Habana
Phone: (53 7) 866-8812

**Rincón Cubano**

*Lobby bar*

Hotel Comodoro.
Playa. La Habana
Phone: (53 7) 204-5551

**El Náutico**

*Pool bar*

Villas Mirador del Mar.
La Habana del Este.
Phone: (53 7) 797-1362

**Rincón del Bolero**

*Nightclub*

Calle 7ma. y 26,
Miramar. Playa. La Habana
Phone: (53 7) 204-2353

**El Patio**

*Bar*

Hotel Habana Libre Tryp. Plaza
de la Revolución. La Habana
Phone: (53 7) 834-6100

**Robaina**

*Cigar-tasting hall*

Hotel Meliá Habana.
Playa. La Habana
Phone: (53 7) 204-8500

**El Polvorín**

*Snack bar*

Ave. Monumental, La Cabaña.
La Habana del Este. La Habana
Phone: (53 7) 863-8295

**Saint John´s**

*Snack bar*

Hotel Saint John´s. Plaza de
la Revolución. La Habana
Phone: (53 7) 833-3740

**El Relicario**

*Cigar-tasting hall*

Hotel Meliá Cohiba. Plaza de
la Revolución. La Habana
Phone: (53 7) 833-3636

**Salón Bohemio**

*Disco*

Hotel Neptuno-Tritón.
Playa. La Habana
Phone: (53 7) 204-1606

**El Tucán**

*Nightclub*

Villa Bacuranao.
La Habana del Este.
Phone: (53 7) 765-7645

**Salón Rojo**

*Cabaret*

Hotel Capri. Plaza de la
Revolución. La Habana
Phone: (53 7) 833-3747

**El Turquino**

*Cabaret*

Hotel Habana Libre Tryp.
Plaza de la Revolución.
Phone: (53 7) 834-6100

**Salón "Benny Moré"**

*Nightclub*

Jardines de la Cervecería
"La Tropical". Marianao.
Phone: (53 7) 206-1282

**Expresso Bar**

*Lobby bar*

Hotel Meliá Cohiba. Plaza de
la Revolución. La Habana
Phone: (53 7) 833-3636

**Salón Verde**

*Bar*

Club de Golf Habana, Carretera
de Vento km. 8, Capdevila.
Boyeros. La Habana
Phone: (53 7) 33-8818

**Galería**

*Bar*

Hotel Nacional de Cuba. Plaza
de la Revolución. La Habana
Phone: (53 7) 836-3564

**Salsa Caliente**

*Nightclub*

Hotel Mariposa.
La Lisa. La Habana
Phone: (53 7) 204-9137

**Gato Tuerto Café Concert**

*Nightclub*

Calle O e/ 17 y 19, Vedado.
Plaza de la Revolución.
Phone: (53 7) 838-2696

**Saoco Bar**

*Bar*

Hotel Tropicoco.
La Habana del Este. La Habana
Phone: (53 7) 797-1371

**Gaviota**

*Bar*

Hotel Kohly. Playa. La Habana
Phone: (53 7) 204-0240

# NIGHTLIFE
## (HAVANA CITY)

**Siboney**
*Piano bar*
Hotel Habana Libre Tryp.
Plaza de la Revolución.
Phone: (53 7) 834-6100

**Gran Añejo**
*Lobby bar*
Hotel Meliá Cohiba.
Plaza de la Revolución
Phone: (53 7) 833-3636

**Snack bar**
*Snack bar*
Hotel La Pradera. Playa.
La Habana
Phone: (53 7) 273-7467

**Guanabo Club**
*Bar*
Calle 468 e/ 13 y 15, Playa
Guanabo. La Habana del Este.
Phone: (53 7) 796-3210

**Snack Bar Piscina**
*Snack bar*
Hotel Habana Riviera.
Plaza de la Revolución.
Phone: (53 7) 836-4051

**Guanabo Club**
*Cabaret*
Calle 468 e/ 13 y 15, Playa
Guanabo. La Habana del Este.
Phone: (53 7) 796-3210

**Tritón**
*Lobby bar*
Hotel Neptuno-Tritón. Playa.
Phone: (53 7) 204-1606

**Guarapera**
*Bar*
Hotel Copacabana.
Playa. La Habana
Phone: (53 7) 204-1037

**Tropicana**
*Cabaret*
Calle 72 e/ 41 y 45.
Marianao. La Habana
Phone: (53 7) 267-1717

**Habana Café**
*Nightclub*
Hotel Meliá Cohiba.
Plaza de la Revolución.
Phone: (53 7) 833-3636

**Vedado**
*VIP bar*
Hotel Meliá Habana.
Playa. La Habana
Phone: (53 7) 204-8500

**Habanos**
*Bar*
Hotel Nacional de Cuba.
Plaza de la Revolución.
Phone: (53 7) 836-3564

**Vedado**
*Lobby bar*
Hotel Vedado. Plaza de la
Revolución. La Habana
Phone: (53 7) 836-4072

**Havana Club**
*Disco*
Calle 1ra. y 86,
Miramar. Playa. La Habana
Phone: (53 7) 204-2902

**Victoria**
*Lobby bar*
Hotel Victoria. Plaza de
la Revolución. La Habana
Phone: (53 7) 833-3510

**Irakere Jazz Club**
*Nightclub*
Calle A e/ 3ra. y 5ta
Miramar. Playa. La Habana

**Victoria**
*Pool bar*
Hotel Victoria. Plaza de la
Revolución. La Habana
Phone: (53 7) 833-3510

**Jardín de la Terraza**
*Nightclub*
Hotel Lincoln.
Centro Habana. La Habana
Phone: (53 7) 862-8061

**Villa Paraíso**
*Snack bar*
Hotel Acuario , Marina
Hemingway. Playa. La Habana
Phone: (53 7) 204-7628

**Jazz Café**
*Nightclub*
Calle Paseo y 3ra., Galerías
Paseo. Plaza de la Revolución.
La Habana
Phone: (53 7) 838-3556

**Vista al Golfo**
*Bar*
Hotel Nacional de Cuba.
Plaza de la Revolución.
Phone: (53 7) 836-3564

# NIGHTLIFE
## (SANTIAGO DE CUBA)

**Alameda**
*Pool bar*
Hotel Meliá Santiago de Cuba.
Santiago de Cuba
Phone: (53 22) 687070

**La Conga**
*Bar*
Hotel Bucanero.
Santiago de Cuba
Phone: (53 22) 68-6363

**Anacaona**
*Bar*
Motel Rancho Club.
Santiago de Cuba
Phone: (53 22) 63-3202

**La Pachanga**
*Disco*
Hotel Carisol-Los Corales.
Santiago de Cuba
Phone: (53 22) 35-6150

**Bar Daiquirí**
*Lobby bar*
Hotel Meliá Santiago de Cuba.
Santiago de Cuba
Phone: (53 22) 687070

**La Pérgola**
*Bar*
Hotel El Saltón. Tercer Frente.
Santiago de Cuba
Phone: (53 225) 6492

**Bello Bar**
*Nightclub*
Hotel Meliá Santiago de Cuba.
Santiago de Cuba
Phone: (53 22) 687070

**La Salsa**
*Pool bar*
Hotel Carisol-Los Corales.
Santiago de Cuba
Phone: (53 22) 35-6150

**Café Cantante Niágara**
*Piano bar*
Ave. de los Desfiles, Teatro
Heredia. Santiago de Cuba

**La Taberna del Ron**
*Bar*
Calle Carnicería e/ San Basilio
y Santa Lucía. Santiago de Cuba

**Calypso**
*Lobby bar*
Hotel Carisol-Los Corales.
Santiago de Cuba
Phone: (53 22) 35-6150

**Las Acacias**
*Bar*
Villa Santiago de Cuba.
Santiago de Cuba
Phone: (53 22) 64 1368

**Centro Nocturno**
*Nightclub*
Hotel Costa Morena.
Santiago de Cuba
Phone: (53 22) 635- 6126

**Club 300**
*Nightclub*
Calle Aguilera No. 302 e/ San
Pedro y San Félix.
Santiago de Cuba
Phone: (53 22) 65-3532

**Lobby Bar**
*Lobby bar*
Hotel San Juan.
Santiago de Cuba
Phone: (53 22) 68-7200

**Club Nocturno**
*Nightclub*
Hotel Versalles.
Santiago de Cuba
Phone: (53 22) 691-016

**Lobby Bar**
*Lobby bar*
Hotel Versalles.
Santiago de Cuba
Phone: (53 22) 691-016

**Club Tropical**
*Disco*
Autopista Nacional km. 1 ½.
Santiago de Cuba
Phone: (53 22) 64-3036

**Marino**
*Bar*
Hotel Costa Morena.
Santiago de Cuba
Phone: (53 22) 635- 6126

**Don Emilio**
*Bar*
Villa Santiago de Cuba.
Santiago de Cuba
Phone: (53 22) 64 1368

**Las Américas**
*Bar*
Hotel Las Américas.
Santiago de Cuba
Phone: (53 22) 64-2011

# NIGHTLIFE
## (SANTIAGO DE CUBA)

**Merengue**
*Pool bar*
Hotel Carisol-Los Corales.
Santiago de Cuba
Phone: (53 22) 35-6150

**El Quijote**
*Nightclub*
Hotel San Juan.
Santiago de Cuba
Phone: (53 22) 68-7200

**Tango**
*Lobby bar*
Hotel Carisol-Los Corales.
Santiago de Cuba
Phone: (53 22) 35-6150

**El Caneysito**
*Snack bar*
Motel Rancho Club.
Santiago de Cuba
Phone: (53 22) 63-3202

**Ranchón**
*Bar*
Hotel El Saltón. Tercer Frente.
Santiago de Cuba
Phone: (53 225) 6492

**La Cascada**
*Bar*
Hotel El Saltón. Tercer Frente.
Santiago de Cuba
Phone: (53 225) 6492

**Mirador**
*Bar*
Hotel El Saltón. Tercer Frente.
Santiago de Cuba
Phone: (53 225) 6492

**Gran Piedra**
*Bar*
Hotel Gran Piedra.
Santiago de Cuba
Phone: (53 22) 686147

**Tropicana Santiago**
*Cabaret*
Autopista Nacional km. 1 ½.
Santiago de Cuba
Phone: (53 22) 64-3036

**El Copero**
*Lobby bar*
Hotel Balcón del Caribe.
Santiago de Cuba
Phone: (53 22) 691-506

**Roof Garden**
*Bar*
Hotel Casa Granda.
Santiago de Cuba
Phone: (53 22) 68-6600

**Rancho Club**
*Cabaret*
Motel Rancho Club.
Santiago de Cuba
Phone: (53 22) 63-3202

**Patio Bar Paticruzao**
*Bar*
Autopista Nacional km. 1 ½.
Santiago de Cuba
Phone: (53 22) 68-7020

**La Bamba**
*Beach bar*
Hotel Carisol-Los Corales.
Santiago de Cuba
Phone: (53 22) 35-6150

**La Caleta**
*Beach bar*
Hotel Bucanero.
Santiago de Cuba
Phone: (53 22) 68-6363

**El Pino**
*Snack bar*
Hotel Versalles.
Santiago de Cuba
Phone: (53 22) 691-016

**San Pedro del Mar**
*Cabaret*
Carretera del Morro km. 7½.
Santiago de Cuba
Phone: (53 22) 69-1287

# NIGHTLIFE
## (HOLGUÍN)

**1492**
*Lobby bar*
Hotel Sol Río de Luna y Mares.
Rafael Freyre. Holguín
Phone: (53 24) 3-0030

**La Niña**
*Lobby bar*
Hotel Atlántico-Guardalavaca.
Banes. Holguín
Phone: (53 24) 3-0195

**Beach Bar**
*Beach bar*
Hotel Playa Costa Verde.
Rafael Freyre. Holguín
Phone: (53 24) 3-0520

**La Dolce Vita**
*Disco*
Hotel Guardalavaca.
Banes. Holguín
Phone: (53 24) 3-0218

**Arenas Nuevas**
*Bar*
Villa Don Lino.
Rafael Freyre. Holguín
Phone: (53 24) 3-0259

**La Santa María**
*Snack bar*
Hotel Atlántico-Guardalavaca.
Banes. Holguín
Phone: (53 24) 3-0180

**Acuabar**
*Bar*
Hotel Guardalavaca.
Banes. Holguín
Phone: (53 24) 3-0218

**La Pinta**
*Pool bar*
Hotel Atlántico-Guardalavaca.
Banes. Holguín
Phone: (53 24) 3-0180

*El Capuccino*
*Bar*
Hotel Guardalavaca.
Banes. Holguín
Phone: (53 24) 3-0218

**La Fuente**
*Lobby bar*
Hotel Blau Costa Verde.
Rafael Freyre. Holguín
Phone: (53 24) 3-0510

**Azúcar**
*Bar*
Hotel Sol Río de Luna y Mares.
Rafael Freyre. Holguín
Phone: (53 24) 3-0030

**La Tinaja**
*Bar*
Hotel Guardalavaca.
Banes. Holguín
Phone: (53 24) 30-218

**Antílope**
*Bar*
Villa Cayo Saetía.
Mayarí. Holguín
Phone: (53 24) 96900

**La Roca**
*Disco*
Playa Guardalavaca.
Banes. Holguín
Phone: (53 24) 3-0167

**El Dorado**
*Lobby bar*
Hotel Sol Río de Luna y Mares.
Rafael Freyre. Holguín
Phone: (53 24) 3-0030

**La Nao**
*Pool bar*
Hotel Sol Río de Luna y Mares.
Rafael Freyre. Holguín
Phone: (53 24) 3-0030

**Bariay**
*Nightclub*
Hotel Sol Río de Luna y Mares.
Rafael Freyre. Holguín
Phone: (53 24) 3-0030

**Laguna Azul**
*Snack bar*
Hotel Blau Costa Verde.
Rafael Freyre. Holguín
Phone: (53 24) 3-0510

**Aquabar**
*Pool bar*
Hotel Playa Costa Verde.
Rafael Freyre. Holguín
Phone: (53 24) 3-0520

**La Rueda**
*Bar*
Playa Guardalavaca.
Banes. Holguín

**El Patio**
*Bar*
Hotel Guardalavaca.
Banes. Holguín
Phone: (53 24) 30-218

# NIGHTLIFE
## (HOLGUÍN)

**Las Guanas**
*Snack bar*
Playa Esmeralda.
Rafael Freyre. Holguín
Phone: (53 24) 30132

**El Ranchón**
*Snack bar*
Hotel Guardalavaca.
Banes. Holguín
Phone: (53 24) 3-0218

**Lobby Bar**
*Lobby bar*
Hotel Playa Costa Verde.
Rafael Freyre. Holguín
Phone: (53 24) 3-0520

**El Saltón**
*Pool bar*
Hotel Paradisus Río de Oro.
Rafael Freyre. Holguín
Phone: (53 24) 3-0090

**Los Amigos**
*Bar*
Playa Guardalavaca.
Banes. Holguín

**El Zaguán**
*Bar*
Hotel Guardalavaca.
Banes. Holguín
Phone: (53 24) 30-218

**Oasis**
*Snack bar*
Playa Esmeralda.
Rafael Freyre. Holguín
Phone: (53 24) 30132

**Fun Pub La Conga**
*Disco*
Hotel Paradisus Río de Oro.
Rafael Freyre. Holguín
Phone: (53 24) 30090

**Palma Real**
*Lobby bar*
Hotel Paradisus Río de Oro.
Rafael Freyre. Holguín
Phone: (53 24) 3-0090

**Galileo**
*Snack bar*
Hotel Sol Río de Luna y Mares.
Rafael Freyre. Holguín
Phone: (53 24) 3-0030

**Yaguajay**
*Snack bar*
Hotel Atlántico-Guardalavaca.
Banes. Holguín
Phone: (53 24) 3-0195

**Pool Bar**
*Pool bar*
Hotel Playa Costa Verde.
Rafael Freyre. Holguín
Phone: (53 24) 3-0520

**Grill Conuco**
*Bar*
Hotel Playa Costa Verde.
Rafael Freyre. Holguín
Phone: (53 24) 3-0520

**El Tejado**
*Lobby bar*
Hotel Guardalavaca.
Banes. Holguín
Phone: (53 24) 3-0218

**Night Club Bar**
*Nightclub*
Hotel Playa Costa Verde.
Rafael Freyre. Holguín
Phone: (53 24) 3-0520

# NIGHTLIFE
## (CAYO LASRGO DEL SUR)

**Aqua-Bar**

*Bar*

Villa Coral, Cayo Largo
del Sur. Isla de la Juventud

Phone: (53 45) 248-111

**Medusa**

*Bar*

Hotel Isla del Sur, Cayo Largo
del Sur. Isla de la Juventud

Phone: (53 45) 248-111

**Bar de Olga**

*Bar*

Villa Capricho, Cayo Largo
del Sur. Isla de la Juventud

Phone: (53 45) 248-111

**Opalino**

*Bar*

Hotel Barceló Cayo Largo Beach
Resort. Isla de la Juventud

Phone: (53 45) 248-080

**Carey**

*Bar*

Villa Iguana, Cayo Largo del
Sur. Isla de la Juventud

Phone: (53 45) 248-111

**Opalino**

*Snack bar*

Hotel Barceló Cayo Largo Beach
Resort. Isla de la Juventud

Phone: (53 45) 248-080

**Cayo Rico**

*Bar*

Marina Cayo Largo del Sur.
Isla de la Juventud

Phone: (53 45) 248-212

**Rent a Car**

*Bar*

Hotel Isla del Sur, Cayo Largo
del Sur. Isla de la Juventud

Phone: (53 45) 248-111

**Chiringuito de Playa**

*Beach bar*

Hotel Sol Cayo Largo.
Isla de la Juventud

Phone: (53 45) 248-260

**Sirena**

*Bar*

Marina Cayo Largo del Sur.
Isla de la Juventud

Phone: (53 45) 248-212

**Daiquirí**

*Bar*

Hotel Barceló Cayo Largo Beach
Resort. Isla de la Juventud

Phone: (53 45) 248-080

**Solazul**

*Pool bar*

Hotel Sol Cayo Largo.
Isla de la Juventud

Phone: (53 45) 248-260

**El Catey**

*Lobby bar*

Hotel Sol Pelícano.
Isla de la Juventud

Phone: (53 45) 248-333

**Taberna del Pirata**

*Bar*

Marina Cayo Largo del Sur.
Isla de la Juventud

Phone: (53 45) 248-212

**El Cayito**

*Lobby bar*

Hotel Sol Cayo Largo.
Isla de la Juventud

Phone: (53 45) 248-260

**Velamar**

*Beach bar*

Hotel Barceló Cayo Largo Beach
Resort. Isla de la Juventud

Phone: (53 45) 248-080

**Karaoke Marimba**

*Karaoke*

Hotel Sol Cayo Largo.
Isla de la Juventud

Phone: (53 45) 248-260

**Zun Zun**

*Bar*

Hotel Sol Pelícano.
Isla de la Juventud

Phone: (53 45) 248-333

**Los Quelonios**

*Bar*

Hotel Sol Pelícano.
Isla de la Juventud

Phone: (53 45) 248-333

# *NIGHTLIFE*
## *(TRINIDAD)*

**1514**
*Bar*
Hotel Trinidad del Mar.
Trinidad. Sancti Spiritus
Phone: (53 41) 99-6500

**Lobby Bar**
*Bar*
Hotel Costasur.
Trinidad. Sancti Spiritus
Phone: (53 41) 99-6174

**Ayala**
*Disco*
Hotel Las Cuevas.
Trinidad. Sancti Spiritus
Phone: (53 41) 99-6133

**Los Cobos**
*Snack bar*
Hotel Trinidad del Mar.
Trinidad. Sancti Spiritus
Phone: (53 41) 99-6500

**Caracol**
*Beach bar*
Hotel Costasur.
Trinidad. Sancti Spiritus
Phone: (53 41) 99-6174

**Los Corsarios**
*Lobby bar*
Hotel Ancón.
Trinidad. Sancti Spiritus
Phone: (53 41) 99-6120

**Caribbean Club**
*Disco*
Hotel Ancón.
Trinidad. Sancti Spiritus
Phone: (53 41) 99-6120

**Los Galeones**
*Lobby bar*
Hotel Trinidad del Mar.
Trinidad. Sancti Spiritus
Phone: (53 41) 99-6500

**Coco Bar**
*Bar*
Hotel Ancón.
Trinidad. Sancti Spiritus
Phone: (53 41) 99-6120

**Los Galeones**
*Pool bar*
Hotel Ancón.
Trinidad. Sancti Spiritus
Phone: (53 41) 99-6120

**Costasur**
*Disco*
Hotel Costasur.
Trinidad. Sancti Spiritus
Phone: (53 41) 99-6174

**Mesón del Regidor**
*Bar*
Calle Simón Bolívar No. 312.
Trinidad. Sancti Spiritus

**El Gallo**
*Bar*
Finca Ma' Dolores.
Sancti Spiritus
Phone: (53 41) 99-6481

**Piano Bar-Karaoke**
*Karaoke*
Hotel Trinidad del Mar.
Trinidad. Sancti Spiritus
Phone: (53 41) 99-6500

**El Potro**
*Bar*
Finca Ma' Dolores.
Trinidad. Sancti Spiritus
Phone: (53 41) 99-6481

**Ranchón Havana Club**
*Bar*
Hotel Ancón. Trinidad.
Phone: (53 41) 99-6120

**La Manta**
*Bar*
Hotel Costasur. Trinidad.
Phone: (53 41) 99-6174

**Ranchón Playa**
*Beach bar*
Hotel Ancón. Trinidad.
Phone: (53 41) 99-6120

**Langostino**
*Pool bar*
Hotel Costasur.
Trinidad. Sancti Spiritus
Phone: (53 41) 99-6174

**Rondeño**
*Bar*
Hotel La Ronda. Trinidad.
Phone: (53 41) 99-4011

**Lina**
*Bar*
Hotel Costasur. Trinidad.
Phone: (53 41) 99-6174

**Taberna La Canchánchara**
*Bar*
Calle Ruben Martínez Villena
esq. a Pablo Pichs. Trinidad.
Phone: (53 41) 99-4345

# NIGHTLIFE
## (SOROA, LAS TERRAZAS & VIÑALES)

**Castillo**
*Bar*
Villa Soroa.
Candelaria. Artemisa
Phone: (53 48) 52-3534

**Salto**
*Bar*
Villa Soroa.
Candelaria. Artemisa
Phone: (53 48) 52-3534

**Centro**
*Bar*
Villa Soroa.
Candelaria. Artemisa
Phone: (53 48) 52-3534

**Snack Bar Piscina**
*Pool bar*
Villa Soroa.
Candelaria. Artemisa
Phone: (53 48) 52-3534

**Lobby Bar**
*Lobby bar*
Villa Soroa.
Candelaria. Artemisa
Phone: (53 48) 52-3534

**Amanecer del Valle**
*Snack bar*
Hotel Los Jazmines.
Viñales. Pinar del Río
Phone: (53 48) 796205

**Bar Piscina**
*Pool bar*
Villa Aguas Claras.
Viñales. Pinar del Río
Phone: (53 48) 27-8426

**Las Arcadas**
*Bar*
Hotel Rancho San Vicente.
Viñales. Pinar del Río
Phone: (53 48) 796205

**Cuevas de Viñales**
*Disco*
Carretera a Puerto Esperanza
km. 36. Viñales. Pinar del Río
Phone: (53 48) 79-3203

**Mirador**
*Bar*
Hotel Los Jazmines.
Viñales. Pinar del Río
Phone: (53 48) 796205

**Discoteca**
*Disco*
Villa Aguas Claras.
Viñales. Pinar del Río
Phone: (53 48) 27-8426

**Ranchón San Vicente**
*Bar*
Carretera a Puerto Esperanza
km. 38. Viñales. Pinar del Río
Phone: (53 82) 79-3200

**Snack Bar**
*Snack bar*
Hotel La Ermita.
Viñales. Pinar del Río
Phone: (53 48) 796072

**La Salsa**
*Disco*
Hotel Los Jazmines.
Viñales. Pinar del Río
Phone: (53 48) 79-6205

**Vista al Valle**
*Bar*
Hotel Los Jazmines.
Viñales. Pinar del Río
Phone: (53 48) 796205

**Jurásico**
*Bar*
Villa Dos Hermanas.
Viñales. Pinar del Río
Phone: (53 48) 93223

**La Terraza**
*Bar*
Hotel La Ermita.
Viñales. Pinar del Río
Phone: (53 48) 796072

# ATTRACTIONS
## (VARADERO)

**Amphitheater of Varadero**
*Theaters*
Vía Blanca y carretera de
Cárdenas. Cárdenas. Matanzas

**Iglesia Presbiteriana
Reformada**
*Churches-Places of Cult*
Calle 34 e/ 1ra. y 2da.
Cárdenas. Matanzas

**Cueva de Ambrosio**
*Caverns*
Varadero. Cárdenas. Matanzas

**Josone Park**
*Places of Interest*
Calle 1ra. y 56. Cárdenas.
Matanzas

**Municipal Museum
of History**
*Museums*
Calle 57 No. 1 esq. a Playa.
Cárdenas. Matanzas
Phone: (53 45) 61-3189

**Iglesia de Nuestra
Señora de Fátima**
*Churches-Places of Cult*
Calle 1ra. No. 801 e/ 8 y 9.
Cárdenas. Matanzas

**Plaza América
Convention Center**
*Institutions*
Autopista Sur km. 11.
Cárdenas. Matanzas
Phone: (53 45) 66-7895

**Iglesia del Inmaculado
Corazón de María
(Santa Elvira)**
*Churches-Places of Cult*
Ave. 1ra. No. 4604 e/ 46 y 47.
Cárdenas. Matanzas

**Varadero Golf Club**
*Places of Interest*
Carretera Las Américas.
Cárdenas. Matanzas
Phone: (53 45) 66-8482

**Cueva de los Musulmanes
(The Cave of Muslims)**
*Caverns*
Cárdenas. Matanzas

# ATTRACTIONS
## (HAVANA COLONIAL)

**Gun Smith's Museum**
*Museums*
Calle Mercaderes No. 157 e/
Lamparilla y Obrapía.
La Habana Vieja. La Habana
Phone: (53 7) 861-8080

**Indian Fountain**
*Places of Interest*
Paseo del Prado y Dragones.
La Habana Vieja. La Habana

**"Santa Clara de Asis"
Convent & Church**
*Places of Interest*
Calle Cuba No. 602 e/ Luz y Sol.
La Habana Vieja. La Habana

**Inglaterra Hotel**
*Monuments*
Paseo del Prado e/ San Rafael y
San Miguel. La Habana Vieja.
La Habana

**"Simón Bolívar" House**
*Museums*
Calle Mercaderes No. 156 e/
Obrapía y Lamparilla.
La Habana Vieja. La Habana
Phone: (53 7) 861-3988

**Instituto Cubano del Libro**
*Institutions*
Calle O'Reilly No. 4 esq. a
Tacón. La Habana Vieja.
Phone: (53 7) 862-8091

# ATTRACTIONS
## (HAVANA COLONIAL)

**Alameda de Paula Promenade**
*Places of Interest*
Alameda de Paula.
La Habana Vieja. La Habana

**José Martí's House**
*Museums*
Calle Leonor Pérez (Paula)
No. 314 e/ Picota y Egido.
La Habana Vieja. La Habana
Phone: (53 7) 861-3778

**Aldama Palace**
*Places of Interest*
Calles Amistad, Reina, Aguila
y Enrique Barnet. La Habana
Vieja. La Habana

**La Acacia Gallery**
*Art Galleries*
Calle San José No. 114 e/
Industria y Consulado.
Centro Habana. La Habana
Phone: (53 7) 861-3533

**Alejo Carpentier Foundation**
*Institutions*
Calle Empedrado No. 215.
La Habana Vieja. La Habana
Phone: (53 7) 861-3667

**La Casona Gallery**
*Art Galleries*
Calle Muralla No. 107 esq. a
San Ignacio. La Habana Vieja.
Phone: (53 7) 862-2633

**La Junta Locomotive**
*Monuments*
Calle Egido, Estación Central
de Ferrocarriles de La Habana.
La Habana Vieja. La Habana

**Aquarium of Old Havana**
*Places of Interest*
Calle Teniente Rey No. 9 e/
Oficios y Mercaderes.
La Habana Vieja. La Habana
Phone: (53 7) 863-9493

**La Merced Church**
*Churches-Places of Cult*
Calle Cuba No. 806 esq. a
Merced. La Habana Vieja.
Phone: (53 7) 863-8873

**Arabian House**
*Museums*
Calle Oficios No. 16 e/ Obispo
y Obrapía. La Habana Vieja.
La Habana
Phone: (53 7) 861-5868

**Lions Fountain**
*Places of Interest*
Plaza de San Francisco de Asís.
La Habana Vieja. La Habana

**Archaeological Park**
*Places of Interest*
La Habana Vieja. La Habana

**Luz y Caballero Park**
*Parks*
La Habana Vieja. La Habana

**Artistic Ceramic Museum**
*Museums*
Calle Mercaderes No. 15 e/
Amargura y Lamparilla. La
Habana Vieja. La Habana
Phone: (53 7) 861-6130

**Marquis de Arcos' House**
*Places of Interest*
Calle Mercaderes No. 16 e/
Empedrado y O'Reilly.
La Habana Vieja. La Habana

**Asian House**
*Museums*
Calle Mercaderes No. 111 e/
Obispo y Obrapía. La Habana
Vieja. La Habana
Phone: (53 7) 863-9740

**Medical Students Memorial**
*Monuments*
Paseo del Prado y Malecón.
La Habana Vieja. La Habana

**Asturian Center**
*Museums*
Calle O'Reilly e/ Zulueta y
Monserrate. La Habana Vieja.

**Monument to Santo Domingo Convent (Royal and Pontifical University of San Geronimo of Havana)**
*Monuments*
Calle Obispo esq. a Mercaderes.
La Habana Vieja. La Habana

# ATTRACTIONS
## (HAVANA COLONIAL)

**Bacardi Building**
*Places of Interest*
Calle Monserrate y San Juan
de Dios. La Habana Vieja.
La Habana

**Museo de las Finanzas**
*Museums*
Calle Obispo No. 26 esq. a Cuba
La Habana Vieja. La Habana
Phone: (53 7) 862-9962

**Basilica of Saint Francis
of Assisi**
*Places of Interest*
Calle Oficios e/ Amargura y
Churruca. La Habana Vieja.
Phone: (53 7) 862-9683

**Museo de los Orishas**
*Museums*
Paseo del Prado No. 615 e/
Monte y Dragones.
La Habana Vieja. La Habana
Phone: (53 7) 863-5953

**Car Museum**
*Museums*
Calle Oficios No. 12 y Callejón
de Jústiz. La Habana Vieja.
Phone: (53 7) 861-5062

**Museo del Naipe**
*Museums*
Calle Muralla No. 101 esq. a
Inquisidor. La Habana Vieja.

**Carlos Manuel de Céspede**
*Monuments*
Plaza de Armas. La Habana
Vieja. La Habana

**Museum of Archaeology**
*Museums*
Calle Tacón No. 12 e/ O'Reilly y
Empedrado. La Habana Vieja.
La Habana
Phone: (53 7) 861-4469

**Castillo de los Tres Reyes
del Morro (Castle of the
Three Kings of El Morro)**
*Places of Interest*
Ribera este del canal de entrada
a la bahía de La Habana.
La Habana del Este. La Habana

**Museum of Cigar**
*Museums*
Calle Mercaderes No. 120 e/
Obispo y Obrapía. La Habana
Vieja. La Habana

**Cathedral of Havana**
*Churches-Places of Cult*
Calle Empedrado No. 158 e/
Mercaderes y San Ignacio.
La Habana Vieja. La Habana
Phone: (53 7) 861-7771

**Museum of Colonial Art**
*Museums*
Calle San Ignacio No. 61 e/
Empedrado y O'Reilly, Plaza
de la Catedral. La Habana Vieja.
La Habana
Phone: (53 7) 862-6440

**Cathedral Square**
*Places of Interest*
Calle Empedrado y San Ignacio.
La Habana Vieja. La Habana

**Museum of Command
Headquarters**
*Museums*
Fortaleza de La Cabaña.
La Habana del Este. La Habana

**Center for Contemporary
Arts "Wilfredo Lam"**
*Institutions*
Calle San Ignacio No. 22 esq. a
Empedrado. La Habana Vieja.
La Habana
Phone: (53 7) 861-3419

**Museum of Religious Art**
*Museums*
Calle Oficios e/ Amargura y
Churruca. La Habana Vieja.
La Habana
Phone: (53 7) 862-9683

**Central Park**
*Parks*
Paseo del Prado. La Habana
Vieja. La Habana

**Museum of Rum**
*Museums*
Calle San Pedro No. 262 e/ Sol y
Muralla. La Habana Vieja.
La Habana
Phone: (53 7) 861-8051

**Central Railroad Station**
*Places of Interest*
Calle Egido y Arsenal.
La Habana Vieja. La Habana

# ATTRACTIONS
## (HAVANA COLONIAL)

**Museum of the City**
*Museums*
Calle Tacón No. 1 e/ Obispo
y O'Reilly. La Habana Vieja.
Phone: (53 7) 861-2876

**Centro Cultural
Pablo de la Torriente Brau**
*Institutions*
Calle Muralla No. 63 e/ Oficios e
Inquisidor. La Habana Vieja.
Phone: (53 7) 66-6585

**Museum of the Revolution**
*Museums*
Calle Refugio No. 1 e/
Monserrate y Zulueta.
La Habana Vieja. La Habana
Phone: (53 7) 862-4091

**Centro Gallego-Great
Theater of Havana**
*Places of Interest*
Paseo del Prado e/ San Rafael
y San José. Centro Habana.
Phone: (53 7) 861-3078

**National Capitol Hill**
*Places of Interest*
Paseo del Prado e/ Dragones
y San José. La Habana Vieja.
La Habana

**Church of the Holy Ghost**
*Churches-Places of Cult*
Calle Cuba e/ Acosta y Jesús
María. La Habana Vieja.
La Habana

**National Center for
Preservation, Restoration
and Museology
CENCREM)**
*Institutions*
Calle Cuba No. 610 e/ Sol y Luz.
La Habana Vieja. La Habana
Phone: (53 7) 861-2877

**Convención Bautista
Cuba Occidental**
*Churches-Places of Cult*
Calle Zulueta No. 502 esq. a
Dragones. La Habana Vieja.

**National Museum of
Fine Arts**
*Museums*
Calle Trocadero e/ Zulueta y
Monserrate. La Habana Vieja.
Phone: (53 7) 862-1643

**De la Real Fuerza Castle**
*Places of Interest*
Calle O'Reilly No. 2 e/ Ave.
del Puerto y Tacón.
La Habana Vieja. La Habana
Phone: (53 7) 861-6130

**National Museum
of Music**
*Museums*
Calle Capdevila No. 1 e/ Aguiar
y Habana. La Habana Vieja.
Phone: (53 7) 861-9846

**El Templete**
*Places of Interest*
Calle Baratillo e/ O'Reilly y
Enna, Plaza de Armas.
La Habana Vieja. La Habana

**National Museum of
Natural History**
*Museums*
Calle Obispo No. 61 esq. a
Oficios. La Habana Vieja.
La Habana
Phone: (53 7) 862-0353

**Fernando VII Monument**
*Monuments*
Calle O'Reilly, Plaza de Armas.
La Habana Vieja. La Habana

**Neptune Fountain**
*Places of Interest*
Avenida del Puerto.
La Habana Vieja. La Habana

**Firemen's House**
*Museums*
Calle Mercaderes No. 162 esq. a
Lamparilla. La Habana Vieja.
La Habana

**Numismatic Museum**
*Museums*
Calle Obispo No. 310 e/ Aguiar
y Habana. La Habana Vieja.
Phone: (53 7) 861-5811

**Forma Gallery**
*Art Galleries*
Calle Obispo No. 255 e/ Cuba
y Aguiar. La Habana Vieja.
La Habana
Phone: (53 7) 862-0123

**Fraternity Park**
*Parks*
Calle Monte.
La Habana Vieja.

# ATTRACTIONS
## (HAVANA COLONIAL)

**Old Havana and its Colonial Fortress System**
*World Heritage Sites*
La Habana Vieja. La Habana

**Francisco Albear Park**
*Parks*
Calle Monserrate e/ Obispo
y O'Reilly. La Habana Vieja.
La Habana

**Old San Francisco de Sales' School**
*Places of Interest*
Calle Oficios No. 6 esq. a Obispo
La Habana Vieja. La Habana

**Old Villa of San Cristobal of Havana**
*Urban Historic Centers*
La Habana Vieja.

**Generals of the Army Palace**
*Places of Interest*
Calle Tacón e/ Obispo y O'Reilly
La Habana Vieja. La Habana

**Plaza de Armas (Parade Ground)**
*Parks*
Calles Tacón, Obispo, Baratillo y
O'Reilly. La Habana Vieja.
La Habana

**Prado Promenade**
*Places of Interest*
Paseo del Prado.
La Habana Vieja. La Habana

**Granma Memorial**
*Museums*
Calle Refugio No. 1 e/
Monserrate y Zulueta. La
Habana Vieja. La Habana

**Plaza Vieja (Old Square)**
*Parks*
Calles San Ignacio, Teniente Rey
Mercaderes y Muralla. La
Habana Vieja. La Habana

**Guayasamin Foundation House**
*Art Galleries*
Calle Obrapía No. 112 e/ Oficios
y Mercaderes. La Habana Vieja.
La Habana
Phone: (53 7) 861-3843

**Havana Customs House**
*Places of Interest*
Calle San Pedro. La Habana
Vieja. La Habana

**Real Fábrica de Tabacos "La Corona"**
*Places of Interest*
Calle Zulueta No. 106 e/ Refugio
y Colón. La Habana Vieja.
La Habana

**Historical Museum of Sciences "Carlos J. Finlay"**
*Museums*
Calle Cuba No. 460 e/ Amargura
y Teniente Rey.
La Habana Vieja. La Habana
Phone: (53 7) 863-4824

**Remains of the Wall of Havana**
*Places of Interest*
La Habana Vieja.
La Habana Vieja. La Habana

**Historical-Military Park Morro-Cabaña**
*Places of Interest*
Carretera de La Cabaña.
La Habana del Este. La Habana
Phone: (53 7) 862-0607

**Roberto Diago Gallery**
*Art Galleries*
Calle Muralla No. 107 esq. a San
Ignacio. La Habana Vieja.
Phone: (53 7) 862-2377

**Horacio Ruíz Gallery**
*Art Galleries*
Calle Tacón No. 4 / O'Reilly y
Empedrado. La Habana Vieja.

**San Agustín Church**
*Churches-Places of Cult*
Calle Cuba esq. a Amargura.
La Habana Vieja. La Habana

**House of Africa**
*Museums*
Calle Obrapía No. 157 e/
Mercaderes y San Ignacio.
La Habana Vieja. La Habana
Phone: (53 7) 861-5798

**House of Alejandro de Humboldt**
*Museums*
Calle Oficios No. 254 esq. a
Muralla. La Habana Vieja.

# *ATTRACTIONS*
## *(HAVANA COLONIAL)*

**San Carlos and San Ambrosio Seminary**
*Places of Interest*
Calle San Ignacio No. 5 e/ Empedrado y Tacón.
La Habana Vieja. La Habana

**San Carlos de la Cabaña Fort**
*Places of Interest*
Ribera este del canal de entrada a la bahía de La Habana.
La Habana del Este. La Habana

**House of Benito Juarez: Distinguished personality of Las Americas**
*Museums*
Calle Obrapía No. 116 esq. a Mercaderes. La Habana Vieja.
Phone: (53 7) 861-8166

**San Francisco de Paula Church**
*Places of Interest*
Calle Paula No. 9 esq. a San Ignacio. La Habana Vieja.
La Habana

**House of Carmen Montilla**
*Art Galleries*
Calle Oficios e/ Amargura y Teniente Rey. La Habana Vieja.
La Habana
Phone: (53 7) 33-8768

**San Francisco Square**
*Parks*
Calles Oficios, Amargura y San Pedro. La Habana Vieja.
La Habana

**House of Count Pedroso**
*Places of Interest*
Calle San Ignacio y Empedrado.
La Habana Vieja. La Habana

**San Salvador de la Punta Castle**
*Places of Interest*
Ave. del Puerto y Paseo del Prado. La Habana Vieja.
La Habana

**House of La Obra Pía**
*Museums*
Calle Obrapía No. 158 esq. a Mercaderes. La Habana Vieja.
La Habana
Phone: (53 7) 861-3097

**Santa Teresa de Jesus Convent & Church (Maria Auxiliadora**
*Churches-Places of Cult*
Calle Compostela esq. a Teniente Rey. La Habana Vieja.
La Habana
Phone: (53 7) 861-1446

**House of Poetry**
*Institutions*
Calle Muralla e/ Oficios e Inquisidor. La Habana Vieja.
La Habana

**Santo Cristo del Buen Viaje Church**
*Churches-Places of Cult*
Calle Villegas e/ Lamparilla y Teniente Rey. La Habana Vieja.
La Habana
Phone: (53 7) 863-1767

**House of Silver Work**
*Museums*
Calle Obispo No. 113 e/ Oficios y Mercaderes. La Habana Vieja.
La Habana
Phone: (53 7) 863-9861

**Segundo Cabo Palace**
*Places of Interest*
Calle O'Reilly No. 4 esq. a Tacón. La Habana Vieja.

**House of the Count Casa Barreto**
*Places of Interest*
Calle Oficios No. 362 esq. a Luz.
La Habana Vieja. La Habana

**Taquechel Pharmacy Museum**
*Museums*
Calle Obispo No. 155 e/ San Ignacio y Mercaderes. La Habana Vieja. La Habana

**House of the Count Casa Lombillo**
*Places of Interest*
Calle San Ignacio No. 364 e/ Teniente Rey y Muralla. La Habana Vieja. La Habana

**Terminal de Cruceros**
*Places of Interest*
Ave. San Pedro.
La Habana Vieja. La Habana

**The Christ of Havana**
*Places of Interest*
Bahía de La Habana.
La Habana del Este. La Habana

# ATTRACTIONS
## (HAVANA COLONIAL)

### House of the Count San Juan de Jaruco
*Places of Interest*
Calle Muralla esq. a San Ignacio.
La Habana Vieja. La Habana

### House of the Marquis of Aguas Claras
*Places of Interest*
Calle San Ignacio No. 54 esq. a
Empedrado. La Habana Vieja.
La Habana

### The Great Statue of the Republic
*Places of Interest*
Capitolio de La Habana, Paseo
del Prado y Teniente Rey.
La Habana Vieja. La Habana

### Victor Manuel Gallery
*Art Galleries*
Calle San Ignacio No. 56, Plaza
de la Catedral. La Habana Vieja.
Phone: (53 7) 861-2955

### Iglesia del Santo Angel Custodio
*Churches-Places of Cult*
Calle Compostela No. 2 e/
Chacón y Cuarteles. La Habana
Vieja. La Habana
Phone: (53 7) 861-0469

### House of the Recio Family
*Places of Interest*
Calle Obispo e/ Mercaderes y
Oficios. La Habana Vieja.
La Habana

### The Traditional Malecon of the City of Havana
*Places of Interest*
Ave. Antonio Maceo. La Habana
Vieja. La Habana

### Iglesia del Sagrado Corazón de Jesús y San Ignacio de Loyola
*Churches-Places of Cult*
Calle Reina No. 463. Centro
Habana. La Habana

# ATTRACTIONS
## (HAVANA CITY)

### "Amadeo Roldan" Theater & Auditorium
*Theaters*
Calle Calzada No. 512 esq. a D,
Vedado. Plaza de la Revolución.
Phone: (53 7) 832-1168

### Iglesia de Jesús de Miramar
*Churches-Places of Cult*
5ta Ave. esq. a 82, Miramar.
Playa. La Habana
Phone: (53 7) 203-5301

### "José Martí" Revolution Square
*Places of Interest*
Calle Paseo. Plaza de la
Revolución. La Habana

### Iglesia de San Antonio de Padua
*Churches-Places of Cult*
5ta. Ave. esq. a 60, Miramar.
Playa. La Habana
Phone: (53 7) 203-5045

### "Abel Santamaria's House" Museum
*Museums*
Calle 25 esq. a O, Vedado.
Plaza de la Revolución.
Phone: (53 7) 870-0417

### Iglesia de San Juan Bosco
*Churches-Places of Cult*
Calle Santa Catalina No. 674 esq.
a Goss. Diez de Octubre.
La Habana
Phone: (53 7) 41-5405

# ATTRACTIONS
## (HAVANA CITY)

**"Buendia" Theater**
*Theaters*
Calle Loma esq. a 39, Nuevo
Vedado. Plaza de la Revolución.
La Habana
Phone: (53 7) 881-6689

**Iglesia del Carmelo**
*Churches-Places of Cult*
Calle Línea No. 1114, Vedado.
Plaza de la Revolución.
La Habana
Phone: (53 7) 833-4789

**Cristobal Colon Cemetery**
*Monuments*
Calle Zapata esq. a 12, Vedado.
Plaza de la Revolución.
La Habana

**Iglesia del Corpus Christi**
*Churches-Places of Cult*
Calle 146 No. 904 esq. a 9na.,
Reparto Cubanacán. Playa. La
Habana
Phone: (53 7) 33-7175

**"El Huron Azul" Museum**
*Museums*
Calle Paz e/ Lindero y
Constancia, Reparto Párraga.
Arroyo Naranjo. La Habana
Phone: (53 7) 57-8246

**Iglesia del Nazareno**
*Churches-Places of Cult*
Ave. 47 No. 5414. La Lisa. La
Habana
Phone: (53 7) 202-2922

**"El Sotano" Theater**
*Theaters*
Calle K e/ 25 y 27, Vedado.
Plaza de la Revolución.
Phone: (53 7) 832-0630

**Iglesia del Nazareno**
*Churches-Places of Cult*
Ave. 56 No. 5112. Marianao.
La Habana

**"Felipe Poey" Natural
History Museum**
*Museums*
Universidad de La Habana,
Edificio "Felipe Poey"
Plaza de la Revolución.
La Habana

**Iglesia del Sagrado
Corazón de Jesús**
*Churches-Places of Cult*
Calle Línea e/ C y D, Vedado.
Plaza de la Revolución.
La Habana
Phone: (53 7) 832-6807

**"Haydee Santamaria"
Gallery of Latin American
Art**
*Art Galleries*
Calle G e/ 3ra. y 5ta., Vedado.
Plaza de la Revolución.
Phone: (53 7) 832-4653

**Iglesia Episcopal de Cuba
(Diócesis Anglicana)**
*Churches-Places of Cult*
Calle 6 No. 273 e/ 11 y 13,
Plaza de la Revolución.

**"Hubert de Blank" Theater**
*Theaters*
Calle Calzada e/ A y B, Vedado.
Plaza de la Revolución.
La Habana
Phone: (53 7) 833-5962

**Iglesia Evangélica
Pentecostal (Asamblea de
Dios)**
*Churches-Places of Cult*
Calle Infanta esq. a Santa Marta.
Centro Habana. La Habana
Phone: (53 7) 870-0350

**"Jose Marti" Memorial
Museum**
*Museums*
Calle Paseo y Ave.
Independencia. Plaza de la
Revolución. La Habana
Phone: (53 7) 882-0906

**Iglesia Metodista**
*Churches-Places of Cult*
Calle 292 No. 309, Santa Fe.
Playa. La Habana

**"Karl Marx" Theater**
*Theaters*
Calle 1ra. e/ 8 y 10, Miramar.
Playa. La Habana
Phone: (53 7) 203-0801

**Iglesia Metodista Central
de La Habana**
*Churches-Places of Cult*
Calle Virtudes No. 152 e/ Crespo
e Industria. Centro Habana.
La Habana

# ATTRACTIONS
## (HAVANA CITY)

### Máximo Gómez Museum
*Museums*
Ave. Salvador Allende, Quinta
de los Molinos. Plaza de la
Revolución. La Habana
Phone: (53 7) 879-8850

### Iglesia Metodista de Cuba
*Churches-Places of Cult*
Calle K No. 502 esq. a 25,
Vedado. Plaza de la Revolución.
Phone: (53 7) 832-0770

### "Mella" Theater
*Theaters*
Calle Línea No. 657 e/ A y B,
Vedado. Plaza de la Revolución.
Phone: (53 7) 833-5651

### Iglesia Presbiteriana Reformada
*Churches-Places of Cult*
Calle Reforma No. 560, Luyanó.
Diez de Octubre. La Habana
Phone: (53 7) 33-9621

### Montane Anthropological Museum
*Museums*
Universidad de La Habana,
Edificio "Felipe Poey"
Plaza de la Revolución.
Phone: (53 7) 879-3488

### Instituto Cubano de la Música
*Institutions*
Calle 15 No. 452 e/ E y F,
Vedado. Plaza de la Revolución.
Phone: (53 7) 832-3503

### "Santa Maria del Rosario" Church
*Churches-Places of Cult*
Calle 24 e/ 31 y 33, Santa María
del Rosario. Cotorro. La Habana

### Jardín Zoológico de La Habana
*Places of Interest*
Ave. 26 y Ave. del Zoológico.
Plaza de la Revolución.
La Habana
Phone: (53 7) 881-8915

### Art Schools
*Places of Interest*
Reparto Cubanacán.
Playa. La Habana

### La Fragua Martiana
*Monuments*
Calle Hospital No. 108 esq. a
Príncipe. Centro Habana.
La Habana

### Artistic and Literary High School of Regla
*Monuments*
Calle Máximo Gómez No. 153 e/
Ambron y La Piedra. Regla.
La Habana

### Lenin Park
*Places of Interest*
Calle 100 y Cortina de la Presa.
Arroyo Naranjo. La Habana
Phone: (53 7) 44-3026

### Calixto García Memorial
*Monuments*
Calle G y Malecón. Plaza de
la Revolución. La Habana

### Municipal Museum of Guanabacoa
*Museums*
Calle Martí No. 108 e/ Versalles y
San Antonio. Guanabacoa.
La Habana
Phone: (53 7) 97-9117

### Callejón de Hammel
*Places of Interest*
Calle Plasencia e/ Concordia
y San Lázaro. Centro Habana.

### Municipal Museum of Regla
*Museums*
Calle Martí No. 158 e/ Facciolo y
La Piedra. Regla. La Habana
Phone: (53 7) 97-6989

### Catedral Episcopal de la Santísima Trinidad
*Churches-Places of Cult*
Calle 13 No. 876 esq. a 6,
Vedado. Plaza de la Revolución.

### Museo de Medicina Tropical "Carlos J. Finlay"
*Museums*
Instituto Medicina Topical
"Pedro Kouri", Autopista Novia
del Mediodia Km. 16. Playa.
La Habana
Phone: (53 7) 202-0430

# *ATTRACTIONS*
## *(HAVANA CITY)*

**Center for Studies on Marti**
*Institutions*
Calle Calzada No. 807 esq. a 4, Vedado. Plaza de la Revolución.
Phone: (53 7) 55-2297

**Museo Municipal de 10 de Octubre**
*Museums*
Calle Vista Alegre esq. a San Lázaro. Diez de Octubre. La Habana
Phone: (53 7) 99-4761

**Building of the Technical Military Institute Jose Marti**
*Monuments*
Calle 45 y 66-A. Marianao. La Habana

**Museo Municipal de Boyeros**
*Museums*
Calle 4 No. 40709 e/ 11 y 13, Santiago de las Vegas. Boyeros. La Habana

**Centro de Investigación de la Cultura Cubana "Juan Marinello"**
*Institutions*
Ave. Boyeros No. 63 e/ Bruzón y Lugareño. Plaza de la Revolución. La Habana
Phone: (53 7) 877-5770

**Museo Municipal de Habana del Este**
*Museums*
Calle 504 No. 5812 esq. a 5ta-C, Guanabo. La Habana del Este.
Phone: (53 7) 96-4184

**Centro Memorial "Dr. Martin Luther King, Jr."**
*Churches-Places of Cult*
Ave. 53 No. 9609. Marianao. La Habana

**Museo Municipal de la Lisa**
*Museums*
Calle 39 No. 208 e/ 206 y 208. La Lisa. La Habana
Phone: (53 7) 26-06942

**Chinese Cemetery**
*Monuments*
Calle 26 e/ 31 y 33, Nuevo Vedado. Plaza de la Revolución.

**Museo Municipal de Marianao**
*Museums*
Ave. 128-B No. 5704 esq. a 57. Marianao. La Habana
Phone: (53 7) 26-09706

**Church of Our Lady of Regla (Nuestra Señora de Regla)**
*Churches-Places of Cult*
Calle Santuario e/ Máximo Gómez y Litoral. Regla.
Phone: (53 7) 97-6228

**Museo Municipal de San Miguel del Padrón**
*Museums*
Calzada de Güines No. 19507 e/ Gabriel y Pepe Prieto. San Miguel del Padrón. La Habana
Phone: (53 7) 91-0780

**City Hall of Regla**
*Monuments*
Calle Guaicanamar e/ Aranguren y Céspedes. Regla. La Habana

**Museo Municipal del Cerro**
*Museums*
Calzada del Cerro No. 1852 esq. a Peñón. Cerro. La Habana

**Ciudades del Mundo Gallery**
*Art Galleries*
Calle 25 esq. a L, Vedado. Plaza de la Revolución. La Habana
Phone: (53 7) 832-3175

**Museo Nacional de la Alfabetización**
*Museums*
Calle 29-E esq. a 98. Marianao. La Habana
Phone: (53 7) 260-8054

**Cojimar Fort**
*Places of Interest*
Malecón e/ Marcos y Victoria, Cojímar. La Habana del Este. La Habana

# ATTRACTIONS
## (HAVANA CITY)

**Museo Nacional del Ministerio del Interior**
*Museums*
Calle 14 e/ 5ta. y 3ra.,
Miramar. Playa. La Habana
Phone: (53 7) 202-1240

**Cojimar Urban Site and its Natural Environment**
*Urban Historic Centers*
Cojímar. La Habana del Este.

**Museum of Sports History**
*Museums*
Ave. Independencia esq. a
Bruzón. Plaza de la Revolución.
La Habana
Phone: (53 7) 881-4696

**Conjunto Forklorico Nacional**
*Institutions*
Calle 4 No. 103 e/ Calzada y 5ta.
Vedado. Plaza de la Revolución.
La Habana
Phone: (53 7) 833-4560

**Museum of the Air Force**
*Museums*
Ave. 212 e/ 29 y 31, La Coronela.
La Lisa. La Habana
Phone: (53 7) 271-7753

**Consejo Nacional de las Artes Escénicas**
*Institutions*
Calle 4 No. 257 e/ 11 y 13,
Vedado. Plaza de la Revolución.
La Habana
Phone: (53 7) 833-4581

**Napoleon Museum**
*Museums*
Calle San Miguel No. 1159 esq. a
Ronda. Centro Habana.
La Habana
Phone: (53 7) 879-1412

**Consejo Nacional de las Artes Plásticas**
*Institutions*
Calle 3ra. No. 1205, Miramar.
Plaza de la Revolución.
La Habana
Phone: (53 7) 203-8581

**National Aquarium**
*Places of Interest*
Calle 1ra. esq. a 60, Miramar.
Playa. La Habana
Phone: (53 7) 203-6401

**Consejo Nacional del Patrimonio Cultural**
*Institutions*
Calle 4 esq. a 13, Vedado. Plaza
de la Revolución. La Habana
Phone: (53 7) 833-4193

**National Ballet of Cuba**
*Institutions*
Calle Calzada No. 510 e/ D y E,
Vedado. Plaza de la Revolución.
La Habana
Phone: (53 7) 55-5442

**Cuban Ludwig Foundation**
*Institutions*
Calle 13 No. 509, Vedado. Plaza
de la Revolución. La Habana
Phone: (53 7) 832-4270

**National Botanic Garden**
*Places of Interest*
Carretera del Rocío km. 3,
Calabazar. Arroyo Naranjo.
La Habana
Phone: (53 7) 54-4108

**Cuban Postal Museum**
*Museums*
Ave. Rancho Boyeros, Ministerio
de Comunicaciones. Plaza de
la Revolución. La Habana
Phone: (53 7) 57-4150

**National Museum of Decorative Arts**
*Museums*
Calle 17 No. 502 e/ D y E,
Vedado. Plaza de la Revolución.
Phone: (53 7) 830-9848

**Cultural House of Plaza Municipality**
*Institutions*
Calle Calzada esq. a 8, Vedado.
Plaza de la Revolución.
Phone: (53 7) 831-2023

**National Puppet Theater**
*Theaters*
Calle M e/ 19 y 21, Vedado.
Plaza de la Revolución.
Phone: (53 7) 832-6262

**Dance Museum**
*Museums*
Calle Línea No. 365 esq. a G,
Vedado. Plaza de la Revolución.
La Habana
Phone: (53 7) 831-2198

# *ATTRACTIONS*
## *(HAVANA CITY)*

### National Theater of Cuba
*Theaters*
Calle Paseo y 39. Plaza de la
Revolución. La Habana
Phone: (53 7) 879-6011

### Ecological Reserve La Coca
*Places of Interest*
Campo Florida.
La Habana del Este. La Habana

### National Zoo
*Places of Interest*
Carretera de Varona km. 2 ½,
Capdevila. Boyeros. La Habana
Phone: (53 7) 44-7613

### Ermita del Potosi
*Churches-Places of Cult*
Calzada de Guanabacoa y
Potosí. Guanabacoa. La Habana

### Neighborhood No. 1
### Camilo Cienfuegos City
*Places of Interest*
Reparto Camilo Cienfuegos.
La Habana del Este. La Habana

### Ernest Hemingway
### Museum
*Museums*
Finca La Vigía, San Francisco de
Paula. San Miguel del Padrón.
La Habana
Phone: (53 7) 91-0809

### Farm House of the Rosell
### Family
*Monuments*
Calle Martí No. 308.
La Habana del Este. La Habana

### Nuestra Señora de la
### Asuncion Church
*Churches-Places of Cult*
Calle Pepe Antonio e/ Martí y
Cadenas. Guanabacoa.
La Habana

### Expocuba
*Places of Interest*
Carretera del Rocío km. 3,
Calabazar. Arroyo Naranjo.
La Habana
Phone: (53 7) 44-6251

### Old Villa of Asunncion
### de Guanabacoa
*Urban Historic Centers*
Villa de Guanabacoa.
Guanabacoa. La Habana

### Parque Almendares
*Places of Interest*
Calle 49-B y 47. Plaza de la
Revolución. La Habana

### Fondo Cubano de Bienes
### Culturales
*Institutions*
Ave. 47 No. 4702 esq. a 36,
Reparto Kohly. Playa.
La Habana
Phone: (53 7) 204-8005

### Parroquia de Nuestra
### Señora del Carmen
*Churches-Places of Cult*
Calle Infanta esq. a Neptuno.
Centro Habana. La Habana
Phone: (53 7) 878-5168

### Fundación "Fernando Ortiz"
*Institutions*
Calle L No. 160 esq. a 27,
Vedado. Plaza de la Revolución.
Phone: (53 7) 832-4334

### Parroquia de San Juan
### de Letrán
*Churches-Places of Cult*
Calle 19 No. 258 e/ J e I, Vedado.
Plaza de la Revolución.
Phone: (53 7) 832-7329

### Fundación de la Naturaleza
### y el Hombre "Antonio
### Nuñez Jiménez"
*Institutions*
Calle 5ta.B No. 661 e/ 66 y 70,
Miramar. Playa. La Habana
Phone: (53 7) 209-2885

### Primera Iglesia
### Presbiteriana de La Habana
*Churches-Places of Cult*
Calle Salud No. 222. Centro
Habana. La Habana
Phone: (53 7) 33-8410

### Fundación del Nuevo Cine
### Latinoamericano
*Institutions*
Calle 212 No. 21254 esq. a 31.
La Lisa. La Habana
Phone: (53 7) 271-8311

### Quinta de los Molinos
### y su delimitación
*Museums*
Ave. Salvador Allende. Plaza de
la Revolución. La Habana

# *ATTRACTIONS*
## *(HAVANA CITY)*

**Gallery 23 and 12**
*Art Galleries*
Calle 12 esq. a 23, Vedado. Plaza
de la Revolución. La Habana
Phone: (53 7) 831-3339

**Real Fábrica de Tabacos
"Partagás"**
*Places of Interest*
Calle Industria No. 520 e/
Dragones y Barcelona. Centro
Habana. La Habana

**Havana Convention
Center**
*Institutions*
Ave. 146 e/ 11 y 13, Reparto
Cubanacán. Playa. La Habana
Phone: (53 7) 203-6011

**Registro Nacional de
Bienes Culturales**
*Institutions*
Calle 17 No. 1009 e/ 10 y 12,
Vedado. Plaza de la Revolución.
La Habana
Phone: (53 7) 833-9658

**Havana Gallery**
*Art Galleries*
Calle Línea No. 460 e/ E y F,
Vedado. Plaza de la Revolución.
Phone: (53 7) 832-7101

**Salones de Convenciones
Hotel Nacional de Cuba**
*Institutions*
Calle O esq. a 21, Vedado. Plaza
de la Revolución. La Habana
Phone: (53 7) 873-3564

**Havana Model**
*Places of Interest*
Calle 28 e/ 1ra. y 3ra., Miramar.
Playa. La Habana

**San Francisco Convent
& Church**
*Churches-Places of Cult*
Calle San Francisco e/ Máximo
Gómez y Corral Falso.
Guanabacoa. La Habana

**House for las Américas**
*Institutions*
Calle 3ra. esq. a G, Vedado.
Plaza de la Revolución.
La Habana
Phone: (53 7) 55-2705

**San Francisco Javier de los
Quemados Church**
*Churches-Places of Cult*
Calle 51 No. 10620 esq. a 108-A.
Marianao. La Habana

**House of Amelia Pelaez**
*Monuments*
Calle Estrada Palma No. 261 e/
Juan Bruno Zayas y Consejal
Veiga. Diez de Octubre.
La Habana

**San Lazaro Tower**
*Places of Interest*
Malecón y Marina. Centro
Habana. La Habana

**Urban area of Regla**
*Urban Historic Centers*
Regla. La Habana

**House of Antonio Castells**
*Monuments*
Calle Flores No. 468 e/ Santa
Emilia y Zapote. Diez de
Octubre. La Habana

**Santa Dorotea de Luna
de La Chorrera Fort**
*Places of Interest*
Malecón e/ 18 y 29, Vedado.
Plaza de la Revolución.

**House of Dulce Maria
Loynaz**
*Museums*
Calle 19 No. 502 e/ E y D,
Vedado. Plaza de la Revolución.
La Habana

**Santiago de las Vegas
Parish Church**
*Churches-Places of Cult*
Calle 190 e/ 409 y 411, Santiago
de las Vegas. Boyeros.
La Habana

**Santuario Nacional San
Lázaro (El Rincón)**
*Churches-Places of Cult*
Calzada de San Antonio km. 23
½, Santiago de Las Vegas.
Boyeros. La Habana

**Santo Domingo Convent
& Church**
*Churches-Places of Cult*
Calle Santo Domingo e/ Roloff y
Lebredo. Guanabacoa.
La Habana

# ATTRACTIONS
## (SANTIAGO DE CUBA)

**"Emilio Bacardi Moreau" Provincial Museum**
*Museums*
Calle Pío Rosado 552 e/ Aguilera y Heredia. Santiago de Cuba
Phone: (53 226) 62-8402

**Metropolitan Cathedral**
*Churches-Places of Cult*
Calles Heredia, Félix Pena, Bartolomé Masó y General Lacret. Santiago de Cuba

**"La Isabelica" Museum**
*Museums*
Carretera de la Gran Piedra km. 14. Santiago de Cuba

**Moncada Barracks**
*Places of Interest*
Calles General Portuondo, Ave. de los Libertadores y Carlos Aponte. Santiago de Cuba

**2da Iglesia Bautista de Cuba Oriental**
*Churches-Places of Cult*
Calle 3ra. No. 455, Reparto Sueño. Santiago de Cuba

**Municipal Historical of Santiago de Cuba**
Monuments
Calle Aguilera esq. a Padre Pico.

**Municipal Museum of the 3rd Front "Mario Muñoz Monroy"**
*Museums*
III Frente. Tercer Frente. Santiago de Cuba

**Abel Santamaría Park**
*Museums*
Calles General Portuondo, Ave. de los Libertadores, Callejón América y Saturnino Lora. Santiago de Cuba
Phone: (53 226) 62-4119

**Acuario Baconao**
*Places of Interest*
Carretera Baconao km 27 1/2. Santiago de Cuba

**Municipal Museum of the Contramaestre "Jesús Rabi"**
*Museums*
Ave. 4 No. 512 e/ 5 y 7, Baire. Contramaestre.
Santiago de Cuba
Phone: (53 226) 69-9339

**Aguilera Park-Dolores Square**
Parks
Calles Aguilera, Mayía Rodríguez y Porfirio Valiente. Santiago de Cuba

**Museum of the Guamá "Combate de La Plata"**
*Museums*
Poblado de La Plata. Guamá. Santiago de Cuba

**Alameda Clock-Tower**
*Places of Interest*
Ave. Jesús Menéndez y Aguilera. Santiago de Cuba

**Municipal Museum of the Palma Soriano**
*Museums*
Calle Martí s/n e/ Villuendas y Lora. Palma Soriano.
Santiago de Cuba
Phone: (53 226) 63802

**Arte Universal Gallery**
*Art Galleries*
Calle C e/ M y Terrazas, Reparto Vista Alegre. Santiago de Cuba

**Municipal Museum of the San Luis "29 de abril"**
*Museums*
Calle Máximo Gómez No. 302 e/ Moncada y Céspedes. San Luis. Santiago de Cuba
Phone: (53 226) 62632

**Arts and Crafts School Major General Antonio Maceo Grajales**
*Historic Sites*
Santiago de Cuba

**Museum of the Songo La Maya "José Maceo"**
*Museums*
Calle Luis Bonne No. 99. Songo-La Maya. Santiago de Cuba

**Bacardí Rum Company**
*Places of Interest*
Calle Peralejo No. 3 e/ Gonzalo Quesada y Narciso López. Santiago de Cuba

# ATTRACTIONS
## (SANTIAGO DE CUBA)

**Museo Arquidiocesano**
*Museums*
Calle Heredia esq. a Santo
Tomás, Catedral Metropolitana
de Santiago de Cuba.
Santiago de Cuba

**Baconao Park**
*Places of Interest*
Carretera de Baconao.
Santiago de Cuba

**Museo de Ciencias
Naturales "Tomás Romay"**
*Museums*
Calle Enramadas s/n e/ Barnada
y Parais. Santiago de Cuba
Phone: (53 226) 62-3277

**Baconao Reserve of the
Biosphere**
*Areas of Natural Interest*
Baconao. Santiago de Cuba

**Museo de Historia Natural
"Valle de la Prehistoria"**
*Museums*
Carretera Baconao km. 6 ½.
Santiago de Cuba
Phone: (53 226) 63-9239

**Birthplace of Antonio
Maceo**
*Museums*
Calle Los Maceo No. 207 e/
Corona y Morúa Delgado.
Santiago de Cuba
Phone: (53 226) 62-3750

**Museo de la Guerra
Hispano-Cubano-
Norteamericana**
*Museums*
Carretera de Siboney km. 13 ½.
Santiago de Cuba
Phone: (53 226) 63-9119

**Birthplace of Frank Pais**
*Museums*
Calle General Banderas No. 226
e/ Habana y Maceo.
Santiago de Cuba
Phone: (53 226) 65-2710

**Museo de La Imagen**
*Museums*
Calle 8 No. 106 e/ 3 y 5, Reparto
Vista Alegre. Santiago de Cuba
Phone: (53 226) 64-2234

**Birthplace of Jose Maria
Heredia**
*Museums*
Calle Heredia No. 260 e/ Pío
Rosado y Hartman.
Santiago de Cuba

**Museo del Transporte
Terrestre**
*Museums*
Carretera Baconao km. 8 ½,
Daiquirí. Santiago de Cuba
Phone: (53 226) 63-9197

**Bofill Gallery**
*Art Galleries*
Calle Heredia e/ Pío Rosado y
Hartmann. Santiago de Cuba

**Museum Dedicated to the
Clandestine Struggle**
*Museums*
Calle General Rabí No. 1.
Santiago de Cuba
Phone: (53 226) 62-4689

**Calle 24 de Febrero**
*Monuments*
Calle 24 de Febrero s/n (Trocha).
Santiago de Cuba

**Museum of Cuban
Historical Background**
*Museums*
Calle Félix Pena No. 612 e/
Aguilera y Heredia.
Santiago de Cuba
Phone: (53 226) 65-2652

**Carlos Manuel de
Céspedes Park**
*Parks*
Calles Aguilera, General Lacret,
Heredia y Felix Pena.
Santiago de Cuba

**Museum of Piracy**
*Museums*
Castillo San Pedro de la Roca del
Morro. Santiago de Cuba
Phone: (53 226) 69-1569

**Carnival Museum**
*Museums*
Calle Heredia No. 303 e/ Porfirio
Valiente y Pío Rosado.
Santiago de Cuba
Phone: (53 226) 62-6955

# *ATTRACTIONS*
## *(SANTIAGO DE CUBA)*

**Museum-Mausoleum Second Forefront (Segundo Frente)**
*Museums*
Ave. de los Mártires s/n, Mayarí Arriba. Santiago de Cuba
Phone: (53 226) 62-5319

**Casa del Caribe**
*Institutions*
Calle 13 No. 154 esq. a 8, Reparto Vista Alegre. Santiago de Cuba
Phone: (53 226) 64-2285

**Old Villa of Santiago de Cuba**
*Urban Historic Centers*
Ciudad de Santiago de Cuba. Santiago de Cuba

**Castle of San Pedro de la Roca**
*World Heritage Sites*
Carretera de El Morro km. 8. Santiago de Cuba
Phone: (53 226) 69-1569

**Oriente Gallery**
*Art Galleries*
Calle Lacret No. 653 e/ Heredia y Aguilera. Santiago de Cuba

**Centro de Estudios "Antonio Maceo"**
*Institutions*
Calle Los Maceo No. 305 e/ San Fermín y Santo Tomás. Santiago de Cuba
Phone: (53 226) 65-2550

**Our Lady of the Caridad Church (Iglesia de Nuestra Señora de la Caridad) (Natural Sanctuary of the Caridad del Cobre)**
*Places of Interest*
Carretera al Cobre. Santiago de Cuba

**Church and Monastery of St. Francis**
*Churches-Places of Cult*
Calle Juan Bautista Sagarra No. 121 e/ Mariano Corona y Callejón del Muro. Santiago de Cuba

**Palace of the Municipal Government**
*Places of Interest*
Calle Aguilera No. 251 e/ General Lacret y Felix Pena.

**Church of the Holy Family**
*Churches-Places of Cult*
Calle 11 No. 53 e/ 6ta. y 4ta., Reparto Vista Alegre. Santiago de Cuba

**Palacio de Gobierno Provincial**
*Places of Interest*
Calle Aguilera No. 355 e/ Pío Rosado y Hartman. Santiago de Cuba

**Church of the Holy Trinity**
*Churches-Places of Cult*
Calle General Moncada No. 259 e/ José M. Gómez y General Portuondo. Santiago de Cuba

**Park of Liberty-Mars Square**
*Parks*
Calles Victoriano Garzón, Pérez Carbó, Aguilera y Plácido. Santiago de Cuba

**College of St. Basil the Great**
*Places of Interest*
Calle Bartolomé Masó No. 203 e/ Félix Pena y Mariano Corona. Santiago de Cuba

**Pico Real del Turquino**
*Places of Interest*
Sierra Maestra. Guamá.

**Command Headquarters of the Second Eastern Front "Frank Pais"**
*Museums*
Ave. Los Mártires s/n. Segundo Frente. Santiago de Cuba

**Promenade of the Alameda Michaelsen**
*Places of Interest*
Ave. Jesús Menéndez e/ Aguilera y Aduana. Santiago de Cuba

**Conjunto de Ruinas de Cafetales Franceses**
*World Heritage Sites*
Sierra Maestra. Santiago de Cuba

**Residence of Adela Babun Selma**
*Places of Interest*
Ave. Pujols No. 108 e/ Aguilera y Taíno. Santiago de Cuba

# ATTRACTIONS
## (SANTIAGO DE CUBA)

**Convención Bautista de Cuba Oriental**
*Churches-Places of Cult*
Calle Carnicería No. 503.
Santiago de Cuba

**Residence of Alomá Family**
*Places of Interest*
Calle Félix Pena No. 352 e/ General Portuondo y Máximo Gómez. Santiago de Cuba

**Customs Building**
*Places of Interest*
Ave. Jesús Menéndez No. 702. Santiago de Cuba

**Residence of Carmen Brauet de Rosell**
*Places of Interest*
Ave. Manduley No. 104 e/ 3ra. y 5ta. Santiago de Cuba

**Dolores Church**
*Places of Interest*
Calle Mayía Rodríguez No. 453 e/ Aguilera y Heredia. Santiago de Cuba

**Residence of Guillermo Castellvi**
*Places of Interest*
Ave. Manduley No. 52 e/ 1ra. y 3ra. Santiago de Cuba

**Dolores School**
*Places of Interest*
Calle Mayía Rodríguez No. 451 e/ Aguilera y Heredia. Santiago de Cuba

**Residence of Rafael Salcedo de las Cuevas**
*Places of Interest*
Calle Heredia No. 206-210 e/ Hartman y General Lacret. Santiago de Cuba

**El Cañón Museum**
*Museums*
Finca San Isidro km 7, carretera de Puerto Boniato a San Luis. San Luis. Santiago de Cuba

**Residence of the De la Torre Family**
*Places of Interest*
Calle Heredia No. 303 e/ Porfirio Valiente y Pío Rosado.

**El Uvero**
*Historic Sites*
Carretera Granma s/n e/ Escuela Simbólica y Campo Deportivo. Guamá. Santiago de Cuba

**Residence of the Gómez Villasana Family**
*Places of Interest*
Calle Bartolomé Masó No. 358 e/ Pío Rosado y Hartman. Santiago de Cuba

**El Viso Fort**
*Parks*
Carretera del Escandel. Santiago de Cuba

**Furnia del Pipe**
*Caverns*
Baire. Contramaestre. Santiago de Cuba

**Residence of the Kindelán Family**
*Places of Interest*
Calle Aguilera No. 468 e/ Mayía Rodríguez y Porfirio Valiente. Santiago de Cuba

**Residence of the Learned Antonio Bravo Correoso**
*Places of Interest*
Calle Félix Pena e/ Castillo Duany y Santa Rita. Santiago de Cuba

**Heredia Theater**
*Theaters*
Ave. de Las Américas e/ Ave. de los Desfiles y Prolongación de Angel Salazar. Santiago de Cuba

**Residence of the Notó Family**
*Places of Interest*
Calle Pío Rosado No. 358 e/ Máximo Gómez y Juan Bautista Sagarra. Santiago de Cuba

**Hermanos La Salle School**
*Places of Interest*
Calle Heredia No. 102 e/ Félix Pena y Corona. Santiago de Cuba

**Residence of the Schueg Family**
*Places of Interest*
Calle Bartolomé Masó No. 354 e/ Pío Rosado y Hartman. Santiago de Cuba

# *ATTRACTIONS*
## *(SANTIAGO DE CUBA)*

### Historical Museum "July 26"
*Museums*
Calle Trinidad e/ Ave. Moncada y Carretera Central. Santiago.
Phone: (53 226) 62-0157

### Residence of the Tejada Brothers
*Places of Interest*
Calle Heredia No. 304 e/ Porfirio Valiente y Pío Rosado. Santiago de Cuba

### Historical Museum of Palma Soriano
*Museums*
Calle Aguilera No. 201 e/ 1ro de Mayo y Quintín Banderas. Palma Soriano.
Phone: (53 226) 63983

### Residence of the Zayas Family
*Places of Interest*
Calle Heredia No. 266 e/ Pío Rosado y Hartman. Santiago de Cuba

### House of Diego Velázquez
*Places of Interest*
Calle Félix Pena No. 612 e/ Aguilera y Heredia. Santiago de Cuba

### Revolution Square "Major Antonio Maceo"
*Monuments*
Calles A, Ave. de las Américas, 9 y Carretera Central. Santiago.
Phone: (53 226) 64-3053

### House of the Norma Family
*Places of Interest*
Calle Joaquín Castillo Duany No. 437 e/ Hartman y General Lacret. Santiago de Cuba

### Royal Bivouac Prison
*Places of Interest*
Calle Aguilera No. 131 e/ Padre Pico y 10 de Octubre. Santiago de Cuba

### Iglesia Adventista del 7mo Día en Cuba
*Churches-Places of Cult*
Calle K esq. a Céspedes. Santiago de Cuba

### Rum Museum
*Museums*
Calle Bartolomé Masó No. 358 e, Pío Rosado y Hartman. Santiago de Cuba
Phone: (53 226) 62-3737

### Iglesia de María Auxiliadora (Don Bosco)
*Churches-Places of Cult*
Calle Lorraine No. 1021.

### San Lorenzo
*Historic Sites*
Terraplén "Los Lajeales", despulpadora "San Lorenzo". Tercer Frente. Santiago de Cuba

### Iglesia Metodista
*Churches-Places of Cult*
Calle Lacret esq. a San Basilio. Santiago de Cuba

### Iglesia de Nuestra Señora del Carmen
*Churches-Places of Cult*
Calle Félix Pena No. 507 e/ Tamayo Fleites y José A. Saco. Santiago de Cuba

### Santa Ifigenia Cemetery
*Places of Interest*
Ave. Raúl Perozo s/n, Reparto Agüero. Santiago de Cuba

### Iglesia del Cristo de la Salud
*Churches-Places of Cult*
Calle 10 de Octubre esq. a San Antonio. Santiago de Cuba

### Santa Lucía Church
*Churches-Places of Cult*
Calle Pío Rosado No. 703 e/ J. Castillo Duany y Eduardo Yero. Santiago de Cuba

### Iglesia del Cristo Rey
*Churches-Places of Cult*
Calle Raúl Perozo No. 130, Reparto Marimón. Santiago de Cuba

### Santo Tomás Church
*Churches-Places of Cult*
Calle Félix Pena No. 314 e/ José Mariano Gómez y General Portuondo. Santiago de Cuba

### Jíbara Cave
*Caverns*
Baire. Contramaestre. Santiago de Cuba

# ATTRACTIONS
## (SANTIAGO DE CUBA)

**Iglesia Evangélica Pentecostal**
*Churches-Places of Cult*
Paseo Martí esq. a Rizal.
Santiago de Cuba

**Serrano Building**
*Places of Interest*
Calle José A. Saco No. 208-212
e/ Félix Pena y M. Corona.
Santiago de Cuba

**Social Centre of the Spanish Community**
*Places of Interest*
Calle Heredia No. 259 e/ Pío Rosado y Hartman.
Santiago de Cuba

**Imperial Hotel**
*Historic Sites*
Calle José A. Saco No. 251 e/ General Lacret y Félix Pena.
Santiago de Cuba

**Sociedad Tumba Francesa La Caridad de Oriente**
*Institutions*
Calle Los Maceos No. 501 esq. a San Bartolomé, Los Hoyos.
Santiago de Cuba

**St. Jerome Housing Complex**
*Places of Interest*
Calle Sánchez Hechavarría No. 469-471-473-477 e/ Porfirio Valiente y Pío Rosado.
Santiago de Cuba

**La Estrella Fortress**
*Places of Interest*
Carretera de Ciudamar km. 8.
Santiago de Cuba

**Teacher-Training School of Oriente (Eastern part of Cuba)**
*Monuments*
Santiago de Cuba

**La Gran Piedra Natural Park**
*Areas of Natural Interest*
La Gran Piedra.
Santiago de Cuba

**The Granjita Siboney (Siboney Farm)**
*Museums*
Carretera de Siboney km. 13 ½.
Santiago de Cuba
Phone: (53 226) 63-9168

**La Milagrosa Church**
*Churches-Places of Cult*
Calle 2da., Reparto Vista Hermosa. Santiago de Cuba

**The Great Rock**
*Monuments*
Carretera de la Gran Piedra km. 14. Santiago de Cuba

**Turquino National Park**
*Areas of Natural Interest*
Sierra Maestra. Guamá.
Santiago de Cuba

**Law Courts**
*Monuments*
Ave. de Los Libertadores s/n e/ A y Victoriano Garzón.

**Mangos de Baragua**
*Historic Sites*
Carretera Mangos de Baraguá-Regina. Mella. Santiago de Cuba

**Velázquez´s Balcony**
*Places of Interest*
Calle Corona No. 660 e/ Heredia y Bartolomé Masó. Santiago

**Mansion of the Bosch Family**
*Places of Interest*
Ave. Manduley No. 254 e/ 9 y 11.
Santiago de Cuba

**Wooden Architecture in Key Granma (Smith) and the vicinity**
*Places of Interest*
Cayo Granma, bahía de Santiago de Cuba. Santiago de Cuba

**Mausoleum of José Martí**
*Monuments*
Cementerio de Santa Ifigenia.
Santiago de Cuba

**Yarayó Fort**
*Monuments*
Ave. Crombet esq. a Juan Gualberto Gómez.
Santiago de Cuba

# ATTRACTIONS
## (HOLGUÍN)

**"Chorro de Maita"**
*Museums*
Cerro de Yaguajay.
Banes. Holguín

**Museo Municipal de Gibara**
*Museums*
Calle Independencia No. 19, bajos, e/ Céspedes y J. Peralta. Gibara. Holguín
Phone: (53 24) 4407

**Bahía de Naranjo Natural Park**
*Areas of Natural Interest*
Bahía de Naranjo. Rafael Freyre. Holguín

**Museo Municipal de Historia**
*Museums*
Calle Thelmo Esperance No. 515 Banes. Holguín
Phone: (53 24) 3555

**Bariay Bay and its natural environment**
*Historic Sites*
Bahía de Baray.
Rafael Freyre. Holguín

**Museo Municipal de Moa**
*Museums*
Calle Mario Muñoz No. 28, Reparto Aserrio. Moa. Holguín
Phone: (53 24) 6-4189

**Portales**
*Caverns*
Rafael Freyre. Holguín

**Battery of Ferdinand VII**
*Historic Sites*
Plaza de la Fortaleza.
Gibara. Holguín

**Museo Municipal de Rafael Freyre**
*Museums*
Calle 10 No. 39 esq. a a 9. Rafael Freyre. Holguín
Phone: (53 24) 0336

**Church of Jesus of the Mountain**
*Churches-Places of Cult*
Carretera Holguín-Gibara km. 17, Poblado Floro Pérez. Gibara.

**Museum of Decorative Arts**
*Museums*
Calle Independencia No. 19, altos, e/ Luz Caballero y J. Peralta. Gibara. Holguín

**Church of Our Lady of Charity**
*Churches-Places of Cult*
Calle Martí No. 11. Banes. Holguín

**Church of St. Lucy**
*Churches-Places of Cult*
Calle B y 3, Santa Lucía. Rafael Freyre. Holguín

**Gran Caverna de Moa**
*Caverns*
Macizo montañoso de Moa. Moa. Holguín

**San Fulgencio de Gibara Parish Church**
*Churches-Places of Cult*
Calles Independencia, Martí, Sartorio y Luz Caballero. Gibara. Holguín

**Gibara "Unión Club" Colonial Theatre**
*Places of Interest*
Calle Sartorio No. 5 e/ Peralta y Luz Caballero. Gibara. Holguín

**Sierra de los Farallones de Gran Tierra de Moa**
*Places of Interest*
Moa. Holguín

**Spanish Casino**
*Places of Interest*
Calle Luz Caballero No. 22 e/ General Soriano e Independencia. Gibara. Holguín

**Indo-Cuban Bani Museum**
Museums
Calle General Marrero No. 305 e/ Ave. José Martí y Carlos M. de Céspedes. Banes. Holguín
Phone: (53 24) 48-2487

**Tanques Azules**
*Caverns*
Caletones. Gibara. Holguín

**The Hierro Hill**
*Monuments*
Carretera Holguín-Gibara km. 17. Gibara. Holguín

# ATTRACTIONS
## (TRINIDAD)

**"Guamuhaya" Archeological Museum**
*Museums*
Calle Simón Bolívar No. 457,
Plaza Mayor. Trinidad.
Phone: (53 41) 9- 3420

**Iglesia y Convento de San Francisco de Paula**
*Places of Interest*
Calle Fernando Hernández esq.
Piro Guinart. Trinidad.

**Architectural Museum of Trinidad**
*Museums*
Calle Ripalda No. 83 e/
Fernando Hernández y Ruben
Martínez Villena. Trinidad.
Phone: (53 41) 9- 3208

**Municipal Museum of Trinidad (Cantero Palace)**
*Museums*
Calle Simón Bolívar No. 423.
Trinidad. Sancti Spiritus
Phone: (53 41) 9-4460

**Cabildo de los Congos Reales o de San Antonio**
*Places of Interest*
Calle Isidro Armenteros No. 168
Trinidad. Sancti Spiritus

**National Museum of the Struggle against Bandits**
*Museums*
Calle Fernando Hernández esq.
Piro Guinart. Trinidad.
Phone: (53 419) 4121

**Casa de la Cultura Trinitaria**
*Places of Interest*
Calle Francisco J. Zerquera No.
406. Trinidad. Sancti Spiritus

**Old Villa of the Holy Trinidad**
*Urban Historic Centers*
Trinidad. Sancti Spiritus

**Galería Amelia Peláez**
*Art Galleries*
Calle Simón Bolívar No. 418.
Trinidad. Sancti Spiritus

**Parish Church of Holy Trinity**
*Churches-Places of Cult*
Calle Francisco J. Zerquera No.
456. Trinidad. Sancti Spiritus
Phone: (53 41) 9-4308

**Historical Center of Trinidad and the Valley of Sugar Cane Mills**
*World Heritage Sites*
Trinidad. Sancti Spiritus

**Romantic Museum (Brunet Palace)**
*Museums*
Calle Fernando Hernández
Echemendía No. 52, Plaza
Mayor. Trinidad. Sancti Spiritus
Phone: (53 41) 9-4363

**House of Aldemán Ortiz (Art Gallery)**
*Art Galleries*
Calle Rubén Martínez Villena
No. 43. Trinidad. Sancti Spiritus
Phone: (53 41) 9-4432

**Santa Ana Church and Square**
*Places of Interest*
Trinidad. Sancti Spiritus

**Iglesia Bautista de Cuba Occidental**
*Churches-Places of Cult*
Calle Antonio Maceo No. 4325.
Trinidad. Sancti Spiritus

**Tower of the Old Sugar Cane Mill Manacas-Iznaga**
*Monuments*
Carretera de Trinidad a Sancti
Spiritus. Trinidad. Sancti Spiritus

**Iglesia de Nuestra Señora de la Candelaria (Ermita de la Popa)**
*Places of Interest*
Trinidad. Sancti Spiritus

**Valle de los Ingenios**
*Monuments*
Trinidad. Sancti Spiritus

# ATTRACTIONS
## (VIÑALES)

**Museo Comunidad Las Terrazas**
*Museums*
Comunidad Las Terrazas.
Candelaria. Artemisa

**Sierra del Rosario Reserve of the Biosphere**
*Areas of Natural Interest*
Sierra del Rosario.
Candelaria. Artemisa

**Orquideario de Soroa**
*Places of Interest*
Carretera de Soroa km. 8.
Candelaria. Artemisa

**Museo Municipal de Viñales "Adela Azcuy Labrador"**
*Museums*
Calle Salvador Cisneros No. 115 e/ Adela Azcuy y Celso Maragoto. Viñales. Pinar del Ríc
Phone: (53 82) 79-3395

**Gran Caverna de Santo Tomás**
*Caverns*
Valle de Santo Tomás. Viñales.
Pinar del Río

**Cueva del Cura**
*Caverns*
Viñales. Pinar del Río

**Palmerito**
*Caverns*
Valle de las Dos Hermanas.
Viñales. Pinar del Río

**Cueva del Garrafón**
*Caverns*
Viñales. Pinar del Río

**Prehistoric Mural**
*Places of Interest*
Valle de Viñales. Viñales.
Pinar del Río

**Cueva del Indio**
*Caverns*
Valle de Viñales. Viñales.
Pinar del Río

**Viñales National Park**
*Areas of Natural Interest*
Viñales. Pinar del Río

**Viñales Town**
*Urban Historic Centers*
Viñales. Viñales. Pinar del Río

**Memorial a Los Malagones**
*Museums*
Comunidad Moncada. Viñales.
Pinar del Río

**Viñales Valley**
*World Heritage Sites*
Sierra de los Organos. Viñales.
Pinar del Río

**Museo Paleontológico**
*Museums*
Base de campismo "Dos Hermanas", Carretera del Moncada al lado del Mural de la Prehistoria. Viñales.

**Cueva de los Portales**
*Caverns*
Valle de Viñales. Los Palacios.
Pinar del Río

**Caverna del Arroyo**
*Caverns*
Viñales. Pinar del Río

# PRIVATE RESTAURANTS
## (HAVANA CITY)

**Paladar la Fontana**
*Grill*
Avenida 3A No 305, Playa
Phone: (537) 202-8337

**Paladar Calle 10**
*Caribbean*
Calle 10 No 314 Entre Ave 3 & 5,
Playa
Phone: (537) 205-3970

**Castas y Tal**
*Caribbean*
Calle E 158B Entre 9 & Calzada,
Vedado
Phone: (537) 833-1425

**Paladar los Cactus de 33**
*Caribbean*
Av 33 No 3405  Entre Calles 34 &
36, Playa
Phone: (537) 203-5139

**Paladar Vista Mar**
*Seafood*
Av 1 Entre Calles 22 & 24, Playa
Phone: (537) 203-8328

**Paladar Torressón**
*Caribbean*
Malecón  Entre Capdevila &
Genios
Phone: (537) 861-7476

**El Hurón Azul**
*Caribbean*
Humboldt # 153, esq. P, Vedado
Phone: (537) 879-1691

**Doña Juana**
*Caribbean*
Calle 19 #909 (altos), % 6 y 8,
Vedado
Phone: (537) 832-2699

**La Palma**
*Caribbean*
Jovellar #305 % M y N, Vedado
Phone: (537) 878-3488

**El Recanto**
Calle 17 #957 Apt 8 % 8 y 10,
Vedado
Phone: (537) 830-4396

**El Helecho**
*Caribbean*
Calle 6 #203 % 11 y Linea,
Vedado
Phone: (537) 831-3552

**Amor**
*Caribbean*
Calle 23 #759, 3rd floor, % B y C,
Vedado
Phone: (537) 833-8150

**Casa Sarasua**
*Caribbean*
Calle 25 #510, Apt. 1, % H y I,
Vedado
Phone: (537) 832-2114

**El Jinete**
*Caribbean*
Infanta #102 esq, 25, Vedado
Phone: (537) 878-2290

**Marpoly**
*Caribbean*
Calle K #154 % 13 y 11, Vedado
Phone: (537) 832-2471

**El Capitolio**
*Caribbean*
Calle 13 #1159 % 16 y 18, Vedado
Phone: (537) 831-9251

**Las 3B**
*Caribbean*
Calle 21 % L y K, Vedado
Phone: (537) 832-9276

**Balcón del Eden**
*Caribbean*
Ave K % 19 y 21, Vedado
Phone: (537) 832-9113

**Divino**
*International*
Calle Raquel e/ Esperanza y
Lindero. Arroyo Naranjo
Phone: (537) 643-7734

**Los Cascabeles**
*Italian*
San Juan No. 2541 e/ Calzada de
Bejucal y Matanzas. Arroyo
Naranjo
Phone: (537) 643-7191

**El Gallo de Oro**
*International*
Callejón de Lucero No. 7 e/
Calzada de Managua y Santa
Hortencia. Arroyo
Naranjo
Phone: (537) 644-4382

# PRIVATE RESTAURANTS
## (HAVANA CITY)

**Rancho Manso**
*International*
Calzada de Managua #163 e/ 1ra
y Miguel Viondi. Arroyo
Naranjo
Phone: (535) 232-9762

**Doña Teresa**
*International*
Avenida 229 No.21011 e/ 210 y
216. Fontanar. Boyeros
Phone: (537) 645-1861

**Villa Bárbara**
*Italian*
Calle 100 No. 15121 e/ 5ta y
Arday, La Fortuna. Boyeros
Phone: (537) 643-9840

**Lacoste**
*Caribbean*
Avenida 225 No. 22506 e/ 210 y
211. Fontanar. Boyeros
Phone: (535) 293-7205

**Tanokura**
*International*
Calle 403 e/ 180 y 184, Santiago
de las Vegas. Boyeros
Phone: (537) 683-2173

**Rancho Blanco**
*International*
Calle 190 e/17 y 19 Reparto
Tessie, Santiago de las Vegas.
Phone: (537) 683-2992

**La Flor de Loto (Lien Fa)**
*Chinese*
Salud No. 313 e/ Gervasio y
Escobar. Centro Habana
Phone: (537) 860-8501

**La Guarida**
*Caribbean*
Concordia No. 418 e/ Gervasio y
Escobar. Centro Habana
Phone: (537) 866-9047

**San Cristóbal**
*International*
Calle San Rafael No.469 e/
Lealtad y Campanario. Centro
Habana
Phone: (537) 867-9109

**Mimosa**
*Italian*
Calle Salud No.317 e Gervasio y
Escobar. Centro Habana
Phone: (537) 867-1790

**La California**
*International*
Calle Crespo No. 5 e/ San Lázaro
y Refugio. Centro Habana
Phone: (537) 863-7510

**Castropol**
*International*
Calle Malecón No. 107 e/ Genio
Crespo. Centro Habana
Phone: (537) 861-4864

**Bellomar**
*International*
Virtudes 169 A e/ Industria y
Amistad. Centro Habana
Phone: (537) 861-0023

**Versalles**
*International*
San Lázaro No.14 e/ Cárcel y
Prado. Centro Habana
Phone: (537) 864-1339

**El Cantonés**
*International*
Manrique No. 564 altos e
Dragones y Salud. Centro
Habana
Phone: (537) 863-2981

**El Levant**
*International*
Águila e/ Reina y Dragones.
Centro Habana
Phone: (535) 805-0696

**Min Chih Tang**
*Chinese*
Manrique No. 513 (bajos) e/
Zanja y Dragones. Centro
Habana
Phone: (537) 863-2966

**Wong Kong Ja Kong**
*Chinese*
Dragones No. 414 esq.
Campanario. Centro Habana
Phone: (537) 863-2068

**El Zarzal**
*International*
Concordia No. 360 altos e/
Lealtad y Escobar.
Phone: (537) 862-5952

**Notre Dame des Bijoux**
*International*
Gervasio No. 218 e/ Concordia y
Virtudes. Centro Habana
Phone: (537) 860-6764

**See Man**
*Chinese*
Zanja No. 306 e/ Lealtad y
Escobar. Centro Habana
Phone: (537) 878-6484

# PRIVATE RESTAURANTS
## (HAVANA CITY)

**Viejo Amigo**
*Chinese*
Dragones 356 e/ San Nicolás y
Manrique. Centro Habana
Phone: (537) 861-8095

**Mango Habana**
*International*
Calle Industria No. 352 entre San
Miguel y San Rafael. Centro
Habana
Phone: (537) 861-4325

**La Gitana**
*International*
San Lázaro No.208 entre Águila
y Blanco. Centro Habana
Phone: (537) 866-6800

**Torresson**
*Vegetarian*
Malecón No. 27 e/ Prado y
Cárcel. Centro Habana
Phone: (537) 861-7476

**Jared**
*International*
Zanja No.165 e/ Manrique y San
Nicolás. Centro Habana
Phone: (537) 867-2063

**El Maguey**
*International*
Amistad No.111 e/ Ánimas y
Virtudes. Centro Habana
Phone: (537) 861-1701

**Casa Miglis**
*Scandinavian*
Lealtad No. 120 e/ Ánimas y
Laguna. Centro Habana
Phone: (537) 864-1486

**Las Delicias de Consulado**
*International*
Consulado No. 309 apto. B
e/Neptuno y Virtudes. Centro
Habana
Phone: (537) 863-7722

**Chang Weng Chung Tong**
*Chinese*
San Nicolás No. 517 e/ Zanja y
Dragones. Barrio Chino. Centro
Habana
Phone: (537) 862-1490

**La Cayetana**
*International*
Calle 20 de Mayo No. 529 e/
Marta Abreu y Línea del
Ferrocarril. Cerro
Phone: (537) 878-1991

**Rancho Verde**
*International*
Santa Catalina #10633 e/ Avenid
de los Ocujes y Palatino. Cerro
Phone: (537) 641-6433

**El Taller**
*International*
Calle 107 No. 2811 e/ 28 y 30.
Cotorro
Phone: (537) 682-2778

**La Taberna**
*International*
Avenida 101 No. 3006 e/ 30 y 32.
Cotorro
Phone: (537) 682-4608

**El Resplandor**
*Caribbean*
Calle 95 No. 3808 e/ 38 y 40.
Phone: (535) 276-8369

**Rancho Coquito**
*French*
San Miguel No. 566 e/ Anita y
Finlay, Víbora. Diez de Octubre
Phone: (537) 641-4463

**La Orquídea**
*Caribbean*
Lagueruela No.252 e/ 5ta y 6ta,
Lawton. Diez de Octubre
Phone: (537) 698-8210

**Villa Hernández**
*Caribbean*
Calle San Miguel, No. 112 e/
Revolución y Gelabert, Sevillano.
Diez de Octubre
Phone: (537) 640-5250

**Melesio Grill**
*Grill*
Calle Juan Delgado No. 676 e/
Freyre Andrade y Aranguren,
Sevillano. Diez de Octubre
Phone: (537) 642-4496

**Snack Bar Mr. Montejo**
*Sandwiches*
Calzada de 10 de Octubre e/
Vista Alegre y San Mariano.
Lawton. Diez de Octubre
Phone: (537) 641-5396

**El Pavo**
*International*
Vía Blanca No. 11 A e/ San Luis
y D. Guanabacoa
Phone: (537) 797-6432

**117**

# PRIVATE RESTAURANTS
## (HAVANA CITY)

**U F C**
*International*
Calle 3ra e/ 10 y 11. Reparto
Chivás. Guanabacoa
Phone: (537) 793-5919

**Mangle Rojo**
*International*
Avenida 1ra No. 2 e/ 11 y 12.
reparto Chivás. Guanabacoa
Phone: (537) 797-8613

**Beti-Jai**
*Italian*
Calle 11 No. 19 e/ 1ra y 3ra. Rptc
Chivás. Guanabacoa
Phone: (537) 793-5579

**La Terracita**
*International*
Villanueva No. 9606 e/ Concha y
Pezuela, Cojímar. Habana del
Este
Phone: (537) 766-6381

**Chicken Little**
*International*
Calle 504 No. 5B15 e/ 5taB y
5taC, Guanabo. Habana del Este
Phone: (537) 796-2351

**Bodega Las Brisas**
*Seafood*
Calle Real, No. 132 esq. Rio,
Cojimar. Habana del Este
Phone: (537) 766-7538

**Don Peppo**
*Italian*
482 #503 e/ 5taA y 5taD,
Guanabo. Habana del Este
Phone: (537) 796-4229

**La Reina del Mar**
*International*
Calle Real No. 110 e/ Chacón y
Focsa, Cojimar.. Habana del Este
Phone: (537) 766-7288

**Califa**
*International*
Calle Real,No. 31 esq. Moret,
Cojimar.. Habana del Este
Phone: (537) 766-7668

**La Terraza de Cojimar**
*Seafood*
Calle Real No. 161 esq
Candelaria, Cojimar.. Habana
del Este
Phone: (537) 766-5150

**Italnova**
*Italian*
5ta Avenida No. 48018 e/ 480 y
482. Guanabo. Habana del Este
Phone: (537) 796-7896

**Luca's Bar & Grill**
*International*
Calle 15 e/ 2da y 4ta. Reparto
Guiteras. Habana del Este
Phone: (537) 767-4279

**Bellavista**
*International*
482 #506 e/ 5taA y 5taD,
Guanabo. Habana del Este
Phone: (537) 796-3064

**Ajiaco Café**
*Caribbean*
Calle Los Pinos No. 267 e/ 3raE y
5ta. Cojímar. Habana del Este
Phone: (537) 765-0514

**Piccolo**
*Italian*
Ave 5ta e/ 502 y 504 Guanabo.
Habana del Este
Phone: (537) 796-4300

**La Indiana**
*International*
Calle 222 A No. 2302 e/ 23 y 23
A, La Coronela. La Lisa
Phone: (537) 272-7624

**Don Francisco**
*International*
Ave. 35 No. 11 411 e/ 114 y 116.
Marianao
Phone: (537) 262-0514

**La Paila**
*Italian*
Calle 88-B esq. a 51-A. Marianao
Phone: (537) 267-0282

**Samaria**
*Caribbean*
Calle 128 No. 6116 e/ 61 y 63.
Marianao
Phone: (537) 265-3393

**Okan Tomi**
*International*
114 No. 7117 e/ 71 y 73.
Marianao
Phone: (537) 260-6107

**4 Palmas**
*International*
Calle 1ra No. 38 e/ Vía Blanca y
Rotaria. Regla
Phone: (537) 794-2236

# PRIVATE RESTAURANTS
## (HAVANA CITY)

**Dulcería Bianchini II**
*Pastry-confectionery*
San Ignacio No. 68 Plaza de la
Catedral. Habana Vieja
Phone: (537) 862-8477

**Doña Eutimia**
*Caribbean*
Callejón del Chorro No.60 C,
Plaza de la Catedral. Habana
Vieja
Phone: (537) 861-1332

**Habana 61**
*International*
Habana No.61 e/ Cuarteles y
Peña Pobre. Habana Vieja
Phone: (537) 861-9433

**Bar Restaurante Art Pub**
*International*
Teniente Rey No. 306 e/
Aguacate y Compostela .
Habana Vieja
Phone: (537) 861-5014

**Los Nardos**
*Spanish*
Paseo del Prado No. 563 e/
Dragones y Teniente Rey. Phone
(537) 863-2985

**Iván Chef Justo**
*International*
Aguacate No.9 esquina a
Chacón. Habana Vieja
Phone: (537) 863-9697

**El Asturianito**
*Italian*
Paseo del Prado No. 563 e/
Dragones y Teniente Rey.
Phone: (537) 863-2985

**El Tablao de Pancho**
*Italian*
Zulueta No. 658 e/ Gloria y
Apodaca. Habana Vieja
Phone: (537) 861-7761

**Mama Inés**
*International*
Obrapía No.60 e/ Oficios y
Baratillo. Habana Vieja
Phone: (537) 862-2669

**La Xana**
*Italian*
Prado No. 309 esq. Virtudes.
Habana Vieja
Phone: (537) 864-1447

**El Viejo Enrike**
*International*
Calle Corrales No.161 e/ Aponte
y Cienfuegos. Habana Vieja
Phone: (537) 861-2989

**Castillo de Farnés**
*Spanish*
Monserrate, esquina a Obrapía.
Habana Vieja
Phone: (537) 867-1030

**La Terraza**
*Brasserie*
Prado No. 309 esq. Virtudes.
Habana Vieja
Phone: (537) 864-1447

**Café Boutique Jaqueline
Fumero**
*French*
Compostela No. 1 esq. Cuarteles
Habana Vieja
Phone: (537) 862-6562

**El Fígaro**
*Caribbean*
Aguiar No.18 e/ Peña Pobre y
Avenida de las Misiones.
Phone: (537) 861-0544

**Casa Vieja**
*International*
Habana No.203 esq. Tejadillo.
Habana Vieja
Phone: (537) 863-2927

**El Mariachi**
*International*
Obrapía No.454 e/ Aguacate y
Villegas. Habana Vieja
Phone: (537) 862-7677

**Boaz**
*International*
Inquisidor, No. 508 e/ Luz y
Acosta. Habana Vieja
Phone: (537) 862-3821

**La Moneda Cubana
(Empedrado)**
*International*
Empedrado No. 152 esq.
Mercader. Habana Vieja
Phone: (537) 861-5304

**La Moneda Cubana
(San Ignacio)**
San Ignacio No.77 e/ O'Reilly y
Empedrado. Habana Vieja
Phone: (537) 867-3852

**Doña Blanquita**
*Caribbean*
Prado No.158 e/ Colón y
Refugio, 1er piso. Habana Vieja
Phone: (537) 867-4958

# PRIVATE RESTAURANTS
## (HAVANA CITY)

**La Julia**

*Caribbean*

O'Reilly No.506 A e/ Bernaza y Villegas. Habana Vieja

Phone: (537) 862-7438

**La Taberna del Pescador**

*Seafood*

Calle San Ignacio, No. 260 e/ Amargura y Lamparilla.

Phone: (537) 867-1629

**Todo en TV**

*Caribbean*

Egido entre Merced y Jesus Maria. Habana Vieja

Phone: (537) 866-1911

**Sevillas**

*Caribbean*

Obispo No. 455 e/ Villegas y Aguacate, 1er Piso, apto 2. Habana Vieja

Phone: (537) 861-3705

**Don Pucho**

*International*

Aguacate No. 262 e/ Obispo y Obrapía. Habana Vieja

Phone: (537) 862-3667

**La Dueña**

*Caribbean*

San Isidro No. 61 e/ Cuba y Damas. Habana Vieja

Phone: (537) 860-0445

**Chez Aimée**

*International*

Compostela No. 157 e/ San Juan de Dios y Empedrado.

Phone: (537) 863-3803

**La Criolla**

*Caribbean*

Calle San Ignacio No.68 e/ O'Reilly y Empedrado. Habana Vieja

Phone: (537) 860-2210

**Taberna El Portón**

*International*

Merced No. 68C e/ San Ignacio y Cuba. Habana Vieja

Phone: (537) 860-2592

**La Deliciosa de la Habana**

*International*

Bernaza No.1 apto. 1 1er piso e/ Obispo y O'Reilly . Habana Vieja

Phone: (537) 862-1534

**Cuba Italia**

*Italian*

Calle Cuba No. 215 e/ Empedrado y O'Reilly. Habana Vieja

Phone: (537) 860-2266

**La Perla de Obispo**

*International*

Obispo No. 307 apto 1 e/ Habana y Aguiar. Habana Vieja

Phone: (537) 861-6276

**Pizzanella/Habana Vieja**

*Italian*

Aguiar No.18 e/ Peña Pobre y Avenida de las Misiones.

Phone: (537) 864-6527

**El Cubano**

*International*

Muralla No. 309 e/ Habana y Compostela. Habana Vieja

Phone: (537) 863-0974

**Las Estaciones**

*International*

Amargura No. 254 e/ Habana y Compostela.. Habana Vieja

Phone: (537) 864-8795

**La Doña**

*International*

Obispo No. 512 altos, e/ Bernaza y Villegas.. Habana Vieja

Phone: (537) 866-2240

**El Coco**

*International*

Obispo No. 312 e/ Habana y Aguiar. Habana Vieja

Phone: (537) 867-2107

**La Gallega**

*International*

Compostela e/ Obispo y O'Reilly No. 255. Habana Vieja

Phone: (537) 867-3981

**Rincón de Pancho**

*International*

San Ignacio No. 68 e/ O'Reilly y Empedrado, Apto 12.. Habana Vieja

Phone: (537) 818-5325

**Rancho Luna**

*International*

San Ignacio, No. 68 e/ O'Reilly y Empedrado apto 2.. Habana Vieja

Phone: (537) 860-2221

**Gonella**

*International*

San Ignacio 68 e/ O'Reilly y Empedrado, apto. 9.

Phone: (537) 867-1686

# PRIVATE RESTAURANTS
## (HAVANA CITY)

**NaO**
*Caribbean*
Obispo No. 1 e/ San Pedro (Ave. del Puerto) y Baratillo. Habana Vieja
Phone: (537) 295-8209

**Don Lorenzo**
*Italian*
Calle Acosta, No. 260 A e/ Habana y Compostela. Habana Vieja
Phone: (537) 861-6733

**Bistró Habana Kohly (BHK)**
*International*
Ave. 45 #2805 e/ 28 y 34. Playa
Phone: (537) 205-2616

**Chino Lam**
*Chinese*
Calle 3ra A e/ 84 y 86 #8410 Miramar. Playa
Phone: (537) 205-4052

**La Proa**
*Grill*
Calle 60 e/ 3ra y 3ra A. No.303 Miramar. Playa
Phone: (537) 205-1039

**Rejoneo**
*International*
11 esq.84 No.8220, Miramar. Playa
Phone: (537) 203-5190

**Tic-Tac Boquitas**
*Snack food*
11 esq.84 No.8220, Miramar
Phone: (537) 203-5190

**Kpricho**
*International*
3ra y 94. Playa
Phone: (537) 206-4167

**Cubata Havana**
*Mexican*
Calle 31 No. 3012 e/ 30 y 34. Playa
Phone: (537) 206-2540

**Café Lavastida**
*International*
Calle 1era e/ 42 y 44 No. 4215. Playa
Phone: (537) 202-7938

**Rio Mar**
*International*
3ra y Final #11, La Puntilla, Miramar. Playa
Phone: (537) 209-4838

**El Palio**
*Snack food*
Calle 1ra No. 2402 e/ 24 y 26, Miramar. Playa
Phone: (537) 202-9867

**La Cocina de Lilliam**
*International*
Calle 48 No. 1311 e/ 13 y 15. Playa
Phone: (537) 209-6514

**Melen Club**
*International*
Calle 1ra e/ 46 y 60, Miramar. Playa
Phone: (537) 203-0433

**El Olivo**
*Spanish*
Calle 36 No.303 e/ 3ra y 5ta. Miramar. Playa
Phone: (537) 203-7445

**Espacios**
*International*
Address: Calle 10 No.513 e/ 5ta y 7ma. Playa
Phone: (537) 202-2921

**BellaHabana**
*International*
Calle 6 No. 512 e/ 5b (calle 31) y 7ma, Miramar. Playa
Phone: (537) 203-8364

**Tabarish**
*Russian*
Calle 20 No. 503 e/ y 5ta y 7ma, Miramar. Playa
Phone: (537) 202-9188

**Hecho en Casa**
*International*
Calle 30 No. 106 e/ 1ra y 3ra, Miramar. Playa
Phone: (537) 203-6151

**Élite**
*International*
Calle 38 e/ 42 y 7ma No. 705. Playa
Phone: (537) 209-3260

**La Buena Vida**
*Vegetarian*
Calle 46 No. 917 e/ 9 y 11. Playa
Phone: (537) 202-5816

# PRIVATE RESTAURANTS
## (HAVANA CITY)

**La Esperanza**
*International*
Calle 16 No. 105 e/ 1ra y 3ra,
Miramar.. Playa
Phone: (537) 202-4361

**El Diluvio**
*Italian*
Calle 72 No. 1705 e/ 17 y 19.
Phone: (537) 202-1531

**La Carboncita**
*Italian*
3ra No. 3804 e/ 38 y 40. Playa
Phone: (535) 290-4984

**Vistamar**
*International*
Ave 1ra e/ 22 y 24, Miramar.
Phone: (537) 203-8328

**Café Fortuna**
*Snack food*
3ra entre 28 y 26, Miramar. Playa
Phone: (537) 203-3376

**El Partenón**
*International*
Calle 50 #1109 e/ 11 y 13. Playa
Phone: (537) 209-0405

**Casa René**
*Italian*
Calle 22 No. 3110 e/ 33 31 A
Miramar. Playa
Phone: (537) 205-3214

**Milano Lounge Club**
*Italian*
Calle 3ra No.2404 e/ 24 y 26
Miramar . Playa
Phone: (537) 203-4641

**Doctor Café**
*International*
28 No. 111 e/ 1ra y 3ra. Playa
Phone: (537) 203-4718

**Chef Gusteau's**
*French*
Calle 7ma A #6609 e/ 66 y 70.
Playa
Phone: (537) 203-4507

**Casa Blanca/Taller de Sueños**
*International*
Ave. 49 No. 3401 esq. a 34.
Reparto Kohly. Playa
Phone: (537) 203-7232

**Cascada**
*International*
Calle cero entre 1ra y 3ra,
Miramar. Playa
Phone: (537) 205-4999

**Din Don**
*Italian*
Calle 11 No. 7816 e/ 78 y 80..
Playa
Phone: (537) 203-0445

**Segundo Piso**
*International*
1ra No. 4407, e/ 44 y 46, apto 3.
Playa
Phone: (537) 205-9241

**Cafesong**
*International*
Calle 13 No. 7007 e/ 70 y 72.
Playa
Phone: (537) 209-3625

**Cubanitos en 3B**
*International*
Calle 9na No. 12018 esq. 130..
Playa
Phone: (535) 291-6983

**Los Compadres**
*Mexican*
Calle 66 A esq 41. Playa
Phone: (537) 203-6908

**Mi Jardín**
*Mexican*
Calle 66 no. 517 entre 5ta B y
7ma, Miramar. Playa
Phone: (537) 203-4627

**Másquenada**
*Italian.*
164 No.112 e/1ra y 5ta. Flores.
Playa
Phone: (535) 358-3198

**Pizzería 22**
*Italian*
Calle 22 No. 3306 A e/ 33 y 35,
Miramar. Playa
Phone: (537) 205-9341

**Bom Apetíte**
*International*
Calle 11 No.7210 e/ 72 y 74,
Miramar. Playa
Phone: (537) 203-3634

**Mamy's**
*International*
Calle 16 No.708 e/ 7ma y 31.
Playa
Phone: (537) 203-6700

# PRIVATE RESTAURANTS
## (HAVANA CITY)

**Parrillada 84 y Quince**
*International*
Ave. 84 esq. a 15 #8402. Playa
Phone: (537) 206-3430

**Ranchón La Mulata**
*Caribbean*
Calle 3ra A No. 9012 e/ 90 y 92.
Playa
Phone: (537) 203-8384

**Real Café**
*International*
Calle 7ma e/ 62 y 66. Playa
Phone: (537) 203-7219

**Monte Barreto**
*International*
Calle 9na, No. 7813, e/ 78 y 80,
Miramar. Playa
Phone: (537) 206-3527

**Complejo Lucecita**
*Caribbean*
Calle 182 esq. 15, Siboney. Playa
Phone: (537) 272-4673

**Mulanché**
*Caribbean*
Calle 19 No. 3602 esq. 36. Playa
Phone: (537) 202-9926

**Chaplin's Café**
*Caribbean*
Calle 8 No. 513 /5ta y 5ta B,
Miramar. Playa
Phone: (537) 202-1795

**Las Marías**
*International*
Calle 48 No. 1107 e/ 11 y 13.
Playa
Phone: (537) 209-2140

**Vigía**
*Italian*
Avenida 5ta No. 25804 e/ 258 y
260. Santa Fé. Playa
Phone: (537) 272-8183

**La Fontana Habana**
*Caribbean*
Calle 3raA esq. 46. Miramar.
Playa
Phone: (537) 202 8337

**La Onda de David**
*International*
Avenida 19 No. 7605 e/ 76 y 78.
Playa. Playa
Phone: (537) 209-5853

**Casa Zule**
*Mediterranean*
Calle 30 No 116 e/ 1ra y 3ra.
Miramar. Playa
Phone: (537) 202-3275

**El Faro**
*Snack food*
Calle 72 A #4106 e/ 41 A y 41 B.
Playa
Phone: (535) 284-4070

**Pizzanella/Playa**
*Italian*
Calle 33 No.4208 e/ 42 y 44. Play
Phone: (537) 203-2625

**Barlovento**
*Mediterranean*
Avenida 9na No. 12018 e 120 y
130, Reparto Cubanacán. Playa
Phone: (537) 208-2437

**Voilá**
*International*
14 No. 511 e/ 5ta y 7ma.
Miramar. Playa
Phone: (537) 202-5392

**Calle Diez**
*International*
Calle 10 No. 314 e/ 3ra y 5ta,
Miramar. Playa
Phone: (537) 209-6702

**La Figura**
*International*
Calle 64 esq. 45 No. 4316. Playa
Phone: (537) 203-0681

**Dulce Habana**
*Italian*
Calle 17 e/ D y E No. 511
Vedado. Plaza de la Revolución
Phone: (537) 830-4185

**Bikos**
*Mediterranean*
Calle 19 No.1010 e/ 10 y 12. Plaza
de la Revolución
Phone: (537) 831-8847

**Razones**
*International*
Calle F No. 63 apto 2 e/ 3ra y 5ta,
Vedado. Plaza de la Revolución
Phone: (537) 830-6055

**El Acertijo**
*International*
Calle 27 No. 510 e/ E y F.,
Vedado.. Plaza de la Revolución
Phone: (537) 831-1744

# PRIVATE RESTAURANTS
## (HAVANA CITY)

**El Litoral**
*Seafood*
Malecón 161 e/ K y L.
Plaza de la Revolución
Phone: (537) 830-2201

**Motivos**
*International*
Calle F No. 63 e/ 3ra y 5ta
Vedado. Plaza de la Revolución
Phone: (537) 832-8732

**El Cocinero**
*International*
Calle 26 S/N e/ 11 y 13, Vedado.
Plaza de la Revolución
Phone: (537) 832-2355

**Abdala**
*Grill*
Calle D e/ 15 y 17. Vedado. Plaza
de la Revolución
Phone: (535) 832-1443

**Starbien**
*International*
Calle 29 No.205 e/ B y C.
Vedado. Plaza de la Revolución
Phone: (537) 830-0711

**Las Tierras del Sol**
*Italian*
Calle 23 esq 8 No. 1604, Vedado.
Plaza de la Revolución
Phone: (535) 298-3379

**La Catedral**
*International*
Calle 8 e/ Calzada y 5ta, Vedado
Plaza de la Revolución
Phone: (537) 830-0793

**Madrigal**
*International*
Calle 17 No. 809 (altos), e/ 2 y 4,
Vedado. Plaza de la Revolución
Phone: (537) 831-2433

**El Jardín de los Milagros**
*Caribbean*
Calle 37 No. 817 e/ 24 y San Juan
Bautista. Nuevo Vedado.
Phone: (537) 881-1053

**Café Presidente**
*Italian*
Calle 25 esq G, Vedado. Plaza de
la Revolución
Phone: (537) 832-3091

**Bar Encuentros**
*Mediterranean*
Línea #112 e/L y M. Plaza de la
Revolución
Phone: (537) 832-9744

**Café-Galería Mamainé**
*Caribbean*
Calle L No. 206 e/ 15 y 17,
Vedado. Plaza de la Revolución
Phone: (537) 832-8328

**Bar Restaurante**
**Mediterráneo Havana**
*Mediterranean*
Calle 13 No. 406 e/ F y G. Plaza
de la Revolución
Phone: (537) 832-4894

**Piso 15**
*Japaneese*
Calle 15 No. 152, piso 15 apto
142 e/ L y K, Vedado.
Phone: (537) 832-4945

**Al frío y al fuego**
*Snack food*
Calle 25 No. 672 e/ E y F,
Vedado. Plaza de la Revolución
Phone: (537) 831-8243

**Bar Bohemio**
*International*
Calle 21 No 1065 entre 12 y 14.
Plaza de la Revolución
Phone: (537) 833-6918

**Atelier**
*International*
Calle 5ta No. 511 e/ Paseo y 2.
Vedado. Plaza de la Revolución
Phone: (537) 836-2025

**Porto-Habana**
*International*
Calle E No.158 B e/ Calzada y
9na Piso 11. Plaza de la
Revolución
Phone: (537) 833-1425

**Piano Bar Restaurante**
**Somavilla**
*International*
Calle 15 No. 313 esq. H, Vedado.
Plaza de la Revolución
Phone: (537) 832-7323

**El Recanto**
*International*
Calle 10, No.401 esq 17, Vedado.
Plaza de la Revolución
Phone: (537) 830-4396

**El Beduino**
*International*
5ta No.607 e/ 4 y 6. Vedado.
Plaza de la Revolución
Phone: (535) 295-2093

# PRIVATE RESTAURANTS
## (HAVANA CITY)

**Café Laurent**
*International*
Calle M No. 257 e/19 y 21.
Vedado. Plaza de la Revolución
Phone: (537) 832-6890

**Brasilerísimo**
*Brasileña*
Calle 3ra No. 261 e/ A y B,
Vedado. Plaza de la Revolución
Phone: (537) 831-6329

**PP's Teppanyaki**
*Japaneese*
Calle 21 No 106 e/ L y M.
Vedado. Plaza de la Revolución
Phone: (537) 836-2530

**Mesón Sancho Panza**
*International*
Calle J e/ 23 y 25. Plaza de la
Revolución
Phone: (537) 831-2862

**La Casona de 21**
*International*
Calle 21 No. 857 e/ 4 y 6, Vedado
Plaza de la Revolución
Phone: (537) 831-6063

**La Onza**
*Spanish*
21 esq B No 615, Vedado. Plaza
de la Revolución
Phone: (537) 830-2939

**El Balcón**
*International*
Calle 28 No. 590, e/ 31 y 33,
Nuevo Vedado. Plaza de la
Revolución
Phone: (537) 831-2959

**Casa Lala**
*International*
Calle 24 e/ 23 y 21. Plaza de la
Revolución
Phone: (537) 830-1410

**Decamerón**
*International*
Línea No.753 e/ Paseo y 2,
Vedado. Plaza de la Revolución
Phone: (537) 832-2444

**Juana la Cubana**
*International*
Calle 19 No. 1101 esq. a 14.
Vedado. Plaza de la Revolución
Phone: (537) 831-9968

**Bollywood Havana**
*Hindi*
Calle 35 No.1361 e/ 26 y 24,
Nuevo Vedado. Plaza de la
Revolución
Phone: (537) 883-1216

**La Chuchería**
*Snack food*
Calle 1ra e/ C y D, Vedado. Plaza
de la Revolución
Phone: (537) 830-0708

**El Idilio**
*Grill*
Avenida de los Presidentes No.
351, esq. 15. Vedado. Plaza de la
Revolución
Phone: (537) 832-8182

**Café Light**
*International*
Calle Línea No. 58 e/ M y N,
Vedado. Plaza de la Revolución
Phone: (537) 831-6351

**23 y 6**
*Italian*
Calle 23 No. 1011 e/ 4 y 6,
Vedado. Plaza de la Revolución
Phone: (537) 835-3293

**El Farallón**
*International*
Calle 22 No. 361, esq. 23,
Vedado. Plaza de la Revolución
Phone: (537) 830-5187

**Q'Rico**
*Italian*
Calle 23 No.1106 e/ 8 y 10,
Vedado. Plaza de la Revolución
Phone: (537) 833-9435

**La Pachanga**
*Snack food*
Calle 28 No. 254 / 21 y 23,
Vedado. Plaza de la Revolución
Phone: (537) 830-2507

**El Quijote**
*International*
23 No.402 e/ I y J, Vedado. Plaza
de la Revolución
Phone: (537) 832-6313

**Snack Bar 911**
*Snack food*
Calle 27 e/ 4 y 6 # 901. Plaza de la
Revolución
Phone: (537) 833-1783

**El Pachanguero**
*International*
San Lázaro 1217 entre Mazón y
Basarrate. Plaza de la Revolución
Phone: (537) 879-9527

# PRIVATE RESTAURANTS
## (HAVANA CITY)

### Black & White
*International*
Calle 12 No. 508 e/ 21 y 23 apto 1
Plaza de la Revolución
Phone: (537) 836-9301

### La Casa
*Japaneese*
Calle 30 No. 865 e/ Avenida 26 y
41.Nuevo Vedado. Plaza de la
Revolución
Phone: (537) 881-7000

### Esencia Habana
*International*
Calle B No. 153 e/ Calzada y
Línea. Plaza de la Revolución
Phone: (537) 836-3031

### Gringo Viejo
*International*
Calle 21 No. 454 e/ E y F.
Vedado. Plaza de la Revolución
Phone: (537) 831-1946

### Don Remigio
*International*
Calle 36 No. 96 e/41 y 43, Nuevo
Vedado. Plaza de la Revolución
Phone: (537) 881-8058

### El Balcón del Edén
*International*
Calle K No. 361 e/ 19 y 21. Plaza
de la Revolución
Phone: (537) 832-9113

### El Loco Loco
*Snack food*
Neptuno No. 1155 esq. Infanta.
Plaza de la Revolución
Phone: (537) 873-2548

### Aries
*International*
Ave. Universidad No. 456 e/ J y
K, Vedado. Plaza de la
Revolución
Phone: (537) 832-4118

### Mamma Mía
*Italian*
Calle 23 e/ 22 y 24, Vedado.
Plaza de la Revolución
Phone: (537) 831-3093

### Toke
*Snack food*
Calle 25 esq Infanta. Plaza de la
Revolución
Phone: (537) 836-3440

### Punto G
*International*
17 No. 360 esq. G. Vedado. Plaza
de la Revolución
Phone: (537) 832-8354

### La Moraleja
*International*
Calle 25 No. 454 e/ J e I. Plaza de
la Revolución
Phone: (537) 832-0963

### La Tarequera
*International*
Calle 24 No. 418 e/ 23 y 25,
Vedado. Plaza de la Revolución
Phone: (537) 836-3636

### Habitania
*International*
Calle 30 No. 964 e/ 26 y 47.
Nuevo Vedado.
Phone: (537) 881-2026

### Nerei
*International*
Calle 19 No 110 esquina a L.
Vedado. Plaza de la Revolución
Phone: (537) 832-7860

### M en A
*International*
Calle 25 No. 158 e/ Infanta y O.
Plaza de la Revolución
Phone: (537) 836-7985

### Donde Dorian
*Snack food*
25 #1616 e/ 26 y 28. Plaza de la
Revolución
Phone: (537) 831-1241

### Le Chansonnier
*International*
Calle J No. 257 e/ 15 y Línea,
Vedado. Plaza de la Revolución
Phone: (537) 832-1576

### Monguito
*International*
Calle L No. 408 e/ 23 y 25. Plaza
de la Revolución
Phone: (537) 831-2615

### Santa Bárbara
*International*
Calle M e/ 17 y Línea No. 162.
Plaza de la Revolución
Phone: (537) 832-7251

### La Antonia
*International*
Calle Mazón No. 4 e/ Neptuno y
San Miguel, Vedado .
Plaza de la Revolución
Phone: (537) 873-5286

# INDEX

CPSIA information can be obtained
at www.ICGtesting.com
Printed in the USA
LVOW13s2235080617
537478LV00010B/461/P